IMAGES
of America

WAUNAKEE AND WESTPORT

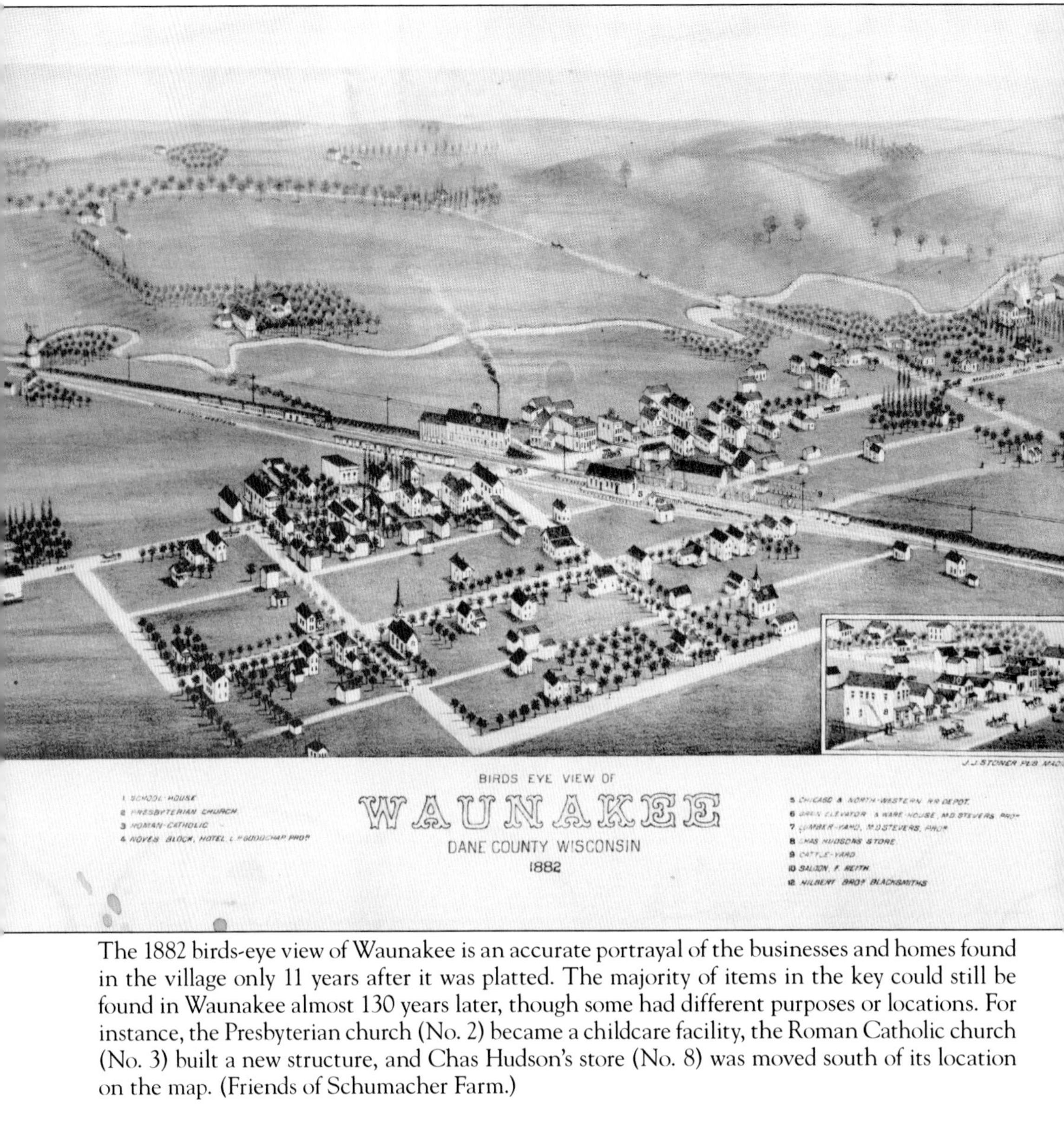

The 1882 birds-eye view of Waunakee is an accurate portrayal of the businesses and homes found in the village only 11 years after it was platted. The majority of items in the key could still be found in Waunakee almost 130 years later, though some had different purposes or locations. For instance, the Presbyterian church (No. 2) became a childcare facility, the Roman Catholic church (No. 3) built a new structure, and Chas Hudson's store (No. 8) was moved south of its location on the map. (Friends of Schumacher Farm.)

On the Cover: The Koltes & Riphahn store remains an iconic symbol of small business success and longevity in Waunakee despite the store's closing in 2010. The full image and description are found on page 23. (James P. Koltes.)

IMAGES
of America

WAUNAKEE AND WESTPORT

Katie Brenner

ARCADIA
PUBLISHING

ISBN 978-0-7385-9174-2

Published by Arcadia Publishing
Charleston, South Carolina

Printed in the United States of America

Library of Congress Control Number: 2011944554

For all general information, please contact Arcadia Publishing:
Telephone 843-853-2070
Fax 843-853-0044
E-mail sales@arcadiapublishing.com
For customer service and orders:
Toll-Free 1-888-313-2665

Visit us on the Internet at www.arcadiapublishing.com

For teachers, especially Mrs. G., Mrs. B., *and* Mrs. D., *from whom I learned to write a photo caption, a history paper, and a sentence*

Contents

Acknowledgments 6
Introduction 7
1. Railroad 9
2. Business 13
3. Farming 37
4. Churches 41
5. Schools 49
6. Houses 61
7. People 77
8. Community 117
Bibliography 126
Index 127

Acknowledgments

For entrusting to me the task of digitizing Waunakee Public Library's (WPL) historical photographs, I thank WPL director Susan Hedrick. I also thank Cynthia Turner and Mary Lynn Liegel for all the hours they scanned to help finish the project. Little did I know what opportunity would present itself from that online photograph album. My coworkers at the library also deserve recognition for all the times they covered the circulation desk while I was scanning or meeting with people. Thank you to my predecessors at Waunakee Public Library who thought it prudent to organize and save these wonderful photographs.

The Waunakee community members who provided photographs for the book and library website shared invaluable time and knowledge. They helped me see through the eyes of their ancestors and completed the story with their photographs. Those people are Paul Bernards, Rev. Msgr. James L. Gunn at St. John the Baptist parish, Mary Ellen Kearney (you came to the rescue with just what the book needed), David and Mary Jean Kennedy (MJ, my genealogic kindred spirit, thank you for your countless hours scanning with me, providing information, and digging for clues), Jim Koltes (your photographs are priceless; thank you for sharing them), Hank Kruschek, Diane Schwartz and Friends of Schumacher Farm, and Hazel Rae Zimbric (I enjoyed all of your anecdotes about life in Waunakee).

In addition to the people listed above, all of whom contributed photographs as well as information, those who helped with research and editing are Judy Borke, Jean Elvekrog, Deb Endres, Ray French, Beth Johnson, Sarah Ottosen, Gay Strandemo, and Tracy Will. The book is higher quality because of you. Sarah—my partner in crime—your knowledge of Waunakee helped get me started, and I appreciate how you always are on the lookout for new contacts and facts.

Lastly, the most profound thanks go to my husband and family, who were patient and understanding of my desire to complete this great task.

INTRODUCTION

The histories of Westport Township and the village of Waunakee are so intertwined that it would be impossible to tell the story of one without the other. Prior to European settlement in the 1840s, the area was occupied by Ho-Chunk Indians (formerly known as Winnebago) who frequently camped along the north shores of Lake Mendota. While their wigwams, camps, and annual villages still dotted the landscape, the first European settlers arrived. The *History of Dane County* (1880) lists Louis Montandon as part of the initial wave of settlers in 1837. Montandon (French Canadian) and Edward Boyles (Irish) are credited in many sources as the first to settle in Westport Township. Joined by Louis's wife, Electa, the men built a log cabin southwest of present-day Waunakee in 1845. However, another family was also present in the township at the time: Thomas O'Malley, who traveled from Ireland with his brother John, built his log cabin in eastern Westport Township in 1843. When the rest of the O'Malley family joined them in 1845 or 1846, they became one of the most prominent family groups. It is said that in the past, one could walk the distance from Waunakee to Madison and never leave O'Malley land.

The Westport landscape was characterized by wide, rolling prairies, as described by early Waunakee businessman E.L. Noyes: "The northern and western parts of the town are principally prairie, beautiful and undulating in hills, valleys and lowland, interspersed with groves of timber, or oak openings, while the southern part of the town is heavily timbered with oak, hickory, and maple, and is familiarly known as the 'Sugarbush.' " The area in the 1840s was home to wolves and bears, though the wolves proved to be more of a nuisance in the presence of fresh pork. The early settlers would let their hogs run freely in the spring until the fattened animals were ready to be collected in the fall. Montandon, Boyles, and O'Malley grew grain, but with the nearest gristmill 18 miles away by foot, their first years in southwest Wisconsin were challenging.

More settlers arrived to the area in 1846, including the Collins and Fitzgibbon families from Ireland, and were joined by additional Irish, including the Tierney, Welsh, and O'Keefe families in 1849 and 1850. Many of those new arrivals were farmers whose land bordered Six Mile Creek or the Catfish River. Before Michael O'Malley named the township after his homeland of Westport, Ireland, the entire section was part of Vienna Township. Once organized and officially recognized by the state legislature as the Town of Westport, the boundaries were chosen, and the town had its first meeting in 1849 at Michael O'Malley's home. Most of the initial town officers were Irish, but by the 1870s, the names of German settlers, including Koltes, Helt, and Schumacher, filled the official posts.

Carl C. Corneliussen, a Norwegian immigrant, built a little sawmill on Six Mile Creek two miles southeast of present-day Waunakee two years before that first 1849 town meeting. Towns would often develop around sawmills, and Corneliussen had great hopes that one would, as he also had a sheep farm and a store in the area. People were already calling it Charlesville in honor of Carl. Unfortunately, Corneliussen died during the Civil War, and his mill was gone by 1877. In 1860, E.D. Churchill built a gristmill on Six Mile Creek just south of the site of Corneliussen's sawmill. Settlers from all over Westport Township brought their grain to be ground there. Churchill sold the mill to William Packham, and 10 years after Corneliussen intended to start his town there, Packham's mill had become the favorite site of the railroad to locate their newest station.

Established before the railroad came through, some English temperance emigration settlements were present around northern Westport and southern Vienna Townships. One village, Leicester, is particularly significant in that it was later favored as namesake for the village of Waunakee. On the 1860 Dane County plat map, it appears in northern Westport as, "LESTER P.O." This is one post office from where famous Victorian poetess and Westport resident Ella Wheeler Wilcox was said to have mailed her early poems to publishers. The remnants of Leicester can be found on the 1873 Dane County plat map in southern Vienna where one can locate the only traces that exist today: School No. 4* (Wilke School on old Highway 113) and W. Plackett Cemetery (now Union Cemetery on Highway 113). Also noted on the 1873 map are C. Hudson and L.P. Goodchap, known general store owners in Leicester, as well as the Episcopal church, which was later converted into a barn. Once Waunakee was established, the post office and many of the buildings were moved to the new village.

Along the old country road that would later become Waunakee's Main Street, one could find Solomon Martin's blacksmith shop and a little district school, as well as land owned by three key people: George C. Fish, Lewis Baker, and Ira P. Bacon. In early 1871, the Baraboo Air Line, part of the Chicago & Northwestern Railroad, completed the route from Madison to Lodi, Wisconsin, and continued it to St. Paul, Minnesota. There was a great celebration in Lodi at the conclusion, yet there was still a question of where to locate a station on the new line. As the railroad was primarily used to transport agricultural goods, it made sense to the railroad to locate the station at Packham's mill on Six Mile Creek. Knowing that railroad stations bring businesses, houses, and settlements, George Fish and Lewis Baker hatched a plan. They made an agreement with the railroad to allow two miles right-of-way on their land in exchange for locating the station where the railroad intersected that old country road, rather than at Packham's mill two miles to the southeast. The railroad required $1,500 in the form of notes and bonds, which Fish and Baker paid with the help of Ira Bacon.

With the railroad station promised, the only remaining need for the new village was a name. Many people supported use of the name *Leicester*, as it was the closest post office. However, the business owners in Leicester refused to give money to bring in the railroad, and so Fish and Baker decided to look elsewhere. Simeon Mills, a Madison banker and railway investor, chose a list of names from which Lewis Baker was said to have selected the name *Waunakee*. The spelling is Mills's own version of the Chippewa or Ojibwa word, which most likely meant "pleasant valley," but also could have been translated as, "I inhabit this place in peace," or even "dark and bloody ground." No one knows for sure. Thus, on January 30, 1871, with a name in tribute to its original inhabitants rather than the homelands of its European settlers, Waunakee was officially platted on the map. And it has since remained the only Waunakee in the world.

* The school building was demolished in March 2012, before this book went to print.

One

RAILROAD

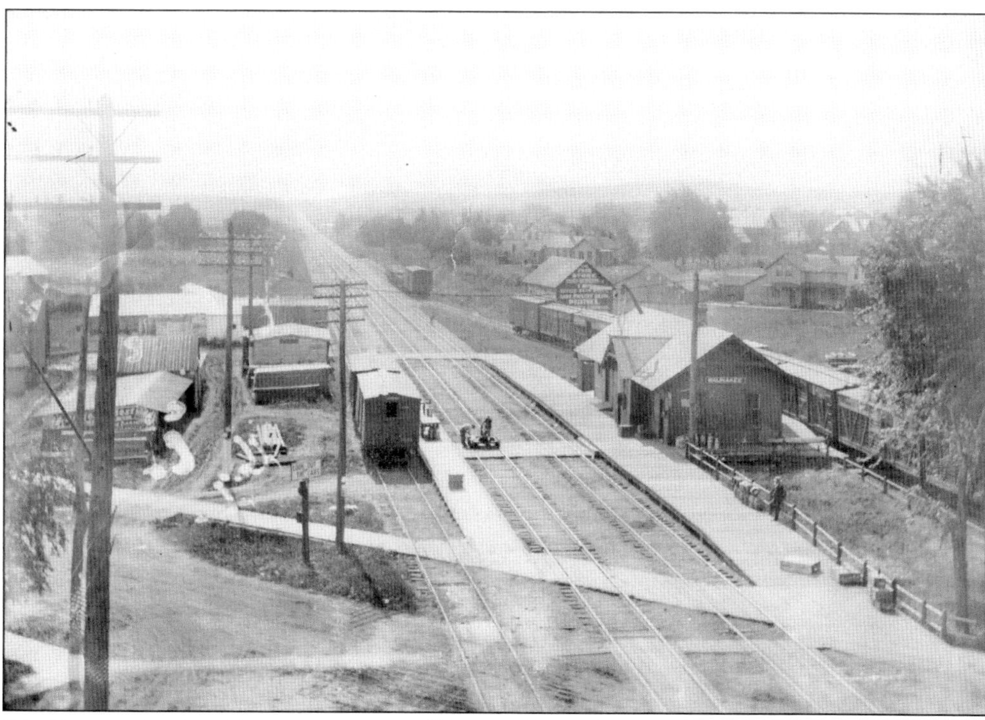

E.L. Noyes, a land and business owner in Westport Township for over 10 years before the railroad arrived, described the tracks cutting through broad, flat prairie land. The railroad tracks were placed in 1871, and the first depot was built the same year. In the 1880s, the depot received a new platform surrounding it, only to be destroyed by fire and completely rebuilt in 1892. (WPL.)

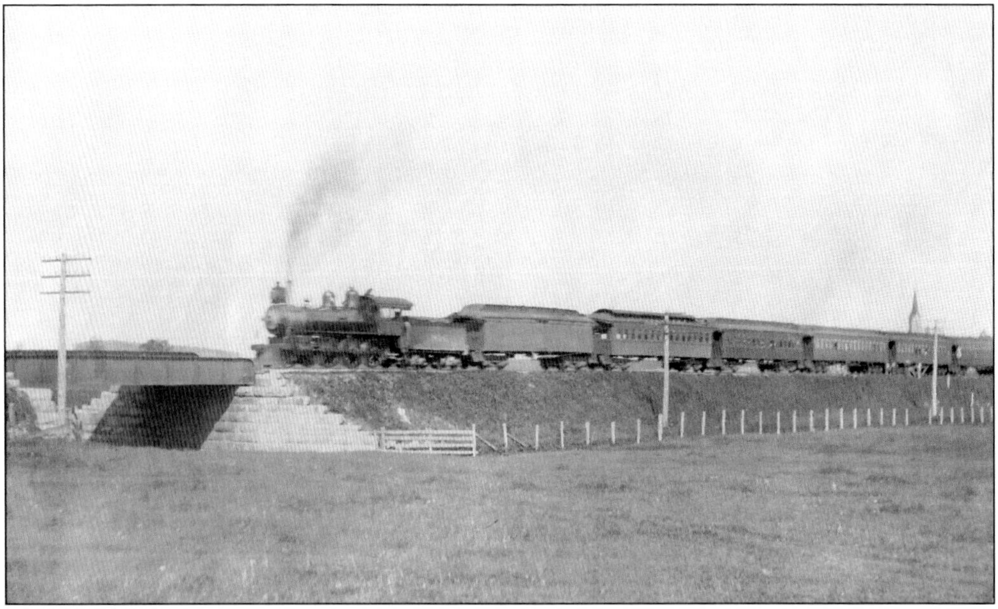

Steam trains rumbled through the peaceful countryside—so many of them that Jerry Paulson wrote in Waunakee's centennial book how his grandfather Math Endres was happy to return to his quiet farm in Springfield after visiting Waunakee because "the trains had kept him awake all night." (James P. Koltes.)

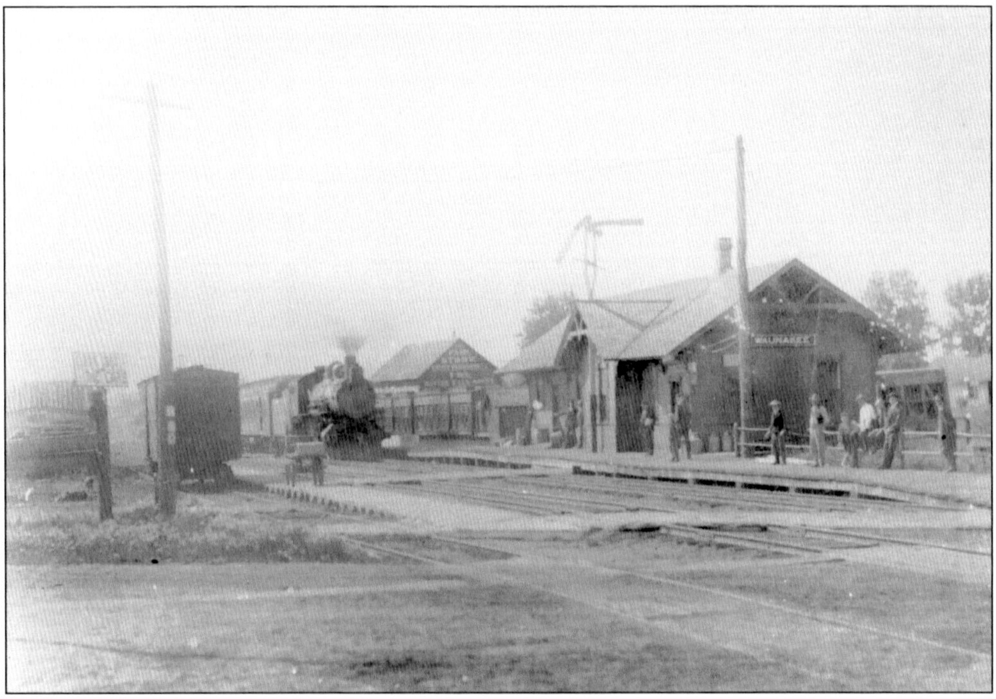

In 1909, one of those steam trains makes its way into Waunakee depot while the onlookers are warned by a small sign that reads, "Look out for the cars." Telephone service was present in the village by 1904, evidenced by the utility wires. Looking to the south, the photograph shows the depot from a dirt-covered Main Street with no sidewalks. (WPL.)

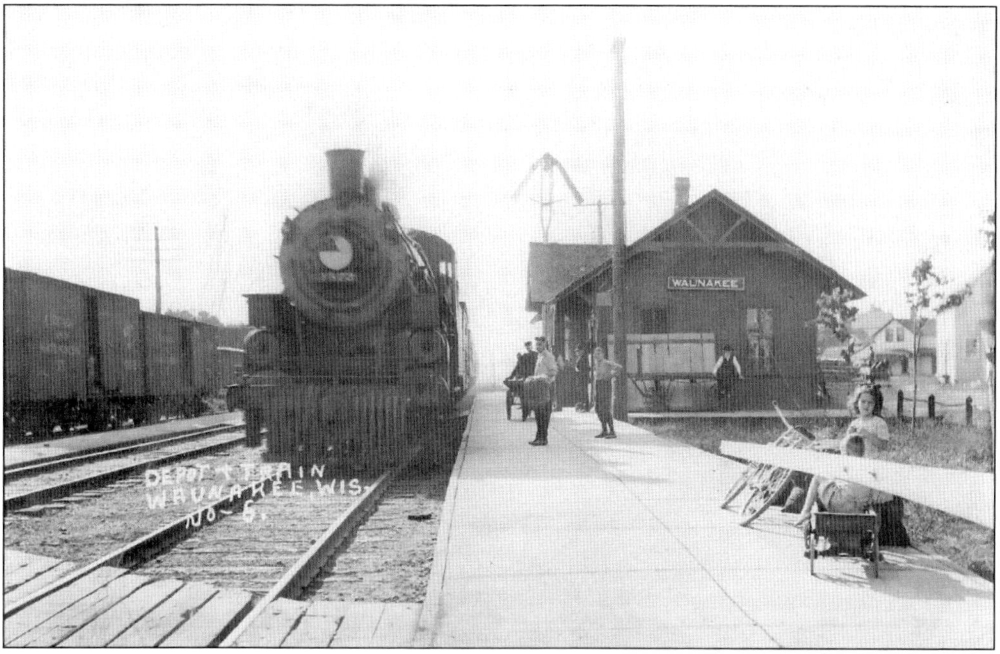

This view of the depot in 1918 shows the progress made since the turn of the century. The wooden platform was replaced with cement, and a pedestrian gate protected people from the 50 trains crossing Main Street each day. Young trees had been planted, and the double-track system placed in 1896 was in full use. (Friends of Schumacher Farm.)

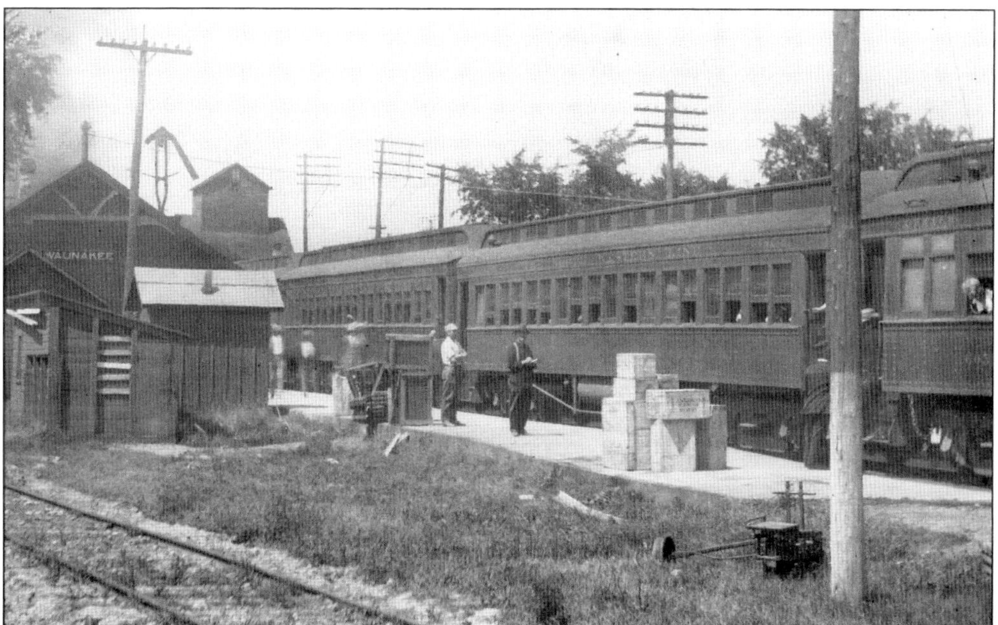

Of the 50 trains daily passing through the station, around 14 were passenger trains. Many of the passenger trains were used by commuters going to work or school in Madison. There was a time before national Prohibition when Waunakee's saloons were open while Madison had a "dry" ordinance, thus making the passenger trains invaluable to Waunakee businesses. (WPL.)

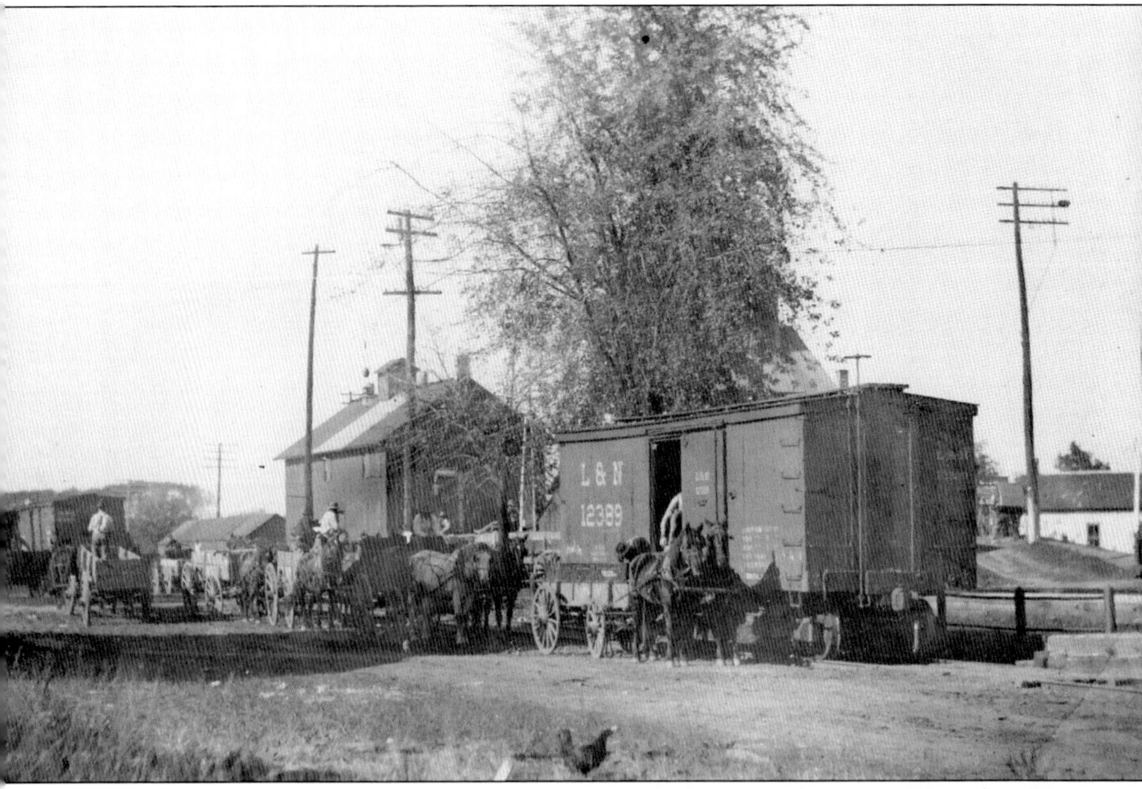

The farming business was one of the primary reasons for locating a depot near Waunakee. Trains were needed to bring agricultural goods to market or to transport crops, as shown here by the farmers in wagons loading sugar beets onto freight cars to deliver to the US Sugar Company. The white village hall building with its triangular bell tower can be seen at the far right. (WPL.)

Two

BUSINESS

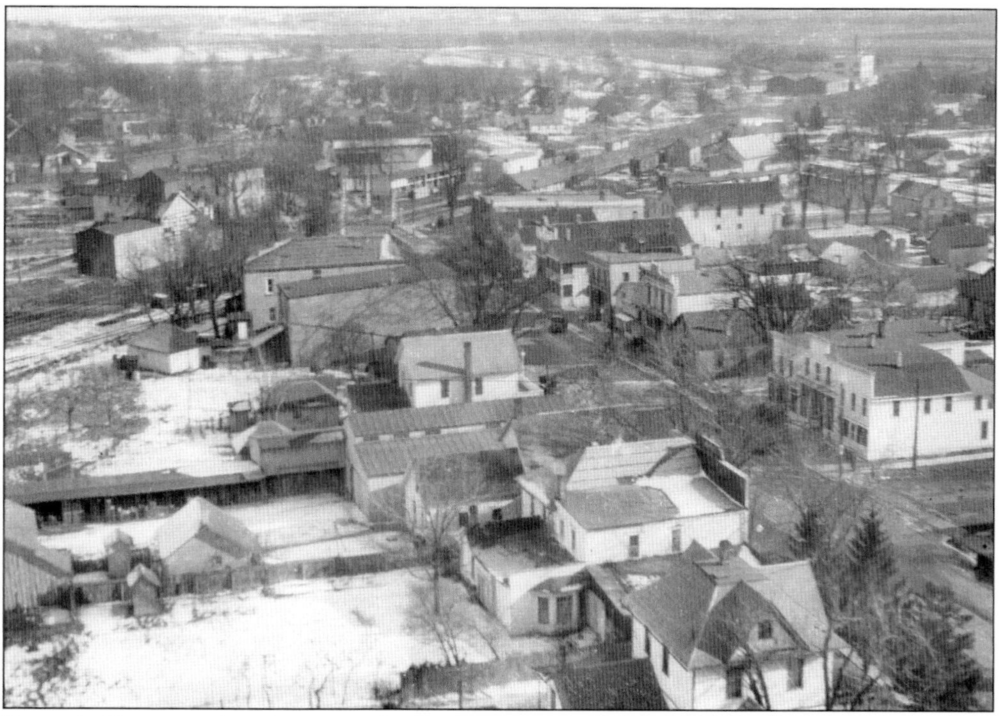

Kenneth Shaw stood at the top of the water tower to take this photograph of Main Street in 1932. From the overhead view of businesses, the false fronts that rose above the rooftops to make businesses look larger and more imposing are visible. Uebersetzig Meat Market is prominent with its wide, white false front on the right side of the photograph. The railroad tracks can be followed from the middle-left side of the photograph where the grain elevator is located to the upper right, which features the cannery with its smokestack. (WPL.)

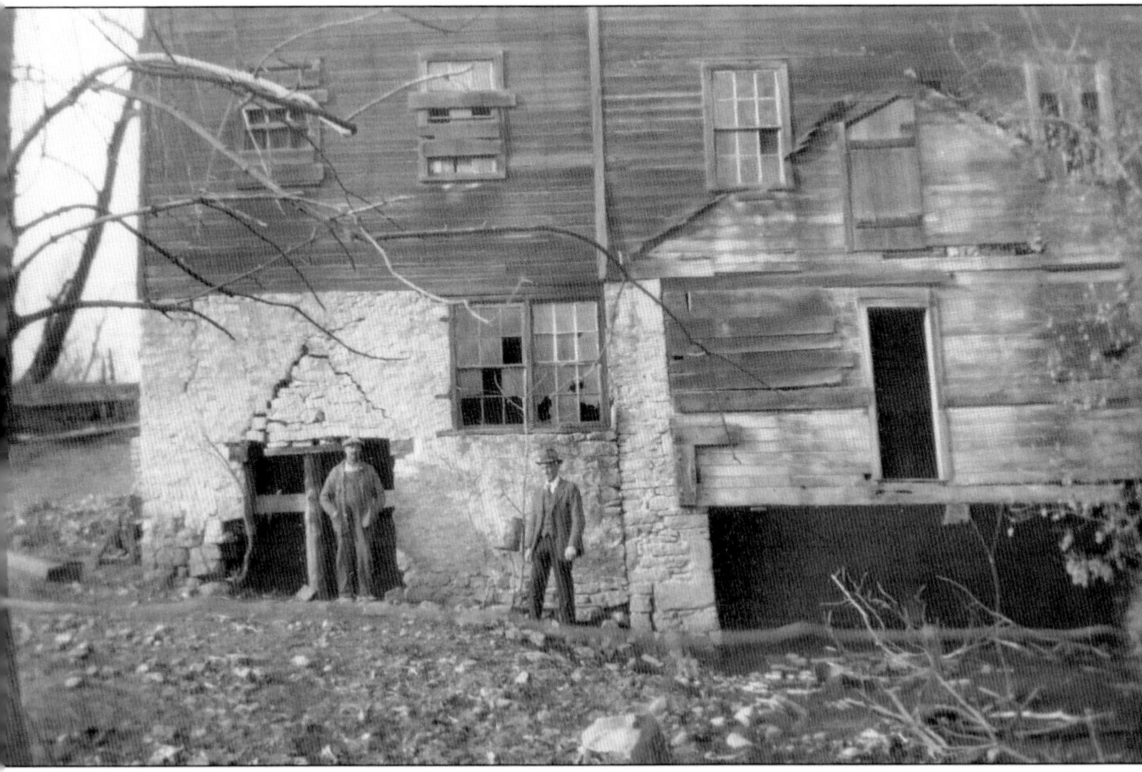

Located two miles south of Waunakee on Six Mile Creek, Packham's mill almost became the village in 1871 when the Chicago & Northwestern Railroad preferred it as a site for their new station. The mill was built in 1860 by E.D. Churchill, and at that time it was referred to as Nettekoven Mill. Early Westport settlers would drive their wagons of grain here to be ground; Ella Wheeler Wilcox described riding on the sacks in her family's wagon. It was reported that Mathias H. Schleck stored his grist upstairs, which caused the building to slump from the weight. The mill changed hands a few times, first sold to William Packham, then run by his sons Raymond and William, and finally sold to John Bowerman in 1876. Prior to when the mill eventually fell into disrepair and was torn down, Harry Koltes (left) and his father, Joseph Koltes, pose for this photograph. The opening on the right side of the structure is where water flowed beneath to power the mill. (James P. Koltes.)

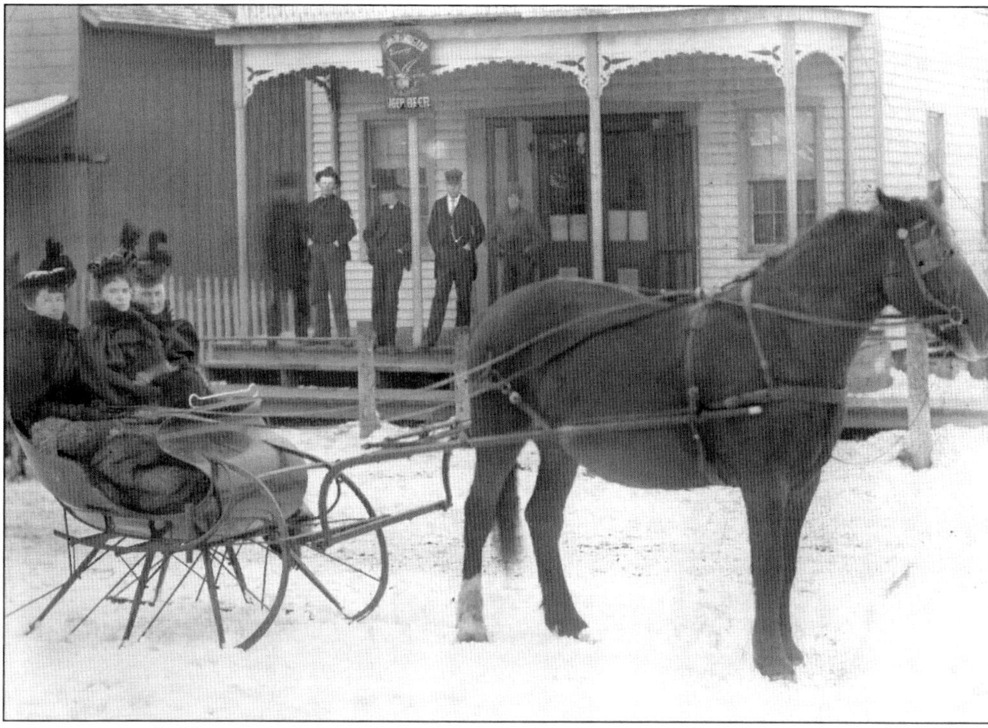

Lucy Tierney (left) sits comfortably with Anna Freney and an unidentified friend under warm buffalo robes, which were necessary in the sleigh during Wisconsin's cold winters. Behind the women is one of Waunakee's first businesses. It was opened by Mathias Schleck in 1871. There were nine bedrooms upstairs originally used to house the railroad workers, whose bills remained unpaid until the railroad was completed. Downstairs was a saloon, as evidenced by the sign advertising lager beer. The saloon was the only one in Waunakee without a back entrance, which hurt the business on Sundays when the other establishments, supposedly closed by ordinance, had open "back-door" policies. The photograph below shows the same business, known years later as Ripp's Bar, and a filling station. (Both, James P. Koltes.)

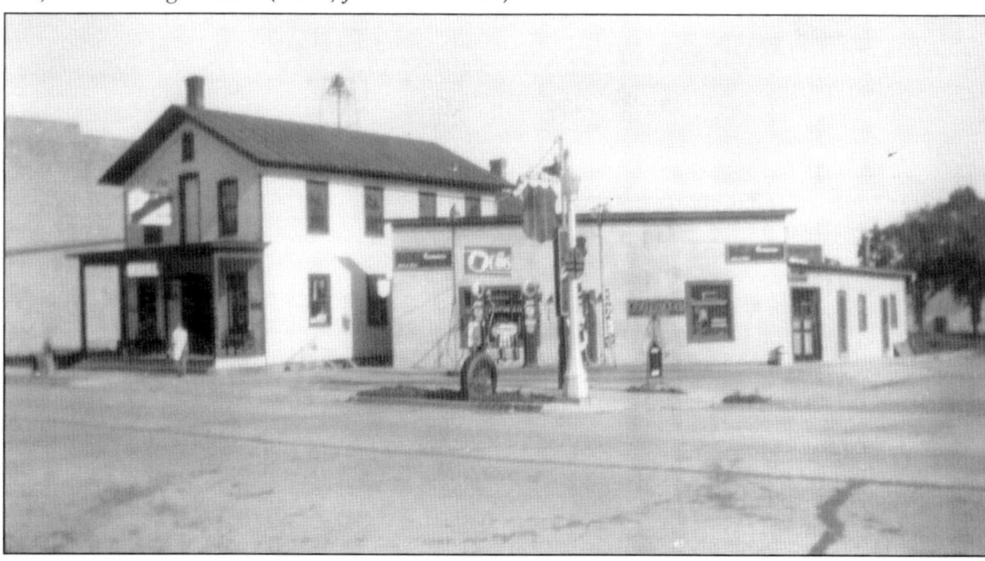

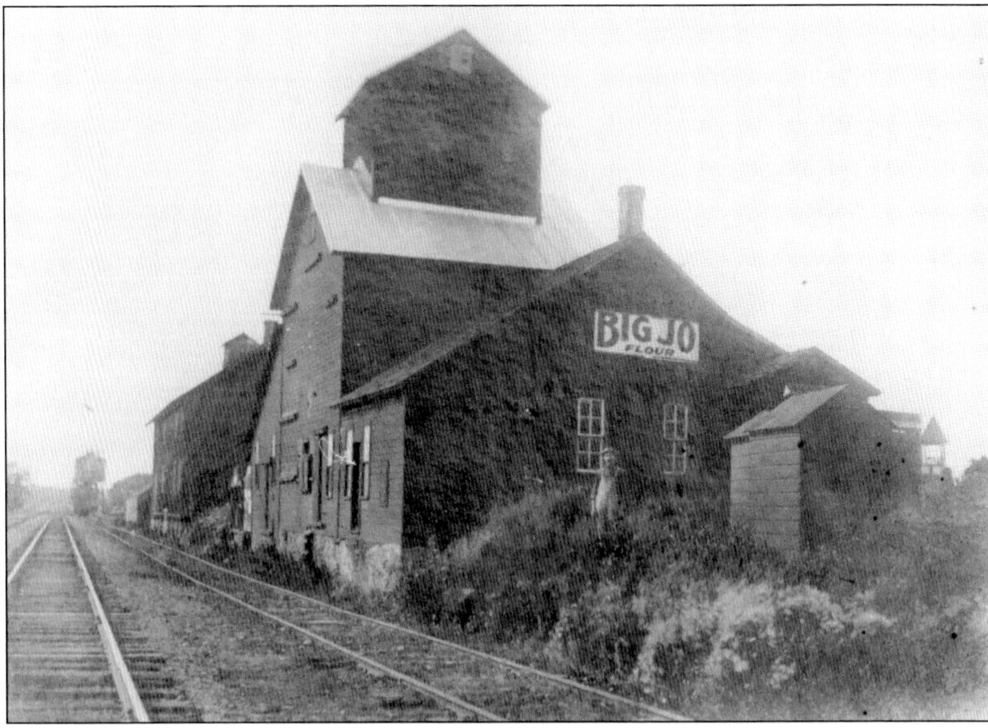

The Packham brothers took over this grain elevator in 1876 after selling their Westport mill. The grain elevator was a great asset to the Waunakee business community, as it was the only steam elevator between Madison and Sparta at the time and could store 10,000 bushels of grain. Through the years, the elevator belonged to various owners: M.D. Stevens in 1883, Henry Heller in 1885, Caldwell and Neill in the 1890s, and C.J. Schmidt (pictured in the 1930s or 1940s). (WPL.)

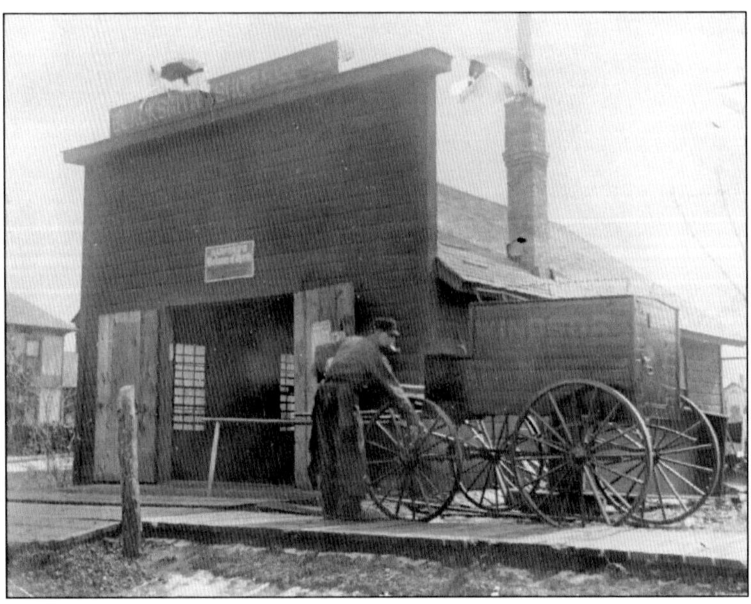

Solomon Martin owned a blacksmith shop in Waunakee even before the village existed. This is most likely not Martin's shop, but it is the building that later became Makken Fur Center on East Main Street. Dr. Austin Blake's house is visible on the left. Herman Doll was blacksmith in the 1890s. Pictured here in 1910, Bob Truehl fixes the Windsor Meat wagon. (WPL.)

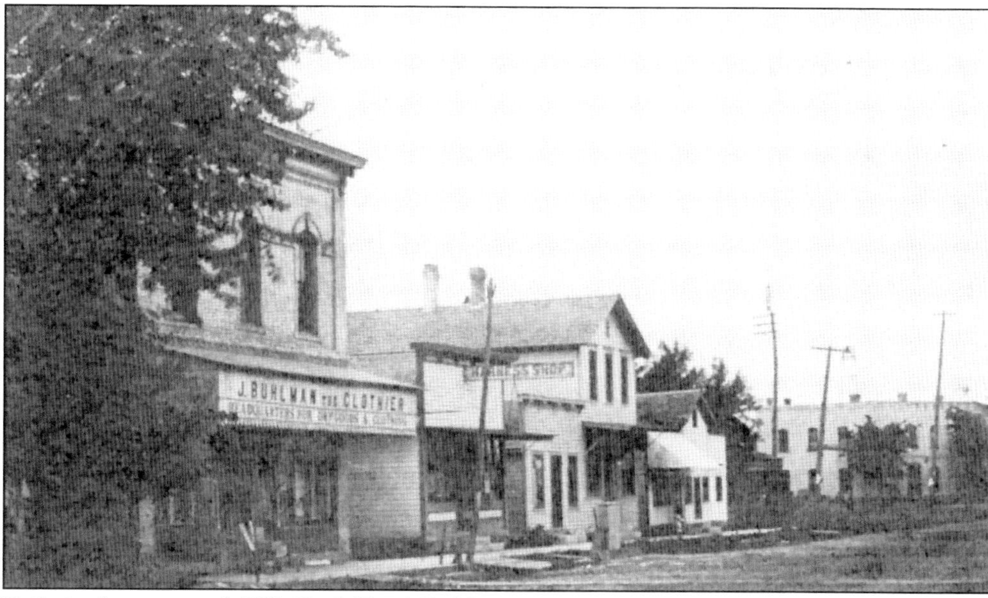

Built in the spring of 1871, Fred (Fritz) Buhlman's store on Main Street was the first business in Waunakee. Soon after that, Fred's brother Jacob joined him from Switzerland. In 1879, the Buhlman brothers built this stone structure across the street from the original frame building. The 1871 location was then used as a creamery, and W. Schmitz later turned it into a soft drink parlor. Next to Buhlman's store are the harness shop, Mathias Schleck's store, and Otto Hohlstein's barbershop with its striped barber pole in front. Far in the distance to the right is the Brausen Hotel, built around 1880. Buhlman's store shown in 1914 (below) includes the sales force, from left to right as follows: Mary Saxer, Mary Koch Wipperfurth, Margaret Feeter, unidentified, Christine Wipperfurth Deans, Margaret Buhlman, and Jacob Buhlman. (Both, WPL.)

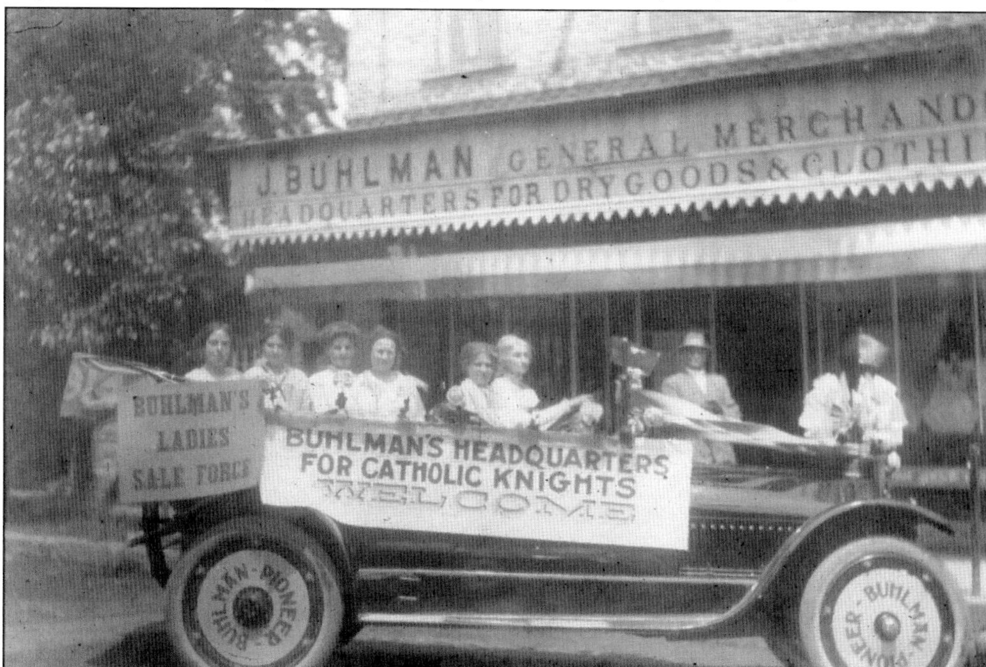

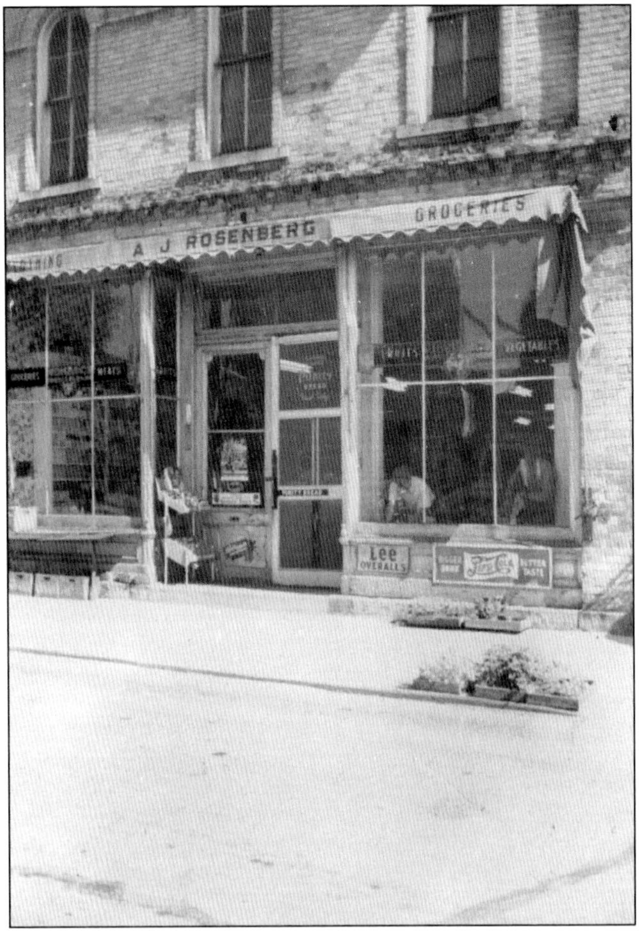

In 1926, A.J. Rosenberg purchased Buhlman's stone building and began A.J. Rosenberg's store, shown in the 1930s. Rosenberg put on an addition in 1948 and another in 1960 after a large fire destroyed much of the upstairs. (WPL.)

Godfrey Schunk and William J. Flatman went into the furniture and undertaking business in the 1890s. Their store was located on Main Street at Madison Street, which is likely the road to the left of the building. As was the custom of the day, the furniture makers were the town woodworkers, so they completed the task of crafting coffins for deceased villagers. (Both, WPL.)

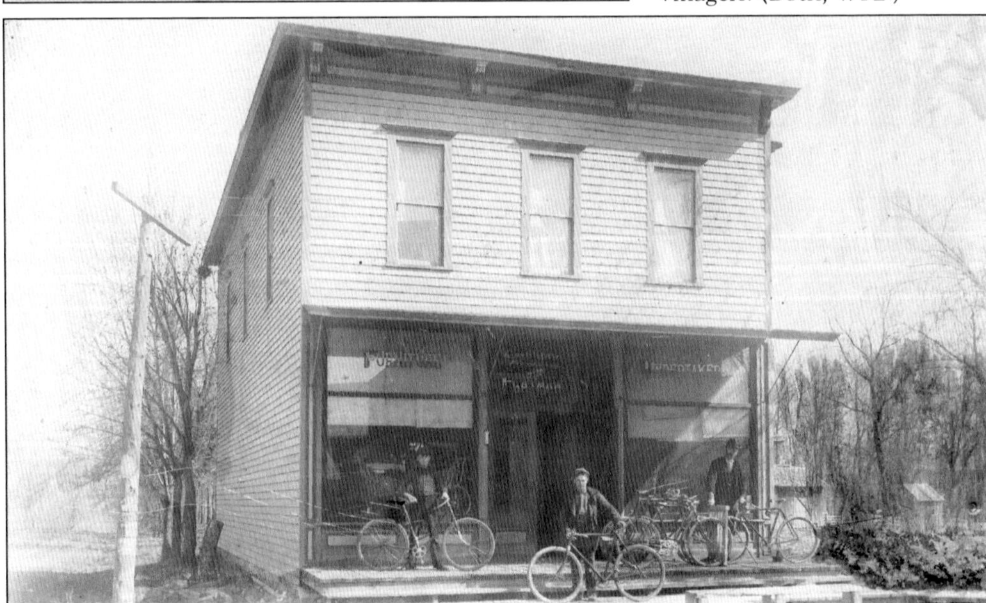

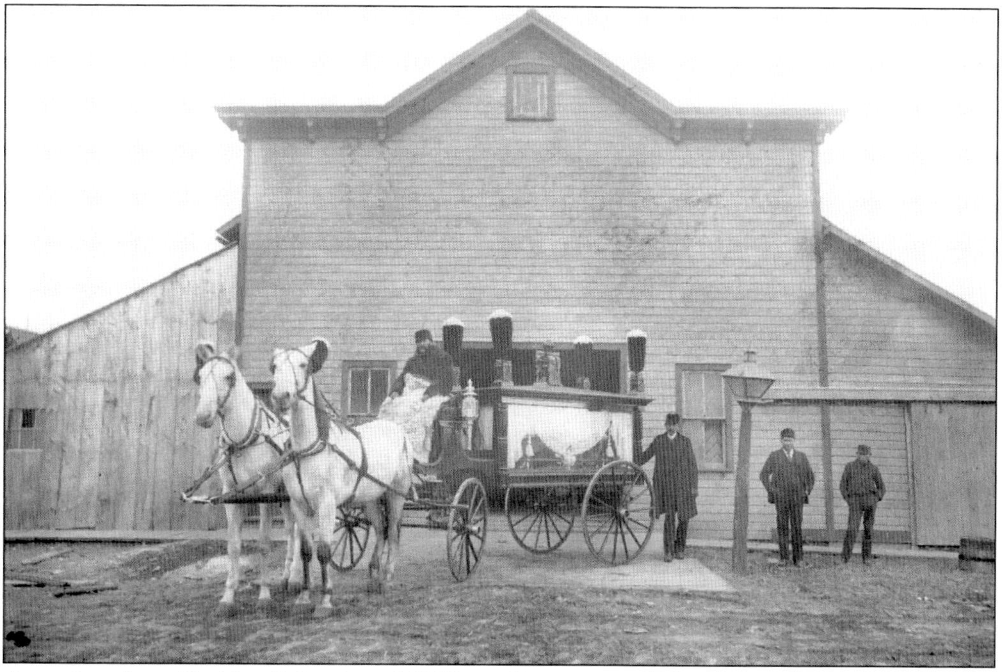

As undertakers, Godfrey Schunk and William Flatman needed to have a hearse to transport coffins and conduct funerals. Their first hearse is displayed in front of their livery stable, later known as Worringer's, which was located on South Madison Street. Flatman stands at the rear of the hearse. (WPL.)

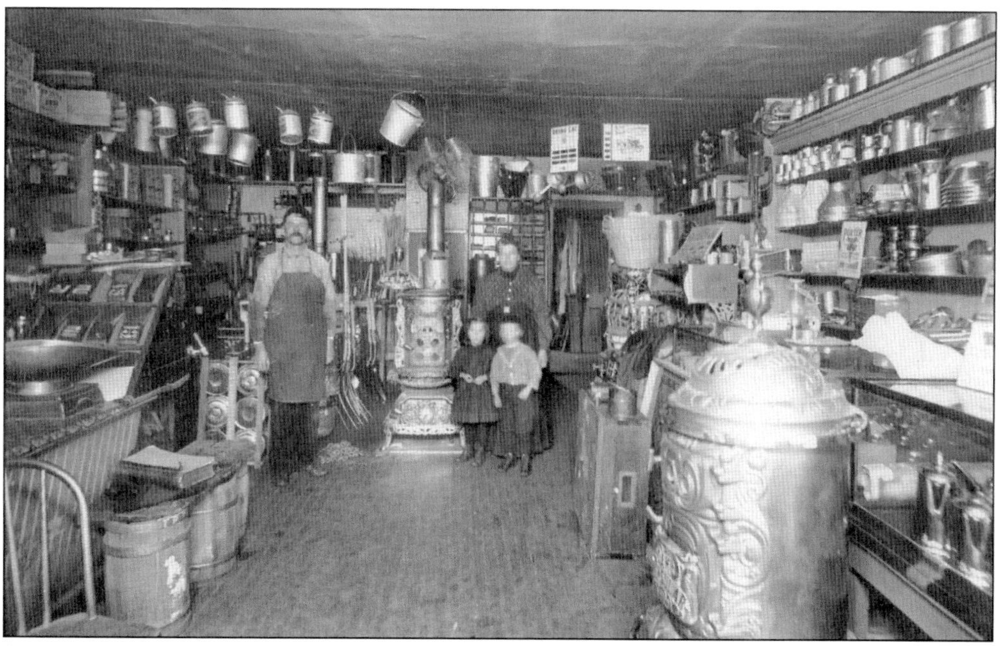

Despite cramped quarters, Gus Fleiner's store contained a variety of merchandise while he was Waunakee's tinsmith in the 1890s. Fleiner stands in his apron—his sleeves darkened with soot from working the metal. His wife and twin children Agnes and Henry join him in the Main Street shop. (WPL.)

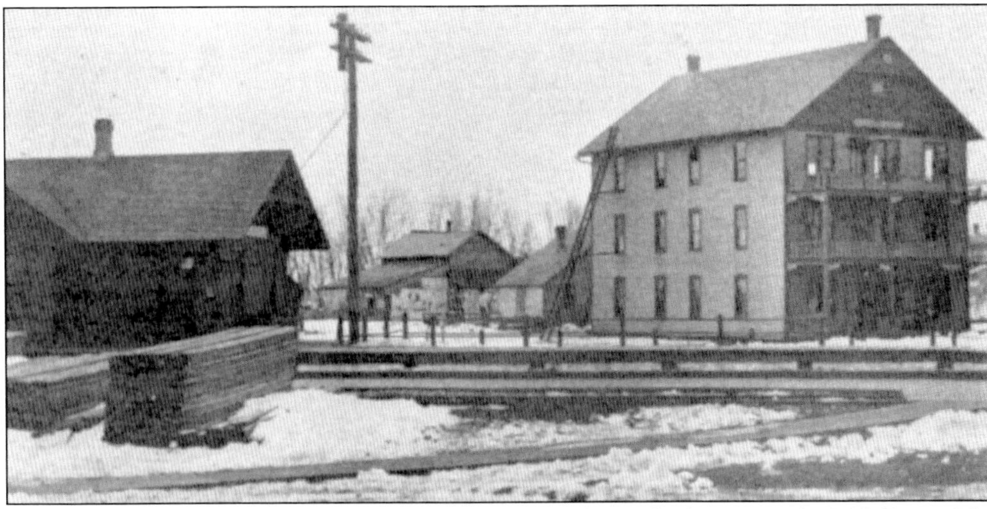

The American House, later known as the Ryan Hotel, was built in 1891 by M.J. Ryan. The three-story frame structure shown west of the railroad depot was once the site of lively dances and parties, which took place in its third-floor ballroom. Mrs. F.E. Baker managed the hotel in the 1890s. (WPL.)

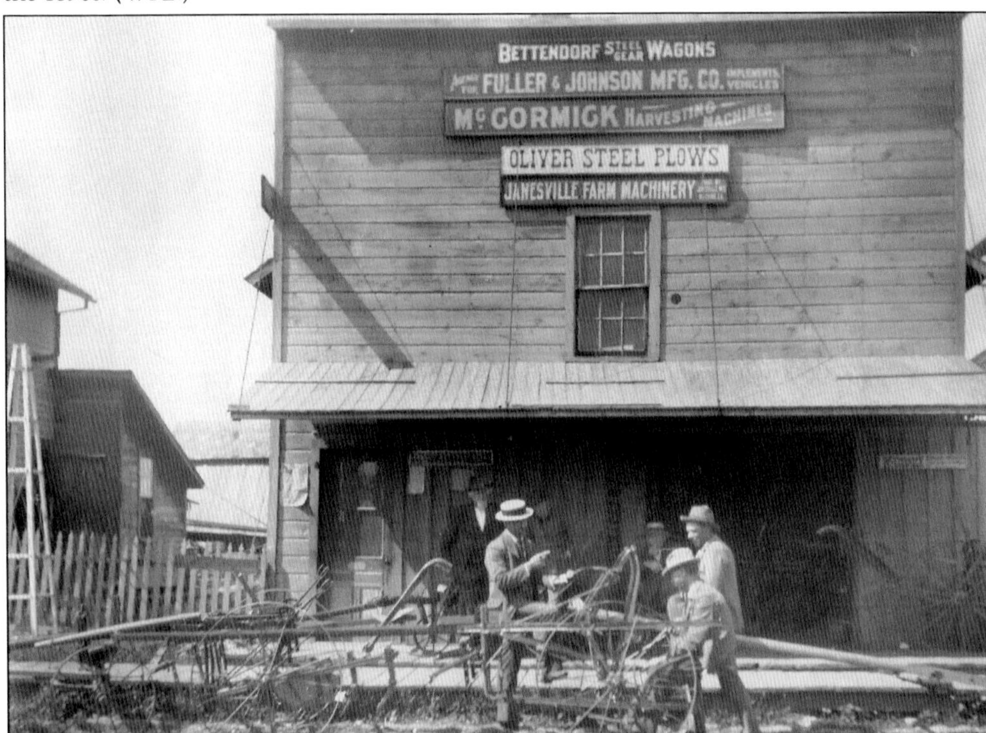

Immediately west of Schleck's tavern was Lawrence Freney's machinery shop where many farm implements of the day, including wagons, plows, and harvesters, were sold and repaired. Freney managed the machinery line for Joseph H. Koltes under the name Koltes, Riphahn & Freney until 1891 when Freney became sole proprietor of the machinery shop. The frame building was later torn down. (James P. Koltes.)

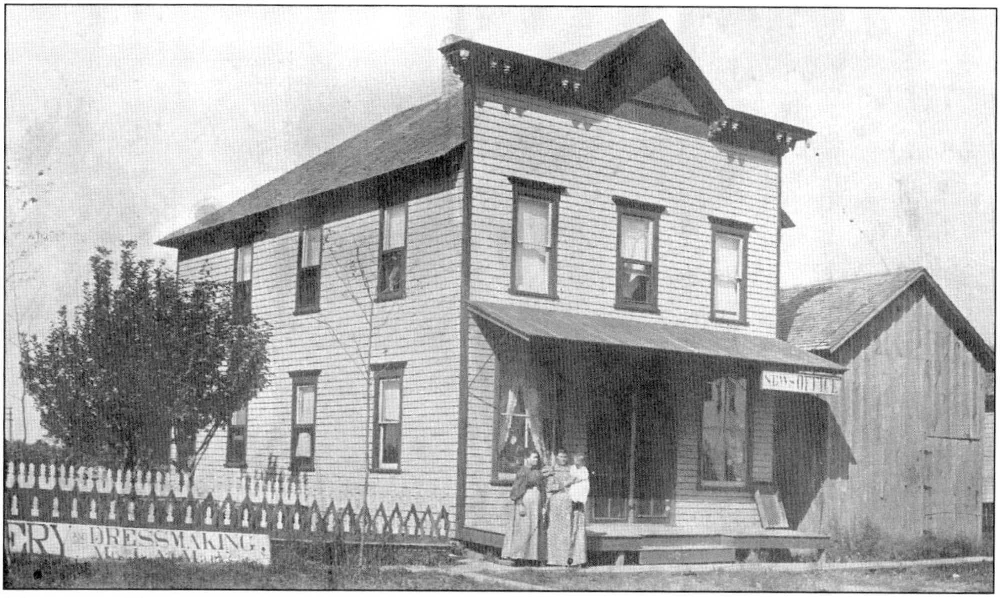

The news office opened in 1896 where the *Waunakee News* was printed for only four years. It was not until 1907 that the *Waunakee Index*, a new newspaper, was begun by L.H. Williams. The *Index* was printed until 1918. (James P. Koltes.)

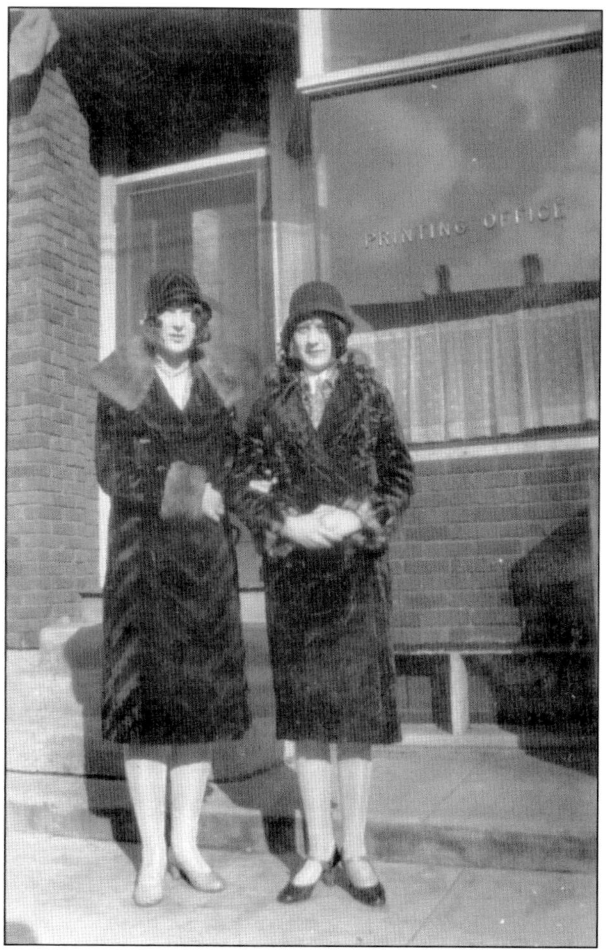

After a two-year break, Albert A. Roessler restarted the newspaper operation under the name *Waunakee Tribune* and built the South Street newspaper office in 1923. Hazel Raemisch took this photograph of Marcella Ripp (left) and her sister outside the new office not long after it was built. (Hazel R. Zimbric.)

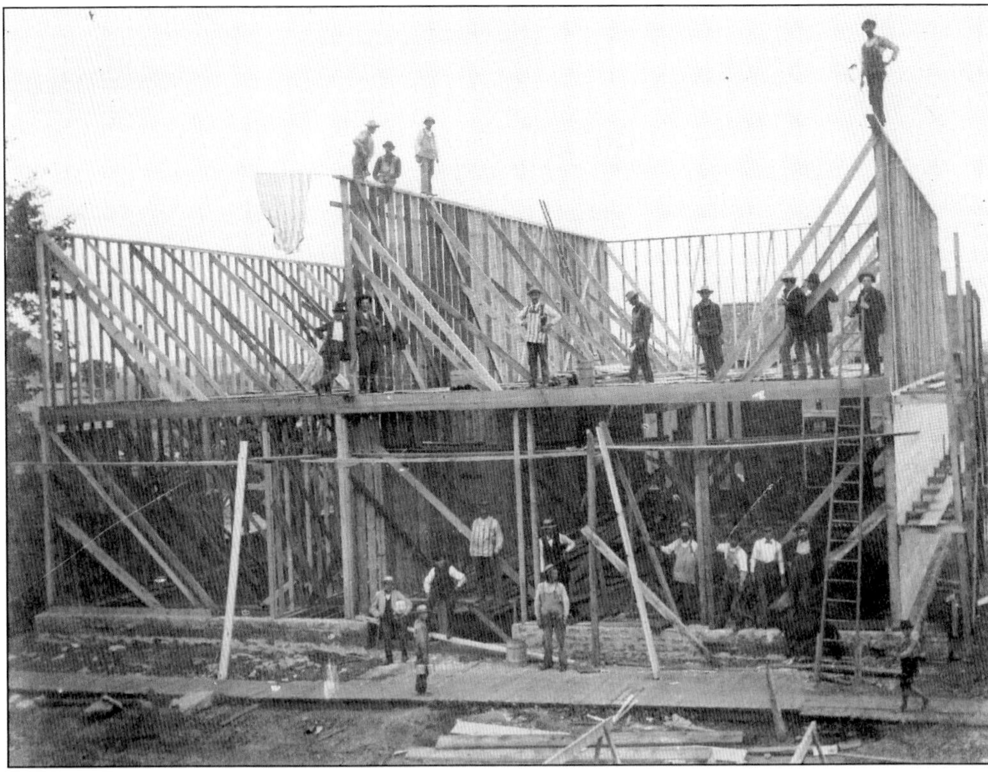

Joseph Koltes stands in a striped apron on the second floor of the Koltes & Riphahn building during its construction in 1898. Joseph Koltes and Peter Riphahn's partnership began in 1888 when they opened a lumberyard, hardware, and grocery store just west of this new location. The Koltes's business history goes further back to Joseph's father, Michael Koltes, a German immigrant who started his Waunakee lumber business with George L. Francis in 1881. (James P. Koltes.)

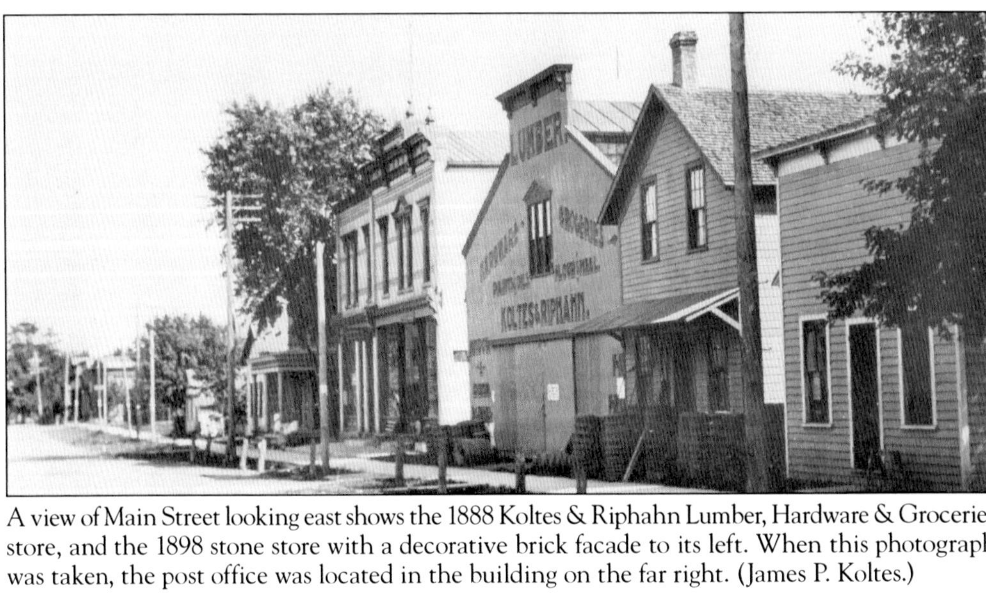

A view of Main Street looking east shows the 1888 Koltes & Riphahn Lumber, Hardware & Groceries store, and the 1898 stone store with a decorative brick facade to its left. When this photograph was taken, the post office was located in the building on the far right. (James P. Koltes.)

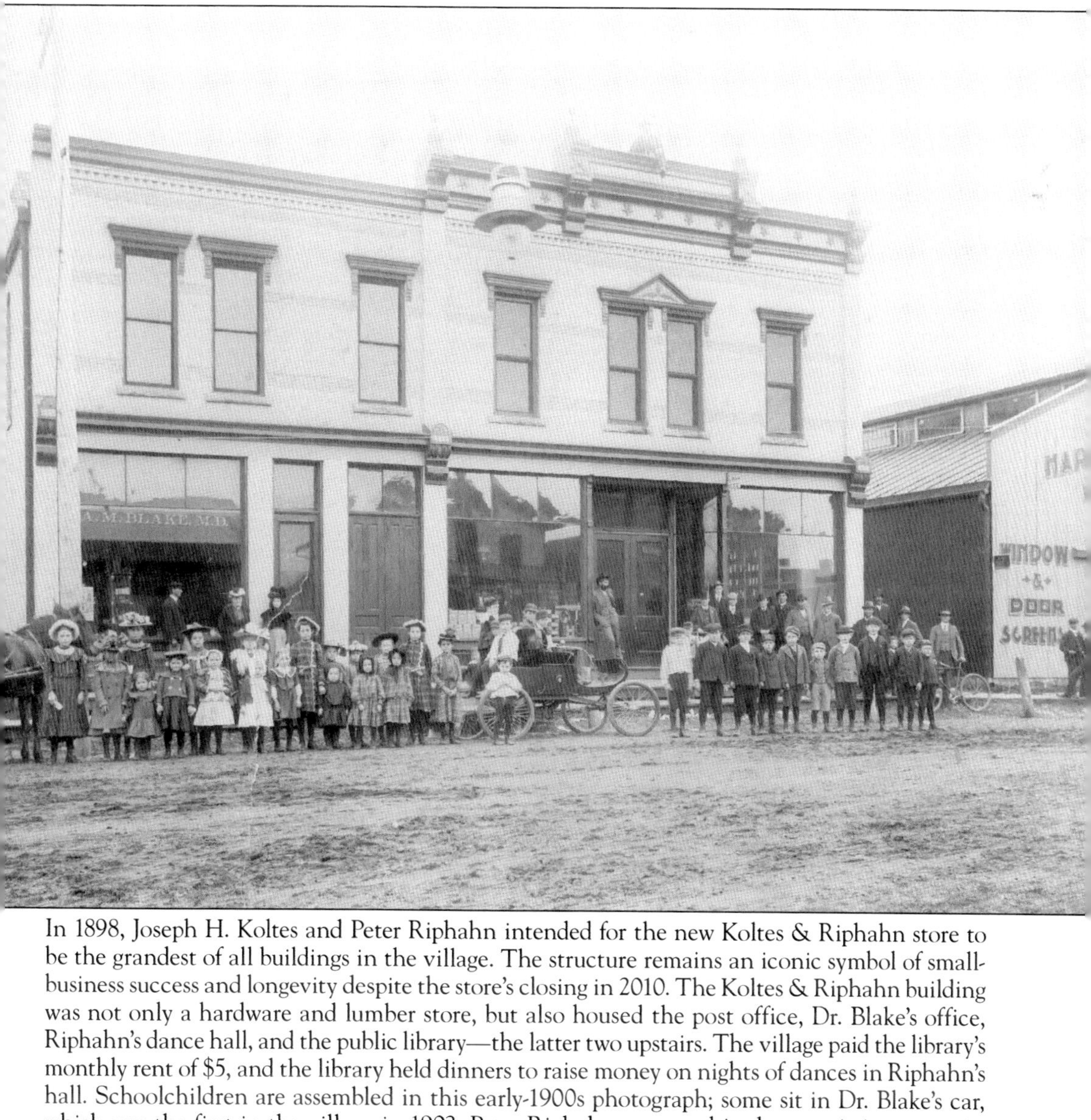

In 1898, Joseph H. Koltes and Peter Riphahn intended for the new Koltes & Riphahn store to be the grandest of all buildings in the village. The structure remains an iconic symbol of small-business success and longevity despite the store's closing in 2010. The Koltes & Riphahn building was not only a hardware and lumber store, but also housed the post office, Dr. Blake's office, Riphahn's dance hall, and the public library—the latter two upstairs. The village paid the library's monthly rent of $5, and the library held dinners to raise money on nights of dances in Riphahn's hall. Schoolchildren are assembled in this early-1900s photograph; some sit in Dr. Blake's car, which was the first in the village in 1902. Peter Riphahn assumes his characteristic posture in the doorway of his mercantile shop and post office, and Joseph Koltes attempts a death-defying trick from the roof. (James P. Koltes.)

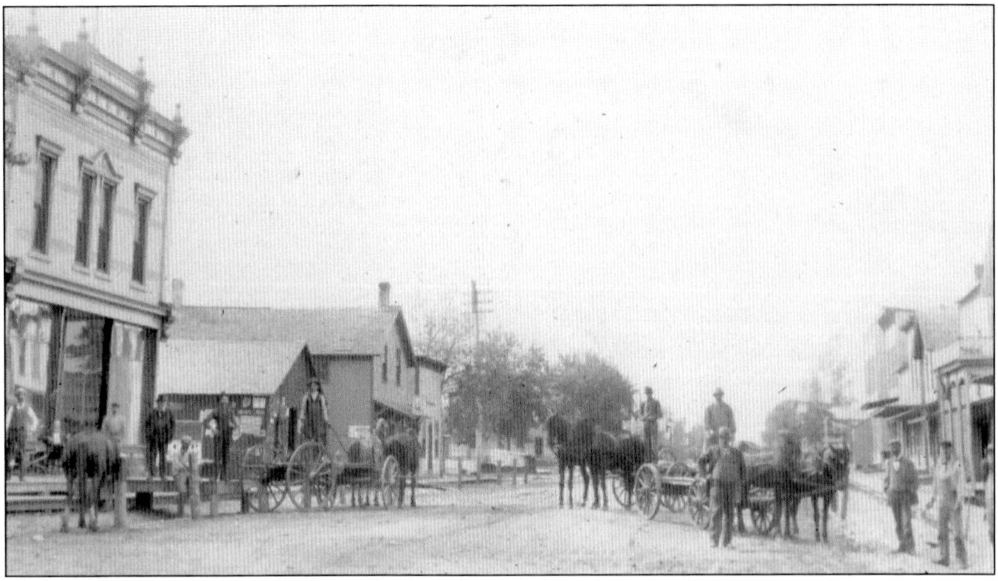

The older wooden Koltes & Riphahn building was replaced with a lumber shed in 1904, as illustrated in this view of Main Street to the west. The boardwalks outside each business were built at varying heights to accommodate different wagons depending on the merchandise that would need to be carried or delivered. (WPL.)

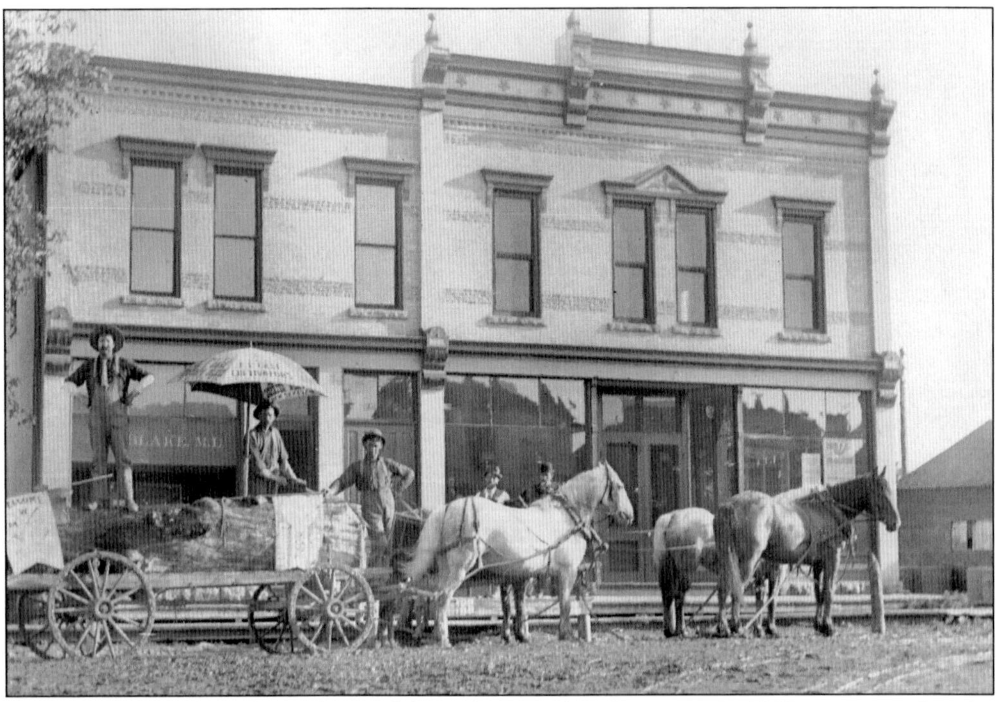

Workers display a large log in front of the Koltes Lumber Company. In 1905, one year after the lumber shed located on the far right was built, Joseph Koltes and Peter Riphahn dissolved their partnership. Riphahn continued the hardware and grocery portion until his retirement when all parts of the business continued under the Koltes name, then passed to Joseph Koltes's sons and eventually to his grandsons. (James P. Koltes.)

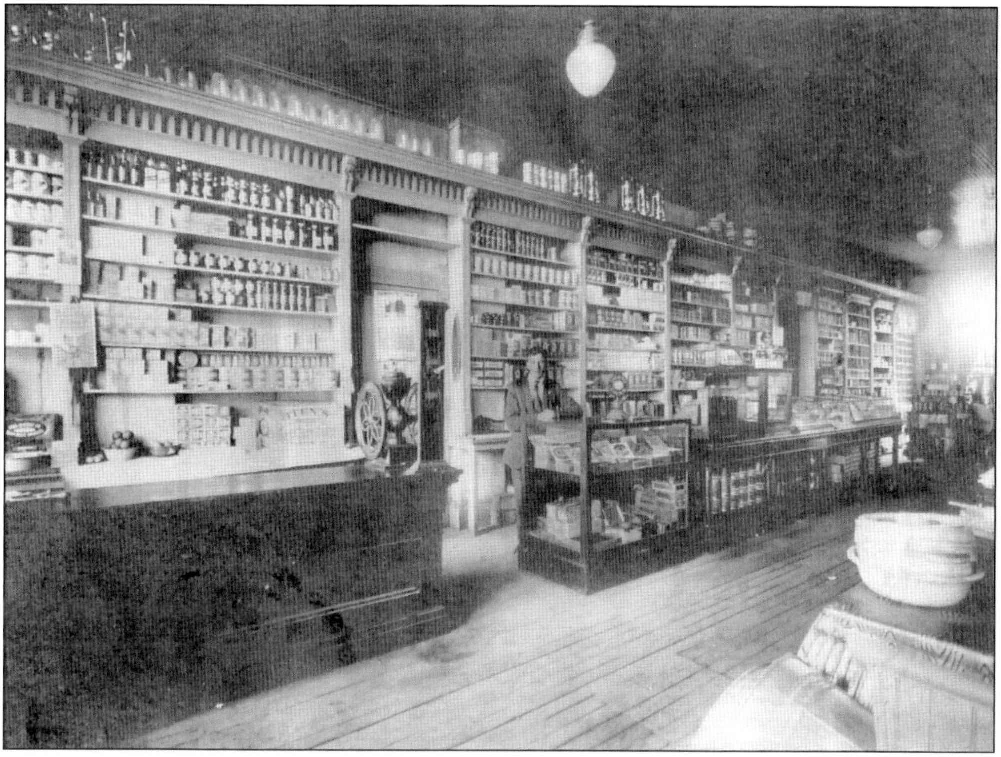

The narrow interior store area pictured was located behind the double wooden doors between Dr. A.M. Blake's office and the Koltes Lumber Company. This photograph was taken some time after Peter Riphahn's retirement, and Martin Kennedy stands behind the counter. Kennedy married J.H. Koltes's daughter Grace. (James P. Koltes.)

Joseph Koltes stands next to the post office, which was housed inside the Koltes & Riphahn store around 1908 or 1909. Riphahn was only the fifth postmaster in Waunakee in 38 years, joining the ranks of Lawrence Freney, Charles Hudson, Jacob Buhlman, and James Clarke. Post offices were political at the time, so the post office location followed the political views of the business owner. (James P. Koltes.)

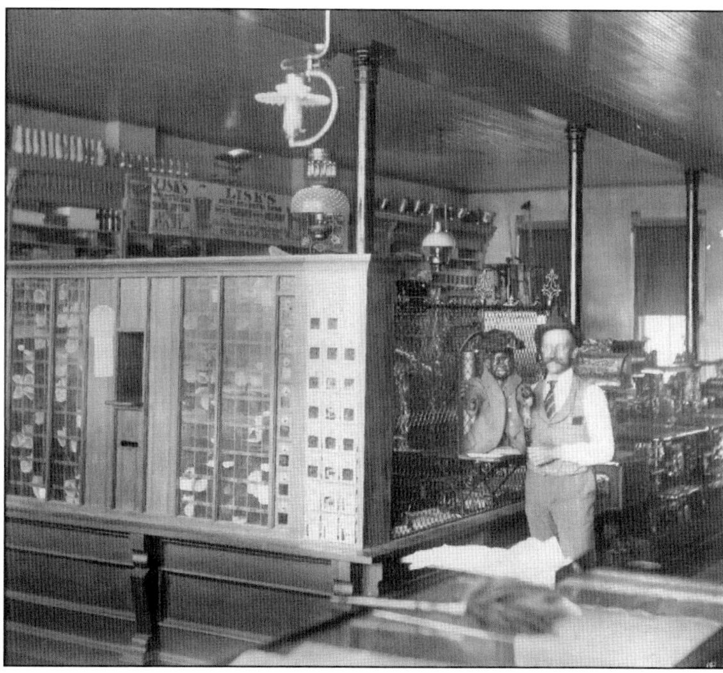

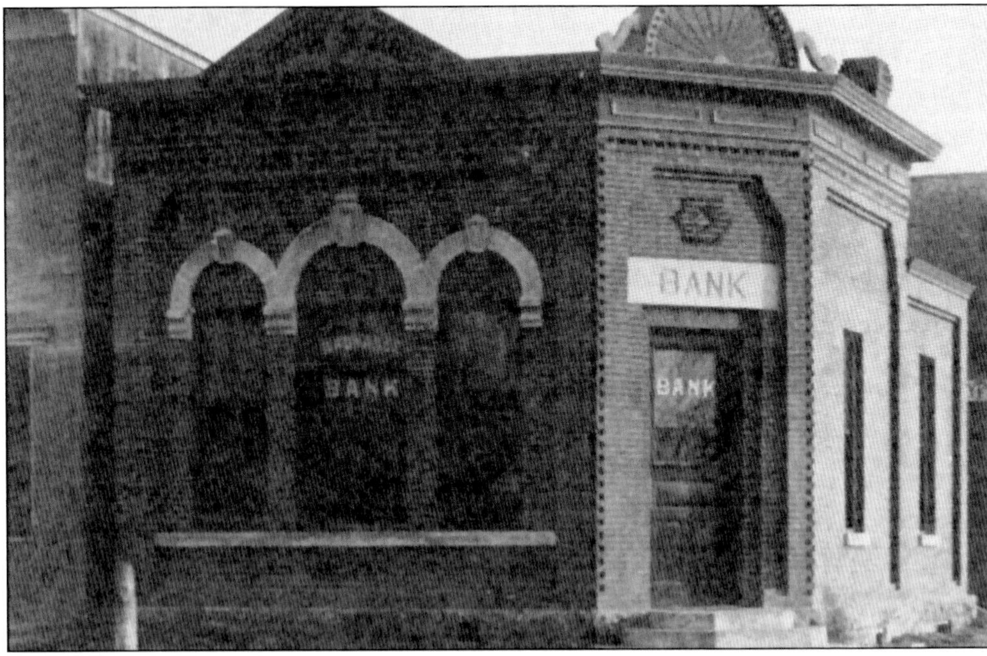

The Waunakee State Bank began as a small brick building on Main and Madison Streets. Ten village residents were involved in forming the bank in 1902 with the O'Malley family being the principal investors. A.P. Kenney was recruited from Ohio to be the cashier, and he remained in the position for 40 years. (WPL.)

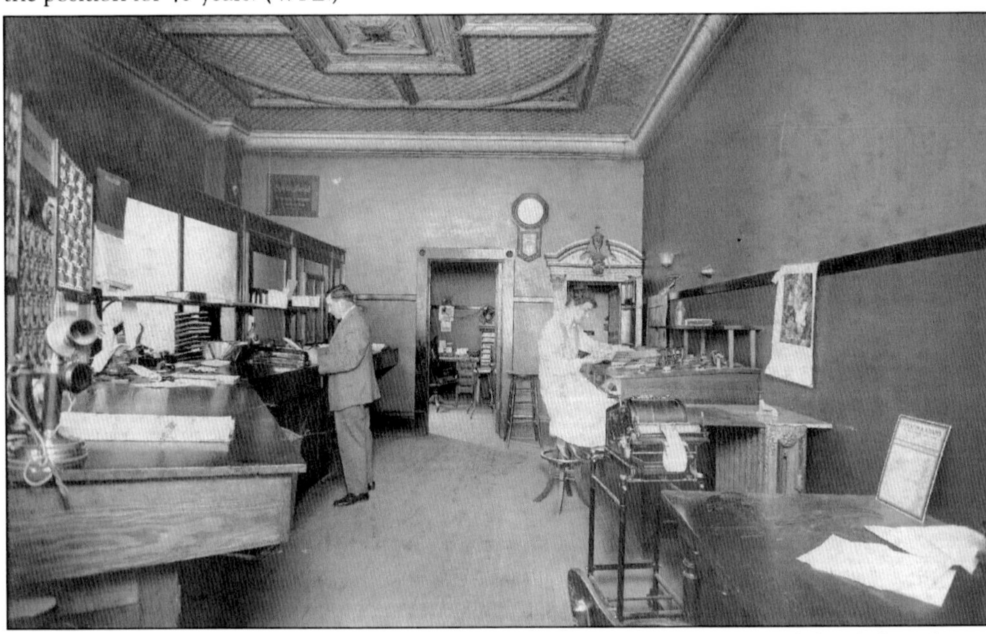

The small bank building was only in business for four years before the board decided to change locations. The large red brick building on Main and South Streets was built in 1908. Charles Hudson's general store was moved back from that location to make room for the new bank. This interior view of Waunakee State Bank features A.P. Kenney (left) and Grace Koltes working in the 1910s. (James P. Koltes.)

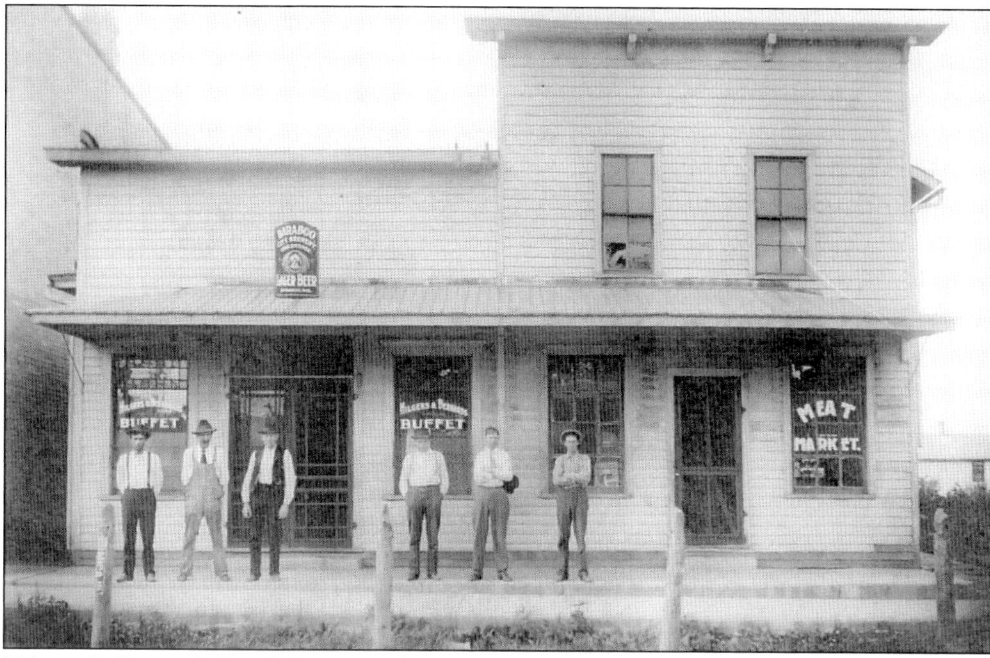

Hilgers & Bernards Bar & Meat Market was one of several taverns in Waunakee at the turn of the century, pictured here in 1909. Standing in front of the business are, from left to right, unidentified, Peter Riphahn, Henry Bernards Sr., Math Hane, Ted Hilgers, and unidentified. The business later became Chambers Bar and then the Gold Nugget. (Paul Bernards.)

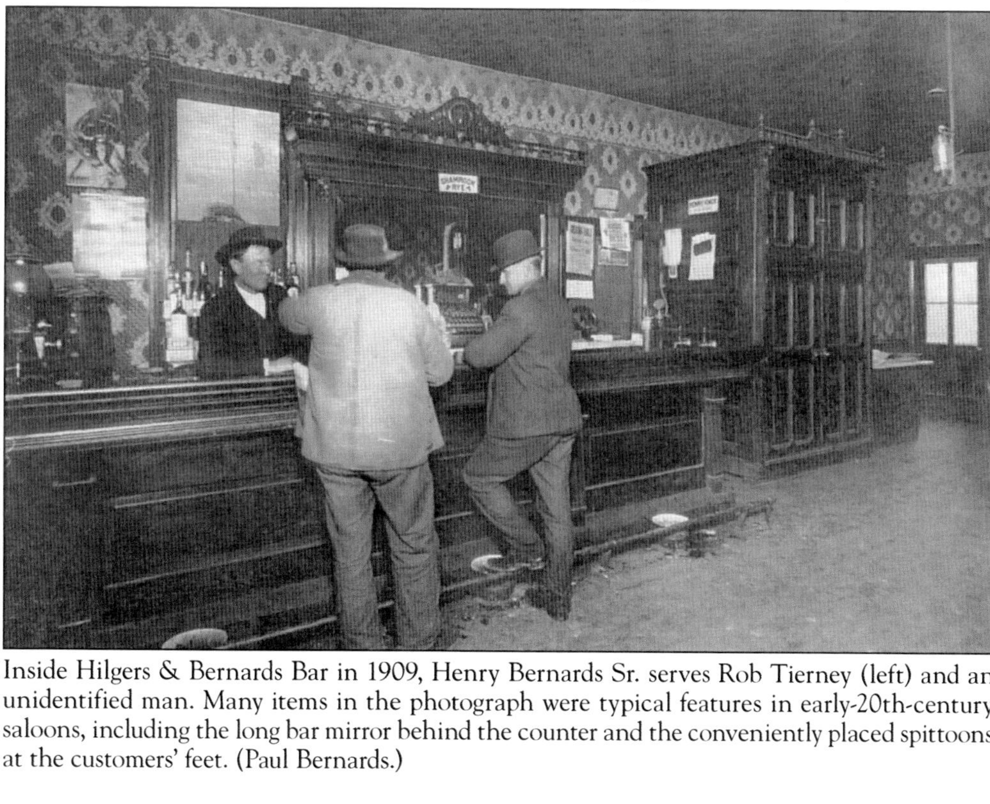

Inside Hilgers & Bernards Bar in 1909, Henry Bernards Sr. serves Rob Tierney (left) and an unidentified man. Many items in the photograph were typical features in early-20th-century saloons, including the long bar mirror behind the counter and the conveniently placed spittoons at the customers' feet. (Paul Bernards.)

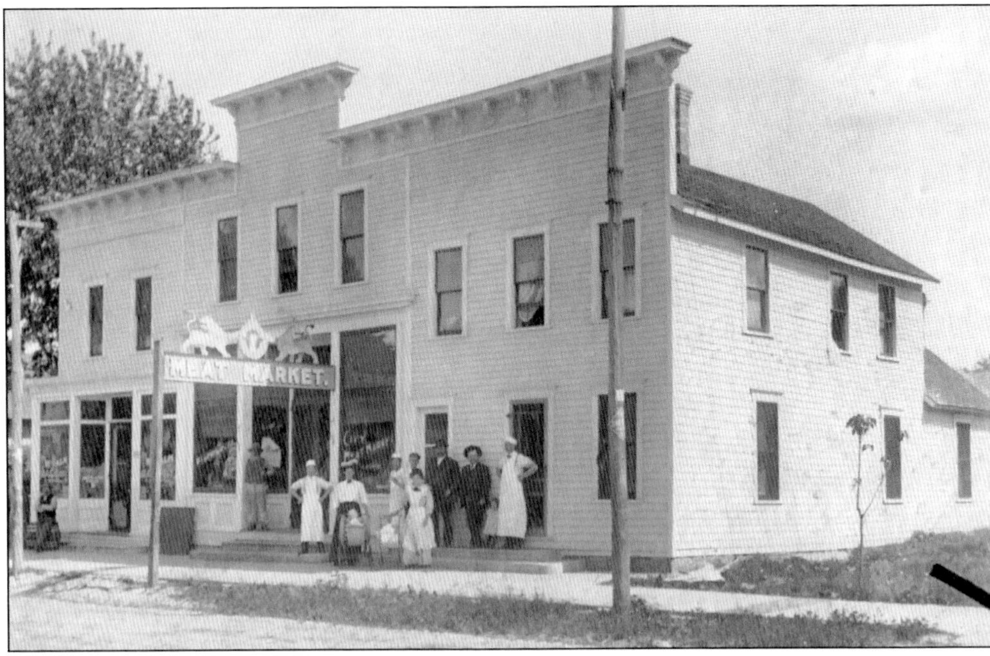

Gathered outside of the Uebersetzig building are owner Peter Uebersetzig (far right) and his daughter Christine (baby buggy), born in 1906. The remaining people are unidentified. Uebersetzig's contained a saloon (left), meat market (middle), and rented retail space (right). There were three apartments upstairs, one with living space for the Uebersetzig family. (Paul Bernards.)

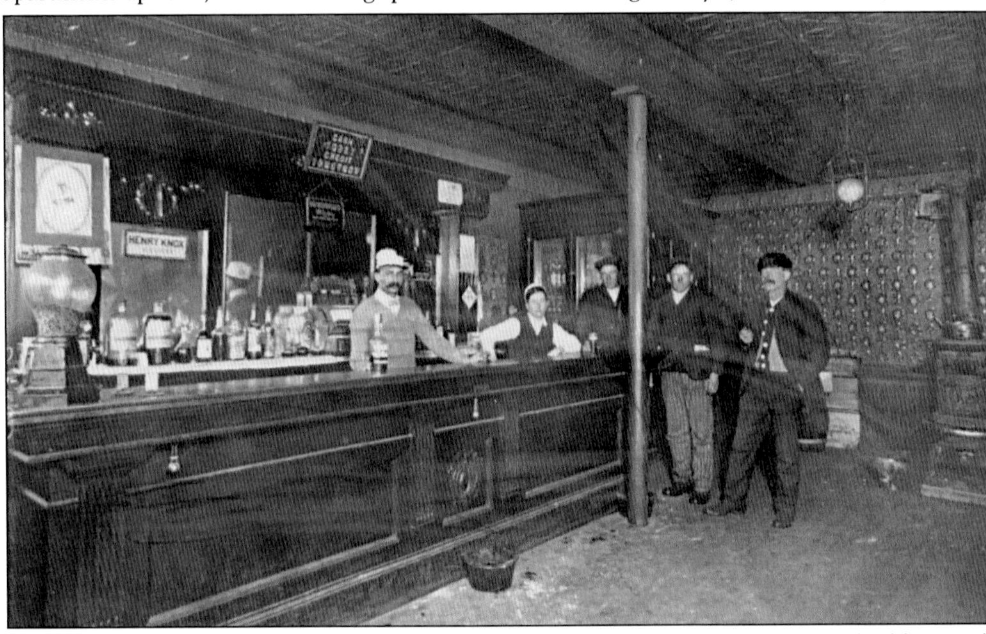

Peter Uebersetzig (far left) stands behind the bar at his saloon in the Uebersetzig building with unidentified others. The business originally belonged to Peter Statz, who started with just a meat market then expanded it in 1898. In 1901, he sold the building, including two acres, a slaughterhouse, tools, and a team of horses, to Peter Uebersetzig for $5,000. In later decades, the outside was renovated leaving little trace of the original design. (Paul Bernards.)

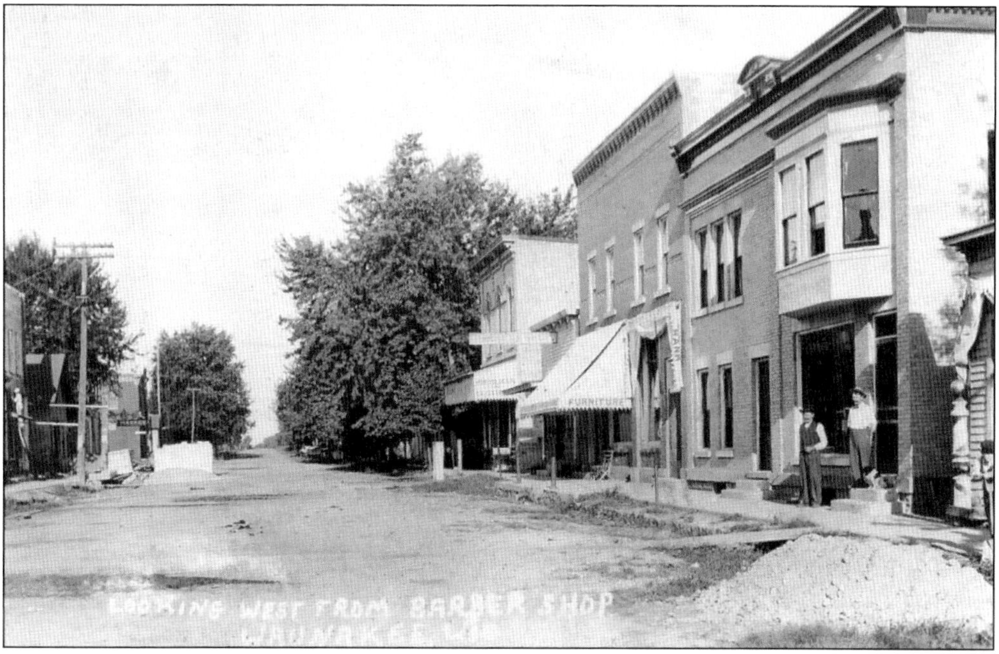

Thriving businesses lining Main Street in 1913 include Uebersetzig Meat Market on the left side of the street with its characteristic lion sign. On the right side of the street are, from left to right, J. Buhlman Clothier, the harness shop, Godfrey and Andrew Schunk's furniture store and bank, and Otto Hohlstein's newly reconstructed barbershop. Many changes are evident from the earlier view of Main Street east of the Buhlman brothers' store, as brick buildings began to replace the original frame structures. (Friends of Schumacher Farm.)

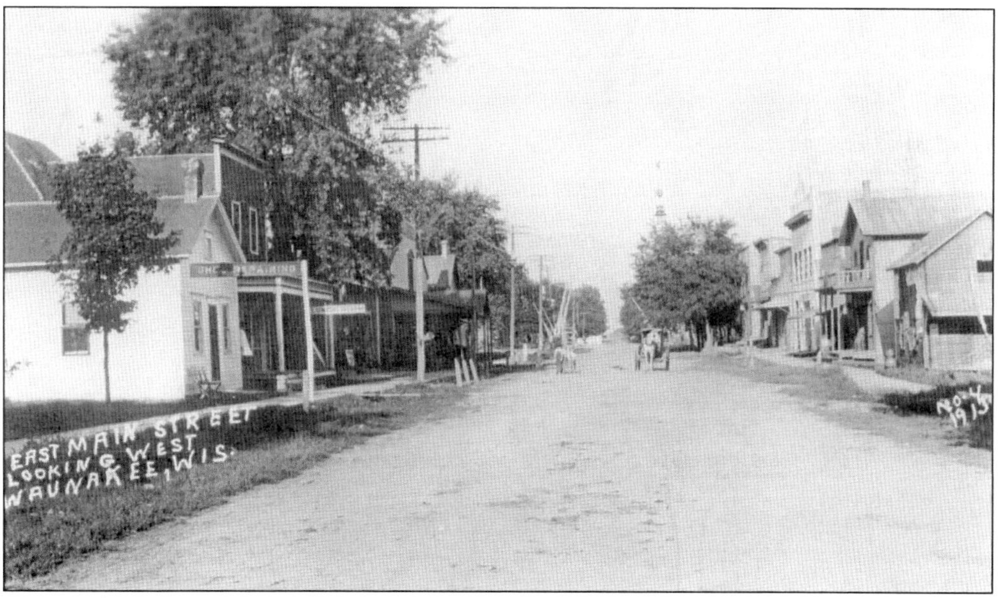

Driving the Fairview Dairy wagon, Victor O'Malley delivers milk on East Main Street in 1913. Fairview Dairy was operated out of the farm owned by Thomas P. O'Malley. The white building on the far left is the first district school, moved to the pictured location by Simon Kirchesch, who operated a shoe repair business there. (Mary Ellen Kearney.)

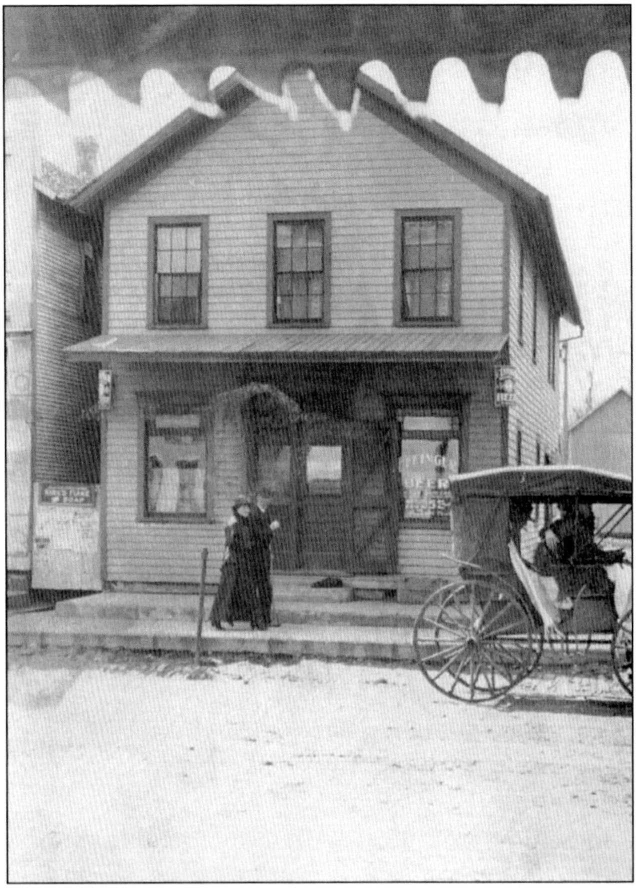

Martha Monks O'Malley and Thomas P. O'Malley walk home from church in the early 1900s. They are passing in front of a tavern on West Main Street that had also been used as the Kuestner family home. The funeral and furniture business across the street was run by the Kuestners and later purchased by Marcel Schwab for his furniture store. (Mary Ellen Kearney.)

Mature trees line West Main Street, changing the landscape looking east in the late 1920s or early 1930s. The tavern and meat market building on the right was later owned by Michael F. Simon Builders and contained their offices, a sample room, and a design center. The company began in Waunakee in 1893 and built a large majority of homes and businesses in the village after that year. (Mary Ellen Kearney.)

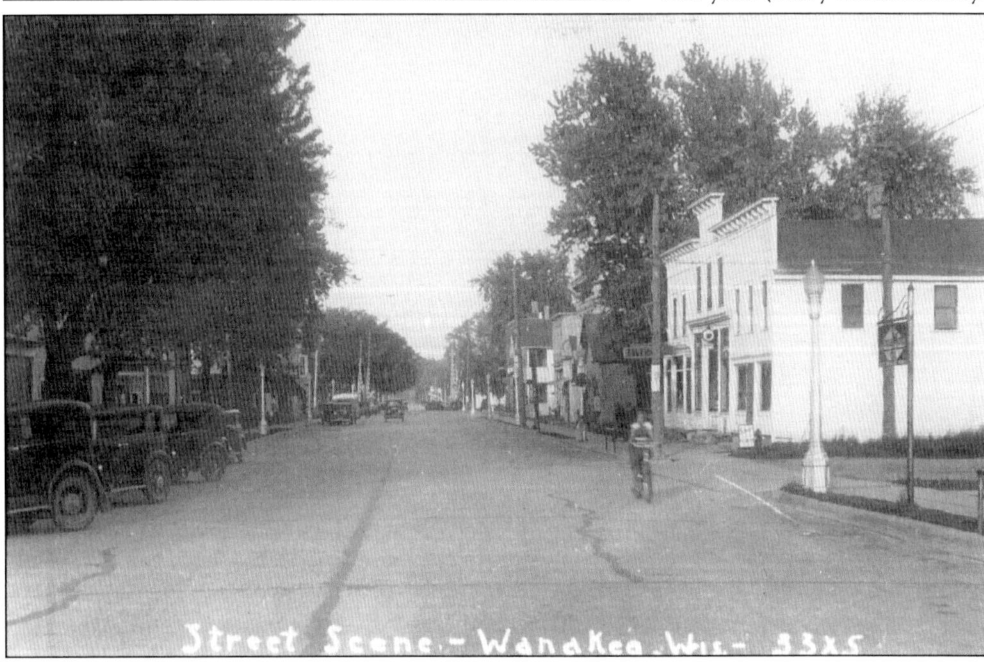

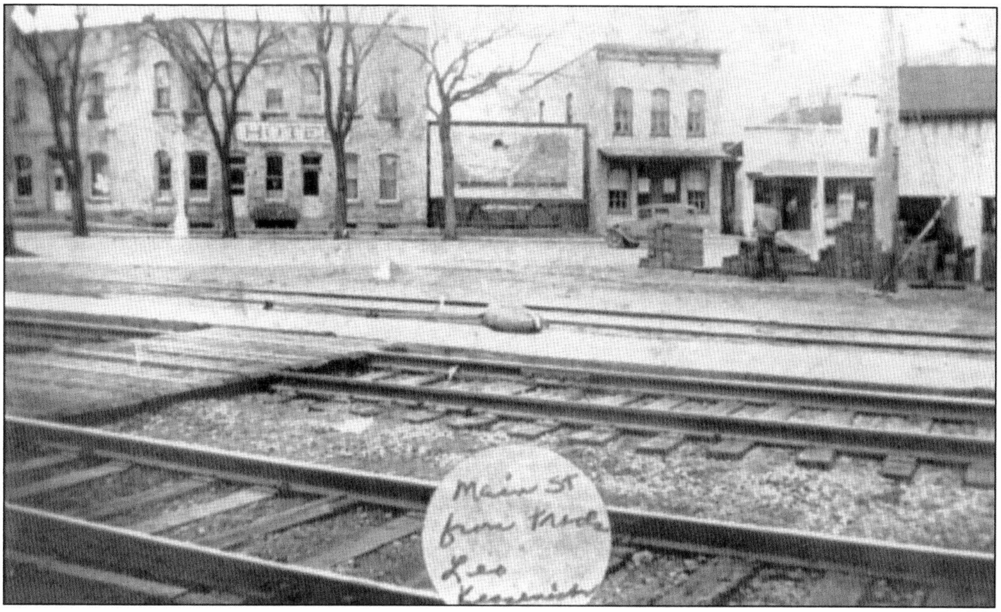

Brausen Hotel (above image, left) occupied land that contained a hotel almost as long as Waunakee was a village. The first hotel on the site was built by E.L. Noyes in the early 1870s. It burned down in the Main Street fire of 1879, and the Noyes family built the brick structure not long after. By 1898, Henry Brausen Sr. had purchased the brick hotel and added on a fancy banquet room and five hotel rooms upstairs. In 1927, when the saloon was closed because of Prohibition, that portion of the hotel was used as the library. The two-story building to the right of the hotel, originally the hall for the International Order of Odd Fellows (IOOF), was bought by the village to house the library after Prohibition ended. The library occupied that space until 1965. Still a thriving business at the time of the parade pictured below in the 1960s or early 1970s, the former Brausen hotel had become Pete Miller's and continued to be a popular gathering spot in the village. (Above, Paul Bernards; below, WPL.)

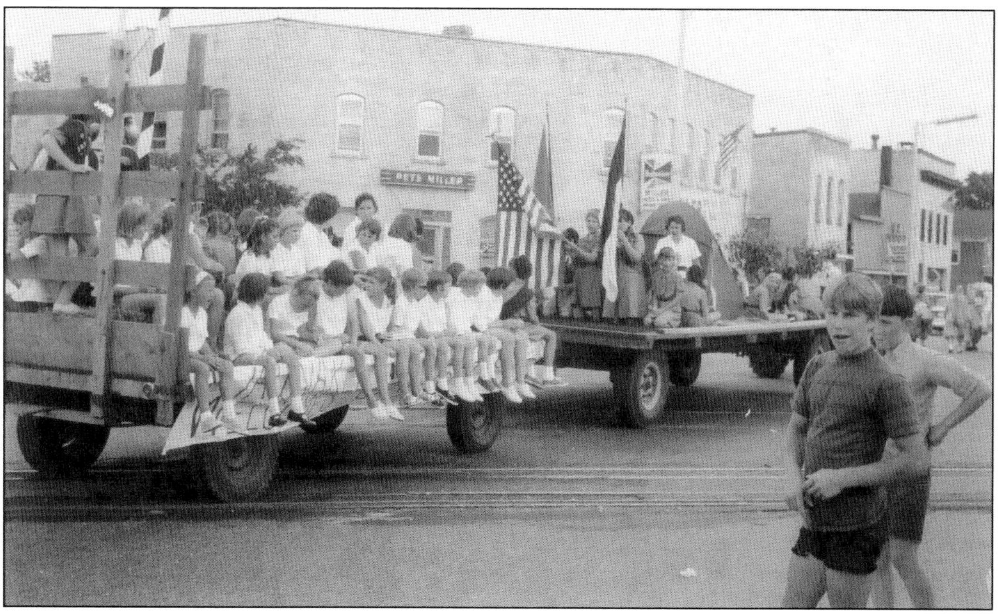

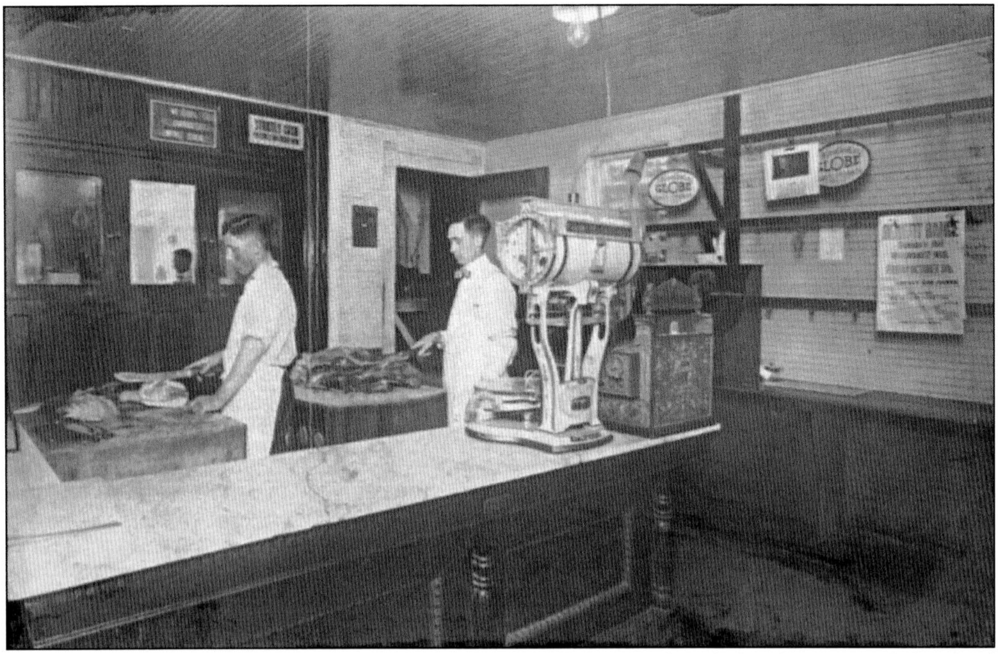

Across Main Street from Otto Hohlstein's barbershop, the Diederich family operated the third meat market in town. Before Diederich's, it was Simonson's, then it was Blau's, and finally Village Market. Based on the advertisement on the wall for a dance at Riphahn's hall, the photograph was likely taken prior to 1931. (Paul Bernards.)

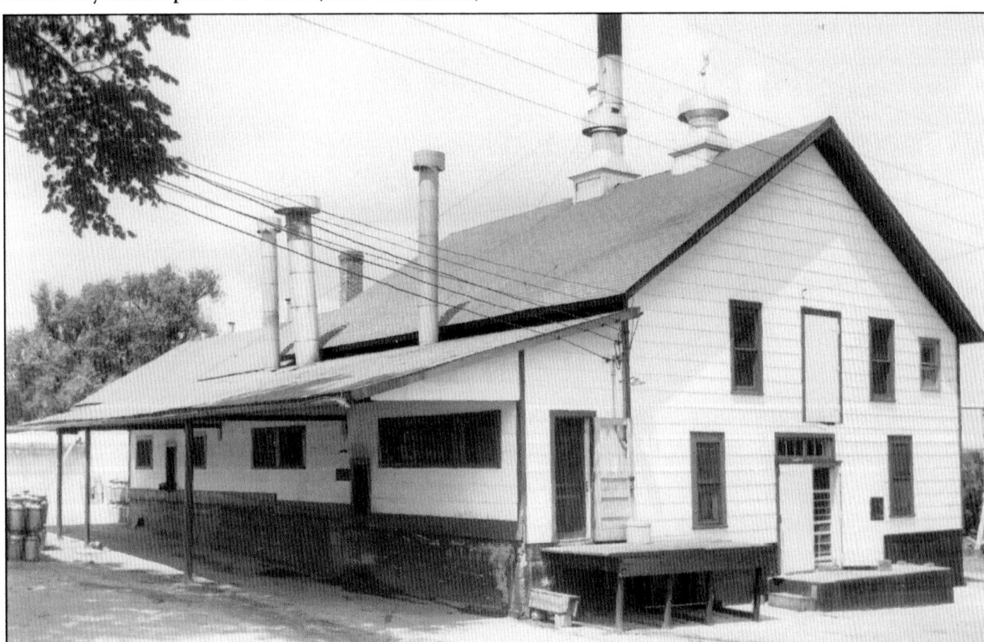

Many of Waunakee's residents still remember when this creamery was located on Madison Street by Six Mile Creek. It was built around 1906 after fire destroyed the previous 1881 building in the same spot. Prior to 1881, a creamery was located in the frame building first erected by Fritz and Jacob Buhlman. (WPL.)

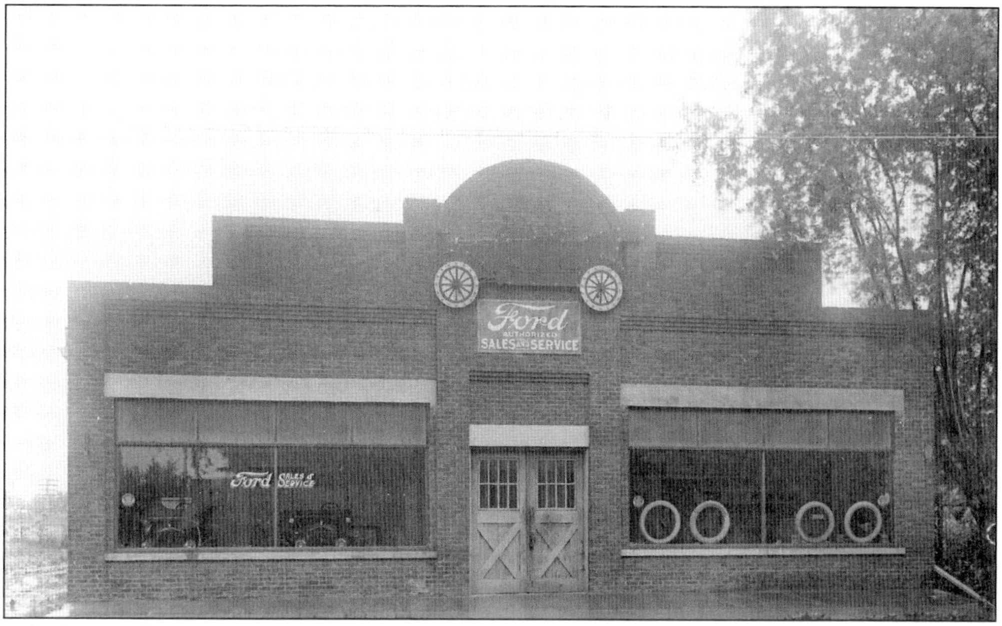

A look into the windows of the A.W. Cameron & Son Ford dealership reveals the early types of cars sold in Waunakee. Before building the location in the photograph in 1917, Cameron used the first floor of the IOOF building. Subsequent owners were Robert Albrecht in 1928 and Bob Scheuerell in the 1950s. Located on the south side of Main Street west of Madison Street, the building housed a bike shop before its demolition. (WPL.)

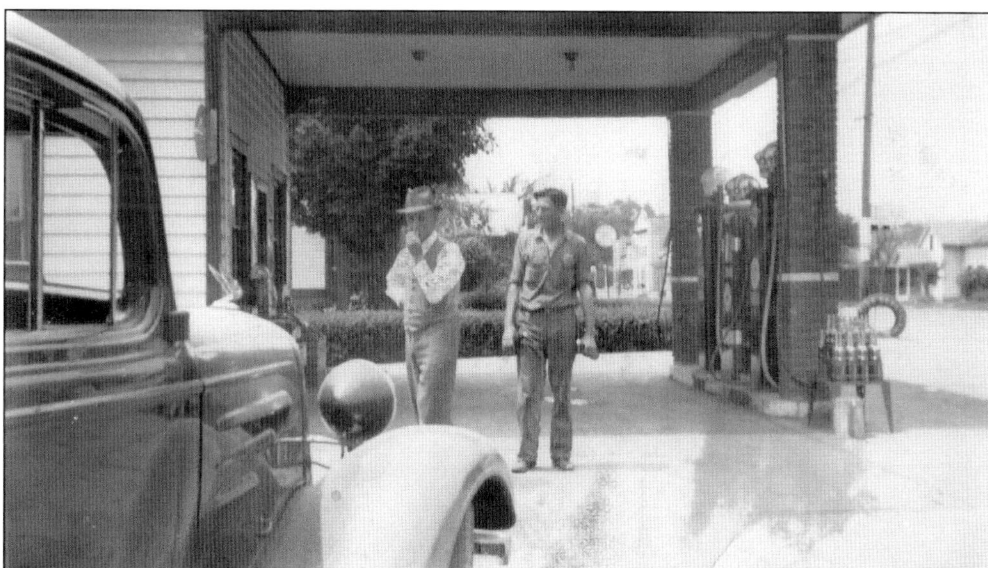

On Main and Madison Streets just east of the Ford dealership, Jinx Corcoran (right) owned the Standard service station. Corcoran's house was between the filling station and the dealership. Corcoran's friend Joseph Koltes (left) ran his lumber business not far west from there. (James P. Koltes.)

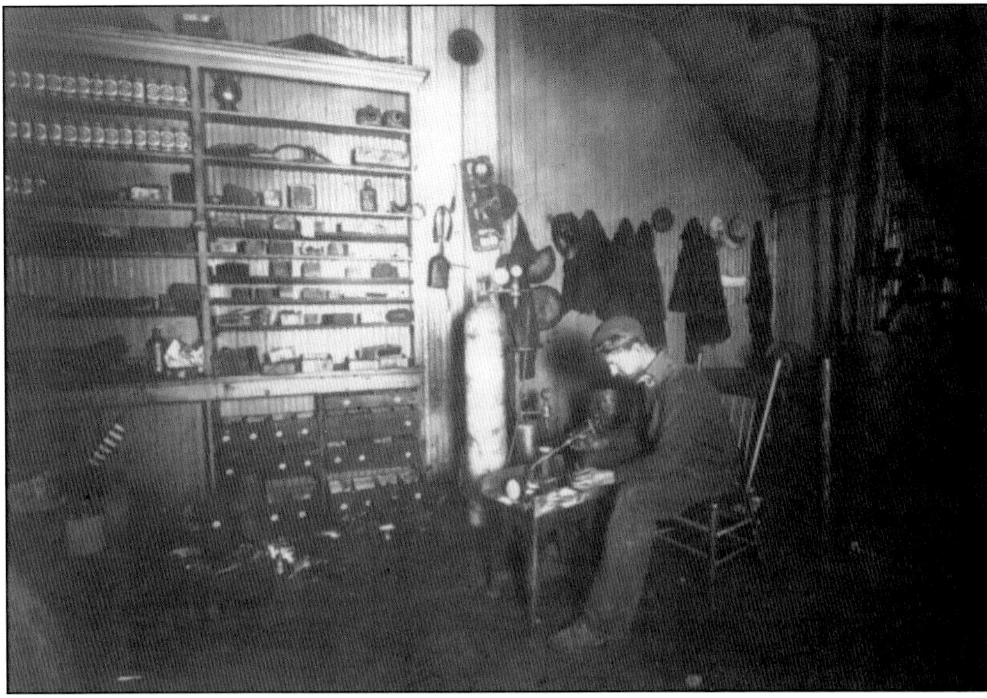

When A.W. Cameron began his Ford dealership in the first floor of the IOOF building, he hired Art Simpson (pictured welding) as a machinist. Simpson later ran the repair department at the 1917 Ford garage. In 1922, Simpson went into business with Sam Blake, son of the local doctor, and patented a battery clip. They called their company Gripx Manufacturing, though the business was not long lived. (WPL.)

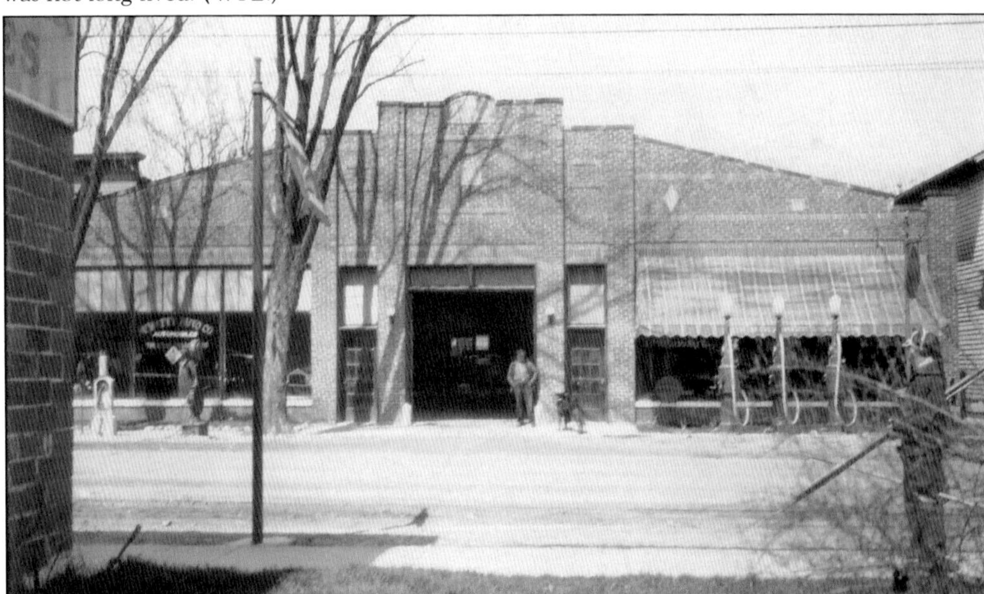

Charles McWatty built his Chevrolet dealership, McWatty Auto Company, in 1924. The building was later Seaman Chevrolet garage, and it was purchased for showroom and warehouse space by Carl F. Statz in 1968. (WPL.)

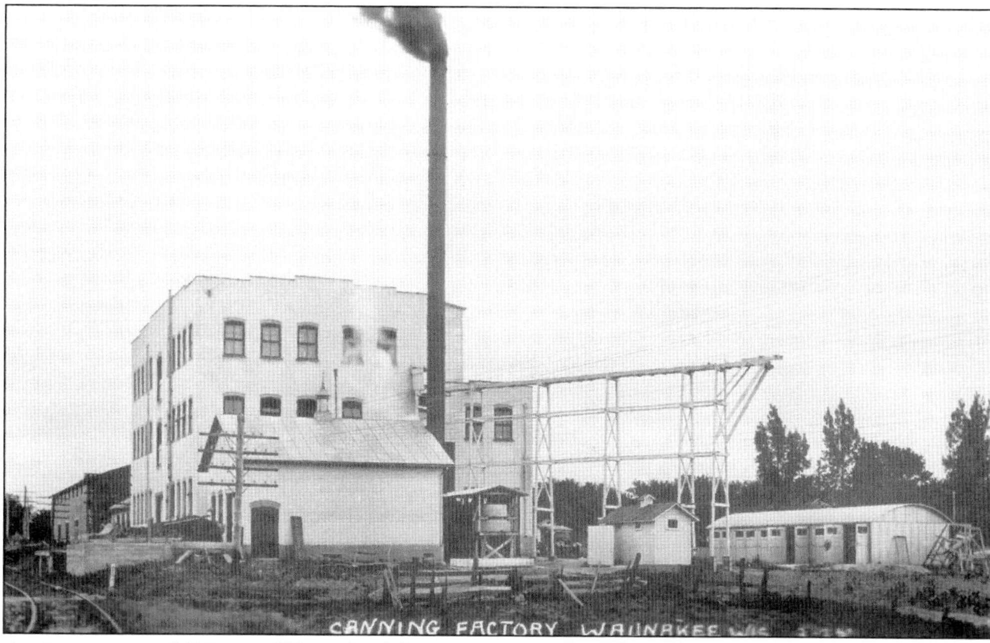

An important addition to Waunakee's businesses was the Waunakee Canning Company built in 1923. Located east of the railroad on East Third Street, the factory provided many jobs packing locally grown peas and corn as well as other food items brought by truck. The cannery operated for almost 75 years; later, it was demolished and the site repurposed for the Waunakee Village Center and senior apartments, aptly named Cannery Row. (James P. Koltes.)

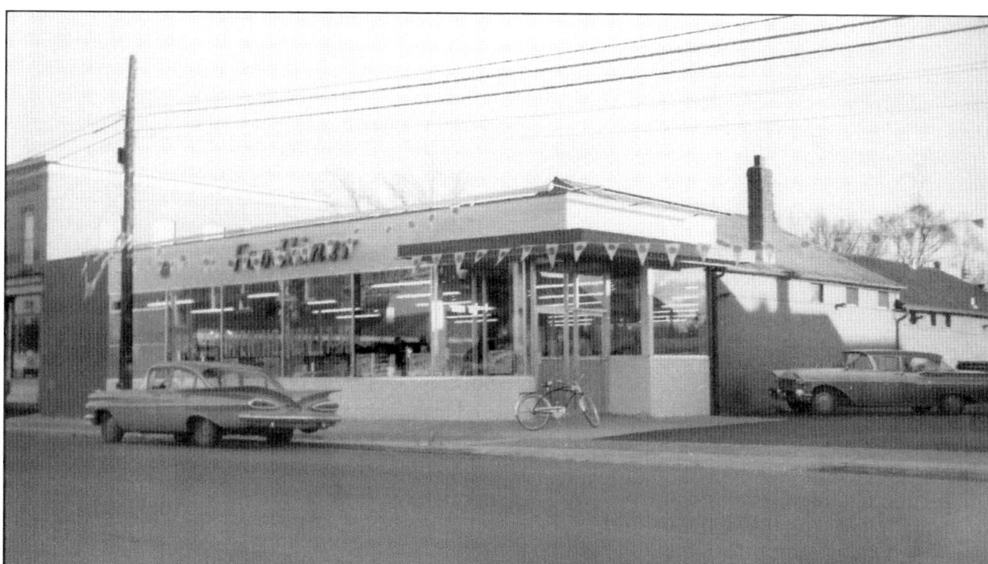

Norbert Miller was nine years old in 1915 when his father, P.B. Miller, first put him to work in their family grocery store. The elder Miller bought the building, which was originally the Math Schmitz general store, in 1911. The younger Miller bought it from his father in 1946. The building was almost entirely lost to a fire in 1949, and within one month Norbert Miller had it completely rebuilt by Simon Builders. The window lettering reads "Grand Opening, Nov. 17." (WPL.)

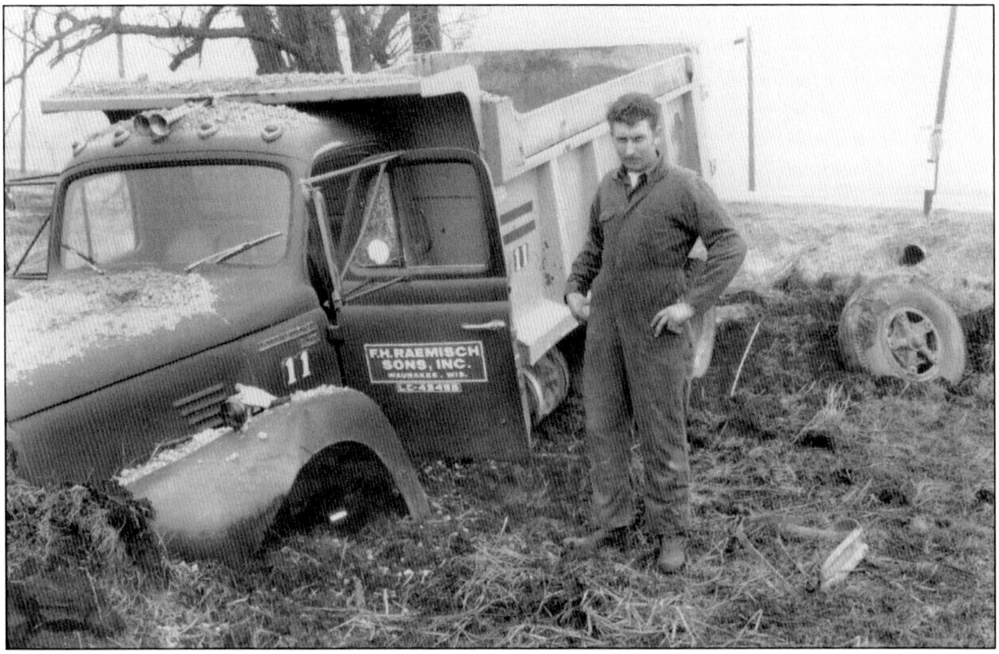

An April 1969 article in the *Waunakee Tribune* described how truck driver Dennis Tuschen of Sun Prairie lost control of his F.H. Raemisch & Sons truck while driving on Easy Street north of Waunakee. Raemisch's business evolved from threshing in the 1920s to road construction and excavating, and its location was moved from Springfield Corners to Waunakee in 1946. (WPL.)

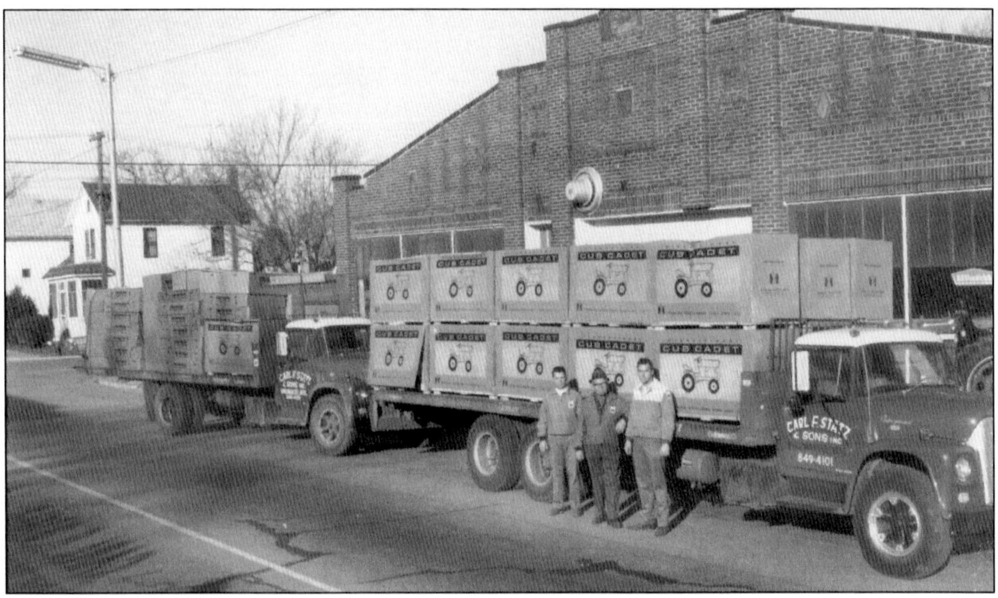

By the time this photograph was taken in 1969, the Schunk & Flatman building was gone, and Carl F. Statz & Sons had adopted the old Chevrolet garage to house excess merchandise and the showroom for their International Harvester franchise, which Carl F. Statz purchased in 1931. Their main office and the parts department were located across the street in the old bank building. From left to right, Ron, Carl F., and Ken Statz stand in front of a large shipment of riding lawn mowers. (WPL.)

Three

FARMING

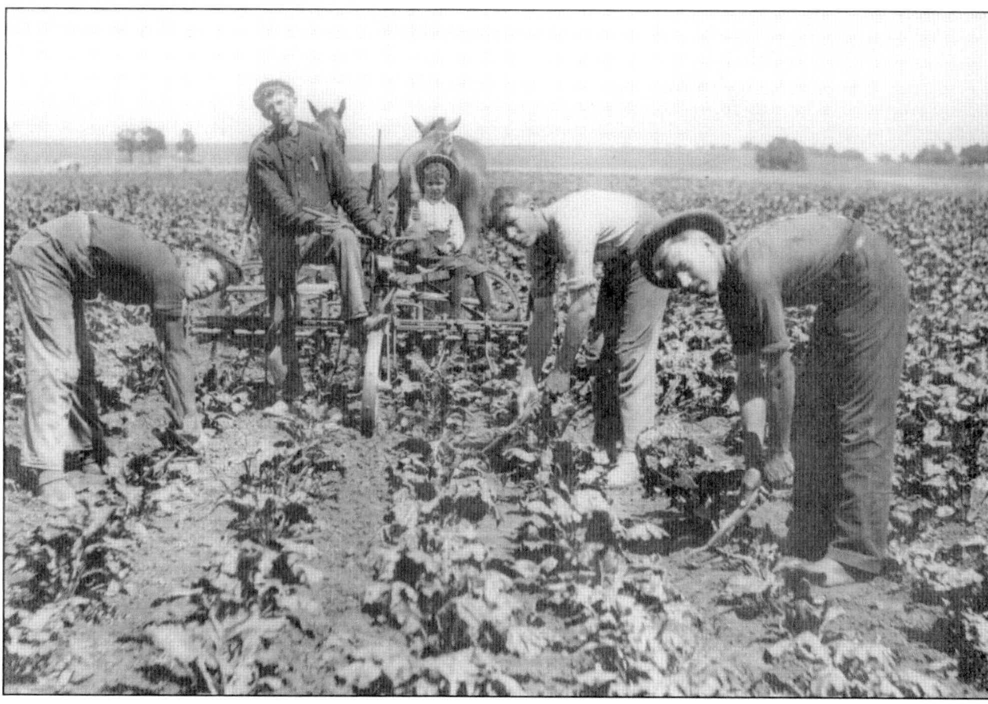

In July 1909 when this photograph was taken, sugar beet farming could be strenuous in the Wisconsin midsummer heat. Sugar beets were a popular commodity, and Charles McWatty capitalized on it by contracting with farmers to grow the beets on their land. Most of the steps involved in sugar beet production required heavy manual labor, and the workers pictured display many of the various hand tools used. (WPL.)

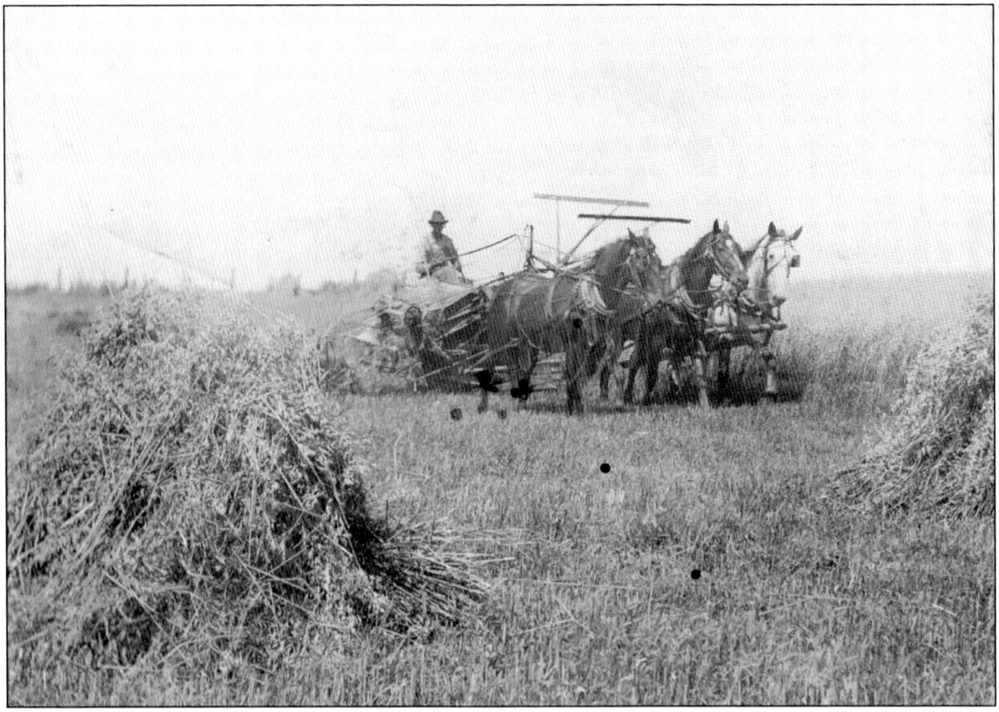

Charles McWatty and his team of horses pull a binder to cut and gather grain. Six to eight bundles of grain from the binder would be collected in the field by hand into shocks (as shown), with one bundle on top to protect from the elements. Then the shocks would be gathered into huge piles until the grain could be threshed. (WPL.)

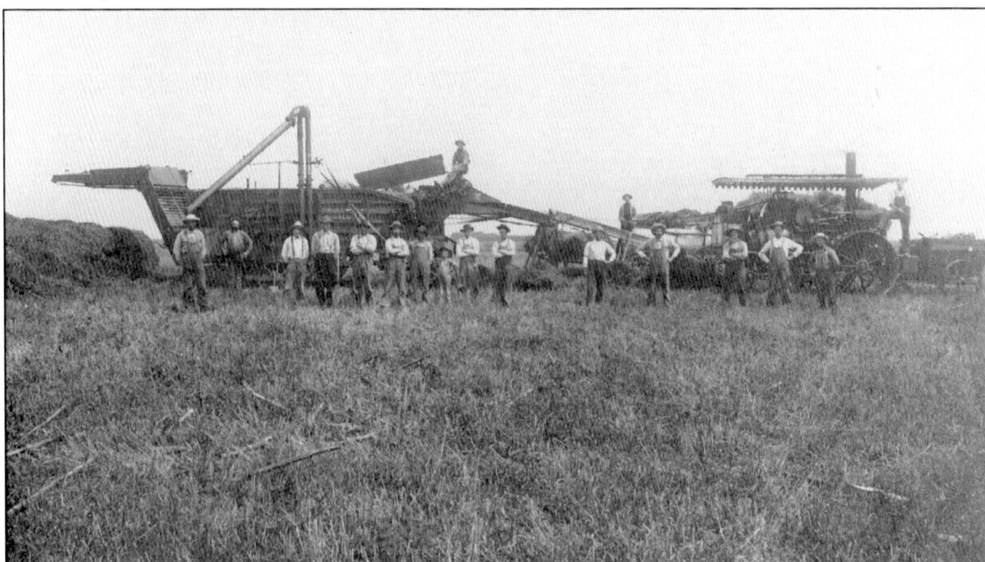

The people in this photograph are unidentified, but they represent one of the many area threshing crews. The crews would be sent out with large steam-powered threshers to area farms where the stacks of grain could be separated into kernels and straw plus chaff. This action was done directly in the fields starting in the 1920s. (WPL.)

Sitting on the steam engine in 1925 are F.C. Raemisch and some of his crew. Threshing was described as a community event where threshers would be sent from farm to farm until all the grain was separated. In 1916, one Westport farmer recorded paying Raemisch $18.78 for threshing oats and barley. (Hazel R. Zimbric.)

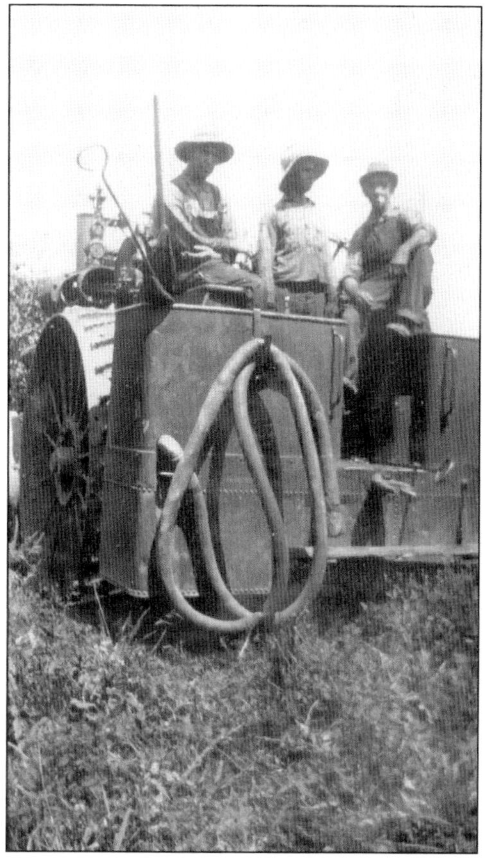

Part of Henry Schumacher's tobacco harvest hangs from a scaffold wagon at Schumacher Farm. The tobacco could be transported on the wagon from field to tobacco shed, or it could be partially cured in the shed and then transferred to the wagon to complete the curing process. Tobacco sheds were common in the township with their open side vents to cure the hanging plants. In 1905, over 523,000 pounds of tobacco were produced in Westport Township. (Friends of Schumacher Farm.)

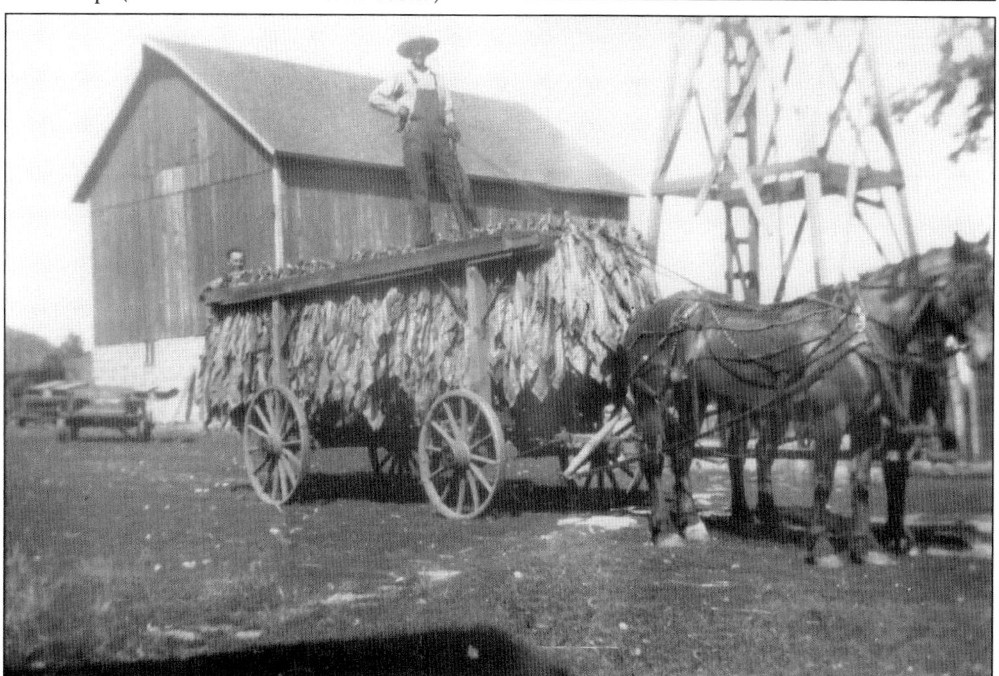

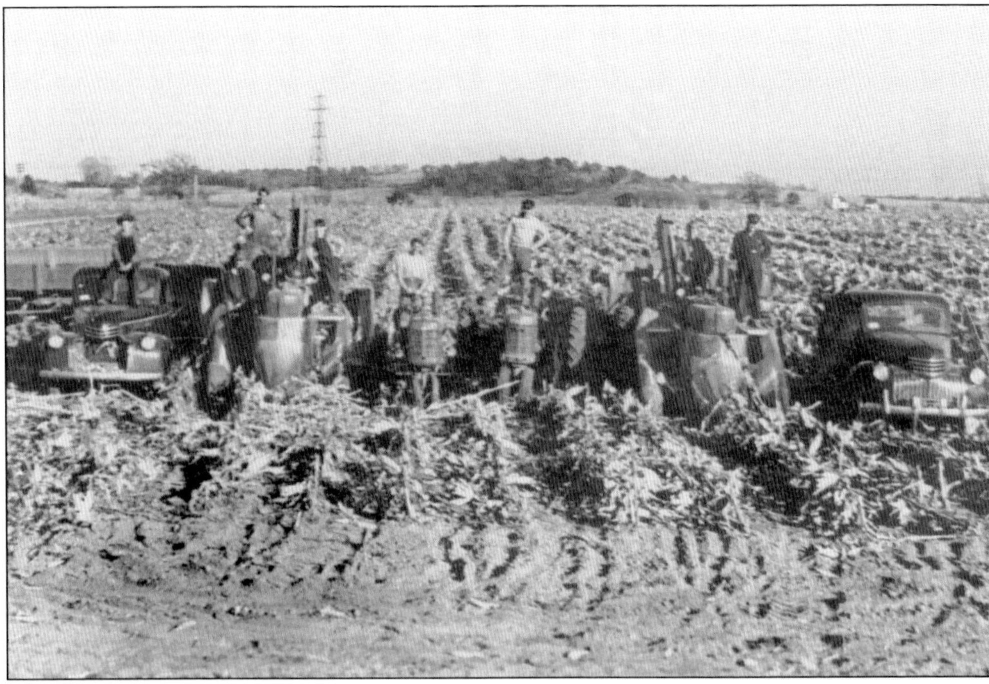

The only information accompanying this photograph reads, "Silo filling." The farm probably belonged to the Fisher or McCloskey families of Westport. Like the methods used by the binders in the grain fields, these workers have cut and bundled the corn, preparing to transport it back to the farm to be placed in the silo. (Kennedy family.)

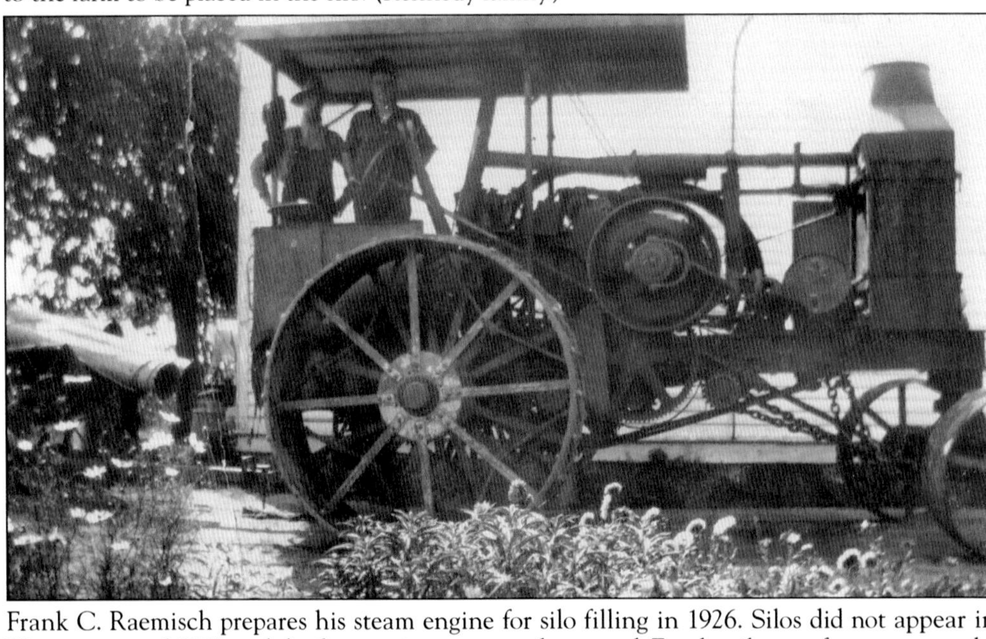

Frank C. Raemisch prepares his steam engine for silo filling in 1926. Silos did not appear in Wisconsin until 1877, and the first versions were underground. For the silage to ferment properly, it requires no air and the perfect amount of moisture in the corn. With the advent of silos and year-round corn storage, farmers were able to feed their dairy cows through the winter, allowing the cows to continue producing milk. (Hazel R. Zimbric.)

Four

CHURCHES

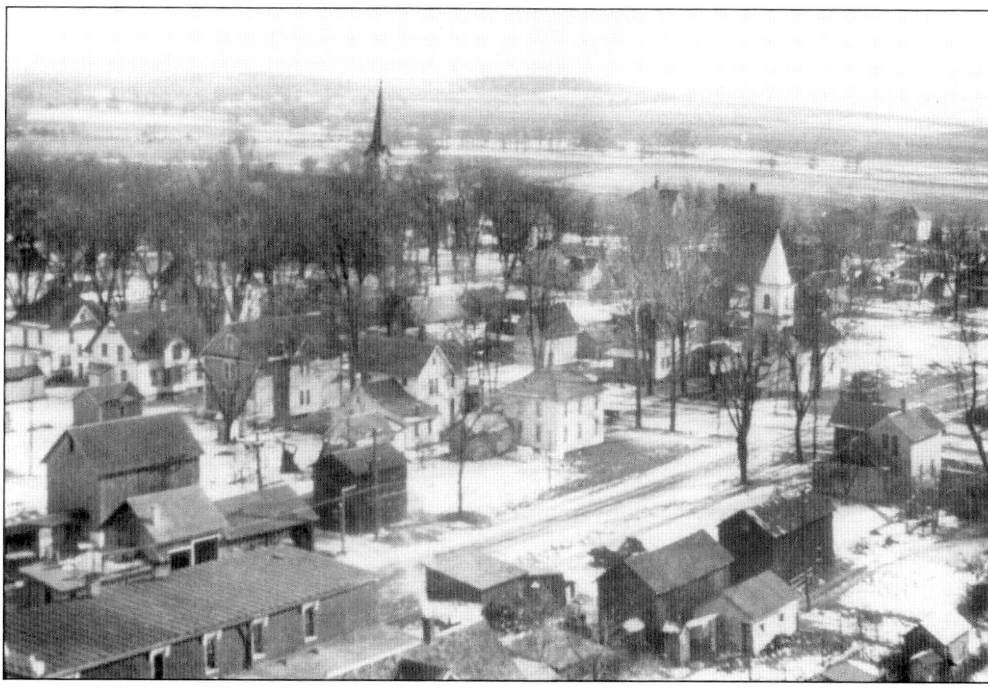

A wintery 1932 view from the water tower features Waunakee's prominent church steeples rising above the bare trees. The white steeple on the right is the Presbyterian church on Second and Fish Streets, and the stone-and-shingle spire at left center is St. John the Baptist Church on Third and South Streets. In Waunakee's early days, church congregations worshipped in barns, the district school, or members' homes. (WPL.)

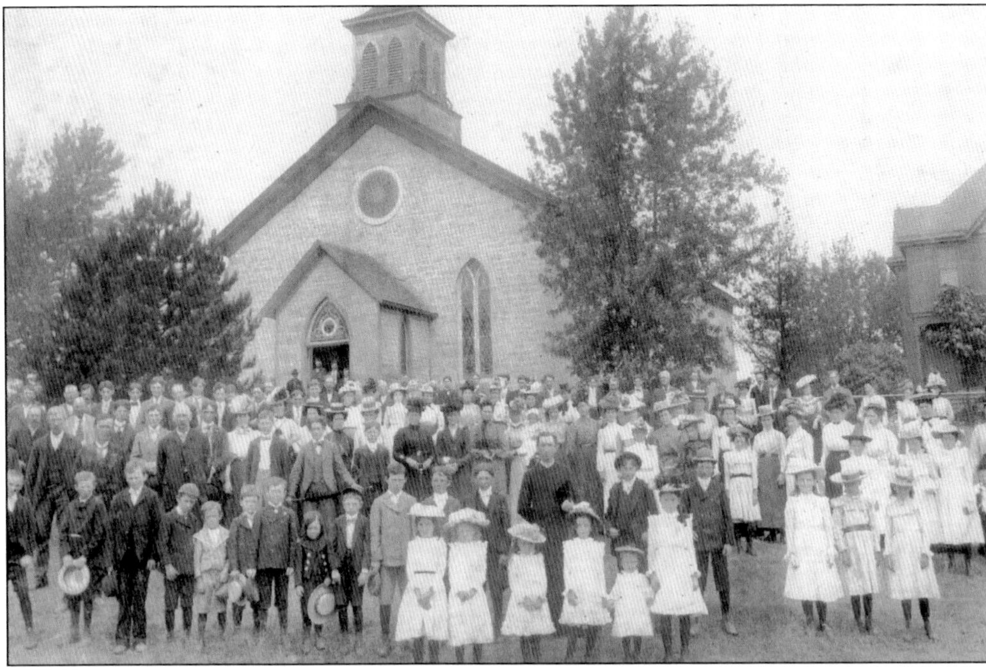

Parishioners of St. Mary of the Lake, Westport, gather outside the Roman Catholic church in 1900. The predominantly Irish congregation dates back to the 1850s when Rev. Etschmann, a missionary priest, would say Mass in members' homes. In 1866, Patrick Tierney donated $100 for four acres of land on which to build a new church. Michael O'Malley brought in limestone from his quarry, and the church was finished in 1869. (Kennedy family.)

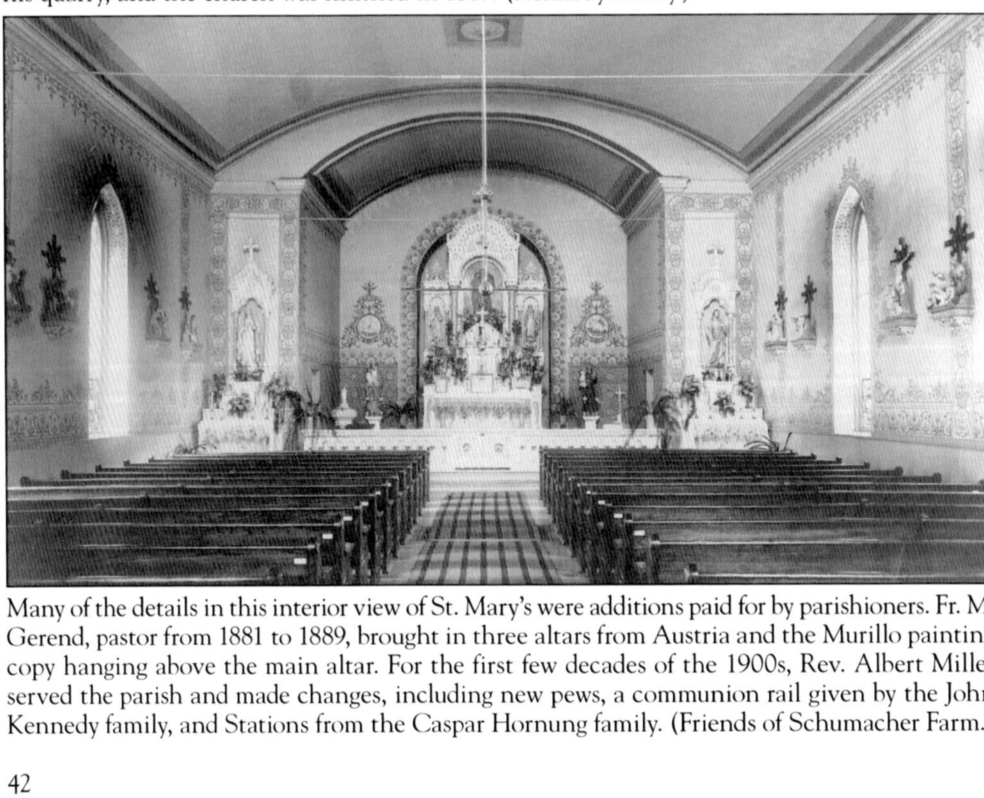

Many of the details in this interior view of St. Mary's were additions paid for by parishioners. Fr. M. Gerend, pastor from 1881 to 1889, brought in three altars from Austria and the Murillo painting copy hanging above the main altar. For the first few decades of the 1900s, Rev. Albert Miller served the parish and made changes, including new pews, a communion rail given by the John Kennedy family, and Stations from the Caspar Hornung family. (Friends of Schumacher Farm.)

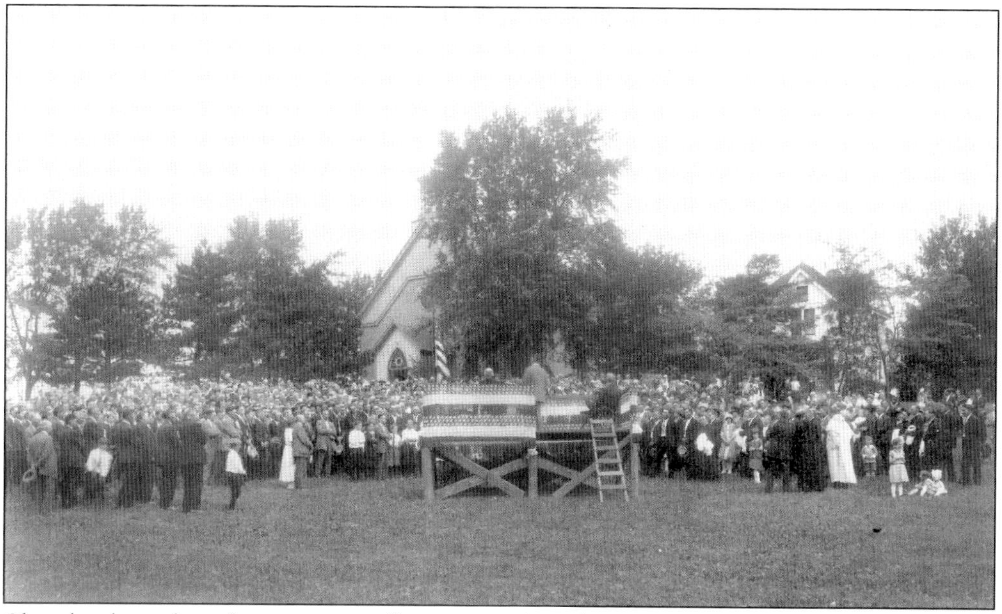

Churches hosted yearly picnics as well as some political events, as seen at St. Mary of the Lake where church members gather for a political rally featuring Wisconsin governor John J. Blaine as the speaker. Blaine proposed the 21st amendment to repeal the 18th amendment that instituted Prohibition. He was governor of Wisconsin from 1920 to 1926, and he died in 1934. (Friends of Schumacher Farm.)

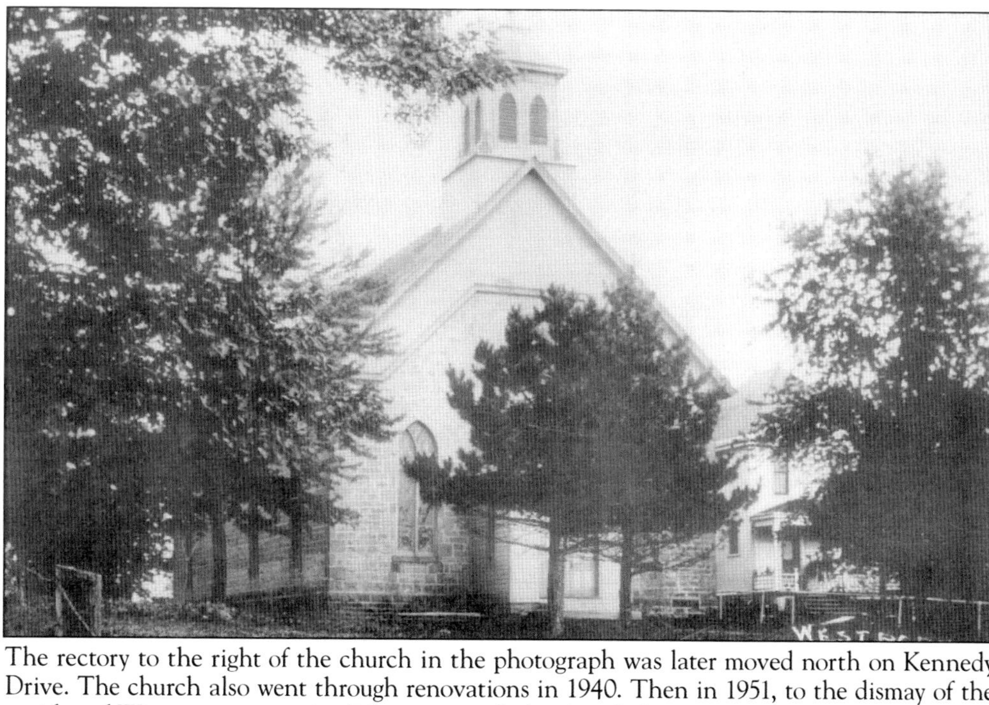

The rectory to the right of the church in the photograph was later moved north on Kennedy Drive. The church also went through renovations in 1940. Then in 1951, to the dismay of the parish and Westport community, lightning struck the church during an early-morning July storm. After the fire, only the limestone shell remained. At the time, 85 families considered St. Mary of the Lake their church home. (Kennedy family.)

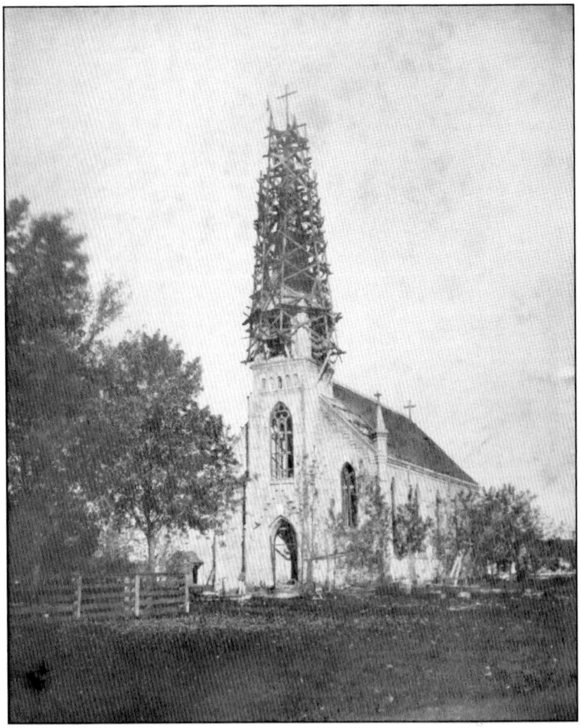

As more German settlers moved into the area, there became a need for a German mission Roman Catholic Church in Waunakee. The parish of 19 families began in 1874 in a wooden church with services twice a month, then incorporated in 1885, and under leadership of Fr. M. Gerend planned to build a stone church. Like St. Mary's, St. John the Baptist Church was built with local quarry stone. This photograph was taken prior to November 1887 when the spire was completed. (St. John the Baptist parish.)

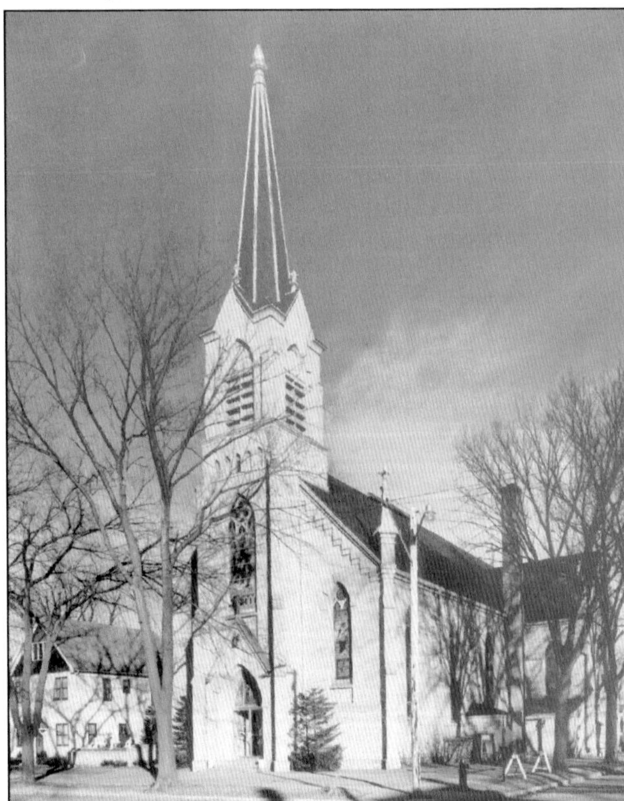

The finished St. John's church was dedicated July 4, 1888. The white rectory north of the church was built in 1889 for Father Siepker and was eventually replaced by the house in this later view. The original 19 families had grown to 125 by 1899. Renovations were made to the church in 1906, including adding the side wings and a choir loft. (St. John the Baptist parish.)

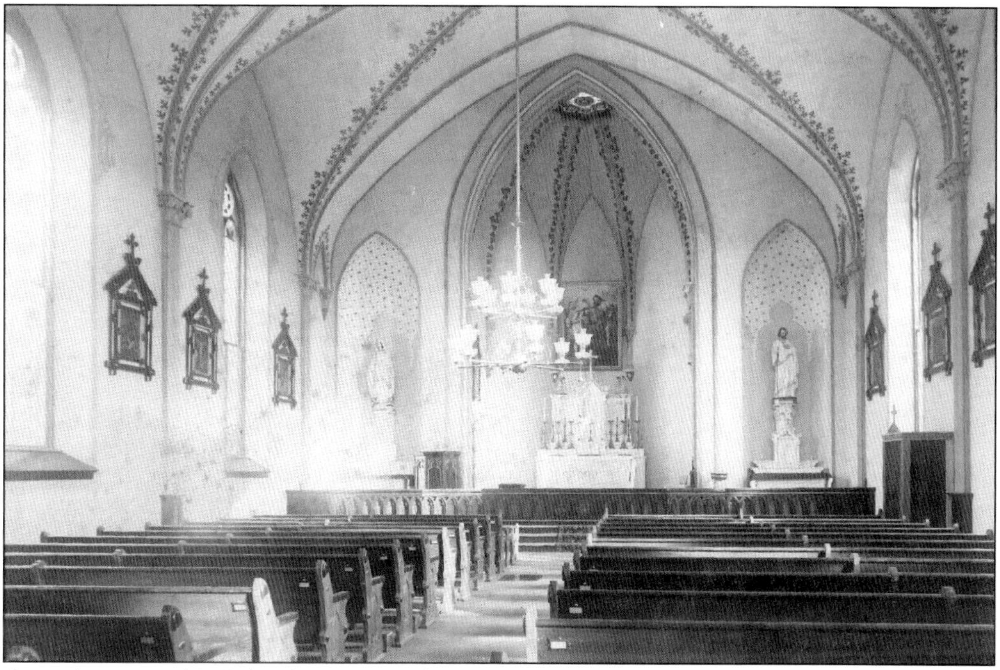

Once the spire of St. John the Baptist Church was finished in 1887, stained-glass windows were brought in from Germany, and local residents helped adorn the interior. The oil painting above the altar, titled *The Baptism of Christ by St. John*, and frescoes were painted by Eben Plackett, a talented young man from Vienna Township. (WPL.)

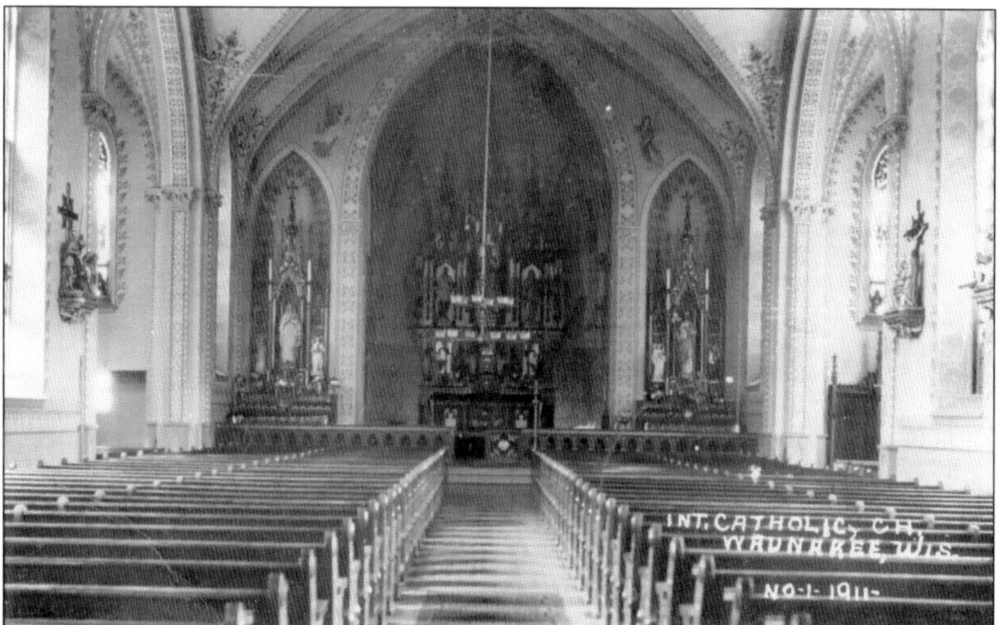

By 1911, few of the original details inside St. John's remained. New statuary, Stations of the Cross, and altars graced the interior, and Eben Plackett's frescoes had been painted over with more elaborate decor. The side wings added a few years prior are visible on the right and left sides of the photograph. (St. John the Baptist parish.)

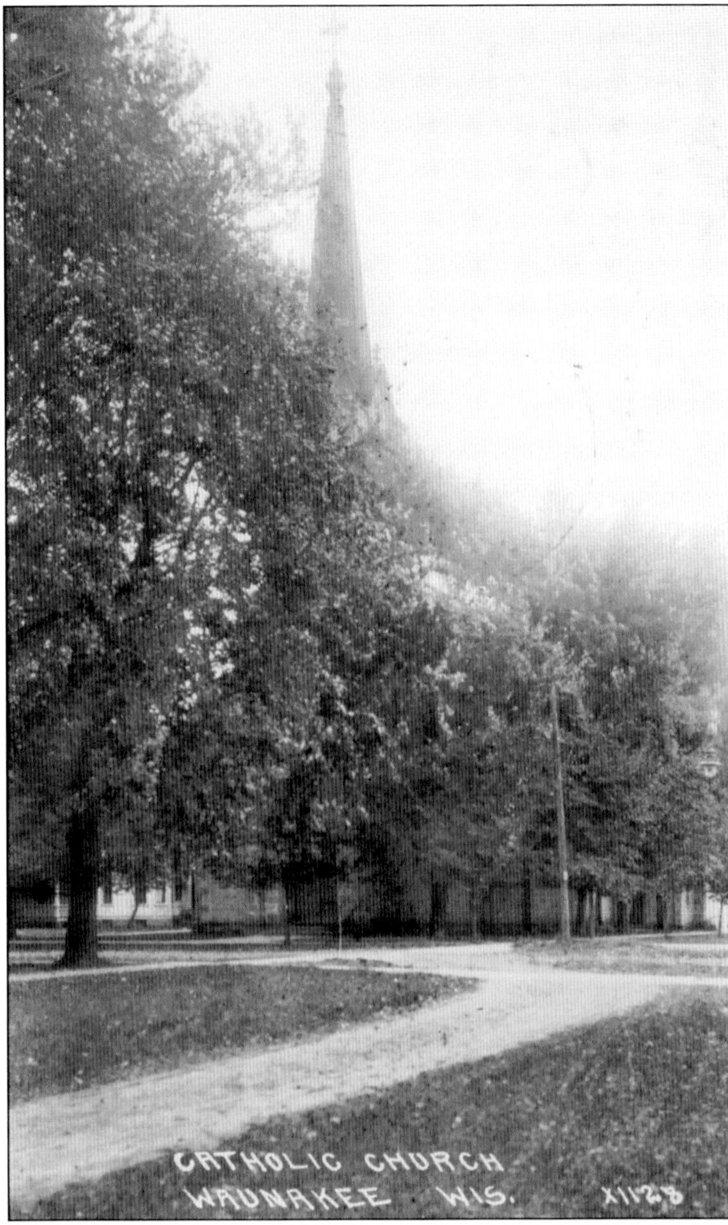

By 1917, when this photograph was taken, it was evident that St. John the Baptist Church was a central fixture in Waunakee society. The dirt road leading to the church is Third Street, and the rectory is partly visible on South Street. The year before, St. John's first resident pastor, Father Siepker, died and was buried in the cemetery east of the church. The land for the cemetery was donated by Ira P. Bacon, who, though not a member of the church, was Father Gerend's friend. Fr. C. Hausner, who served the parish from 1917 until 1935, was instrumental in convincing Waunakee businesses to close from 12:00 p.m. to 3:00 p.m. on Good Friday. Identified as an emphatic speaker, Father Hausner was known for his hour-long homilies. Because of the long sermons and Masses that lasted up to two hours, local farmers worked together to build long, narrow shelters near the church for their horse teams to be protected from the elements during Mass. (St. John the Baptist parish.)

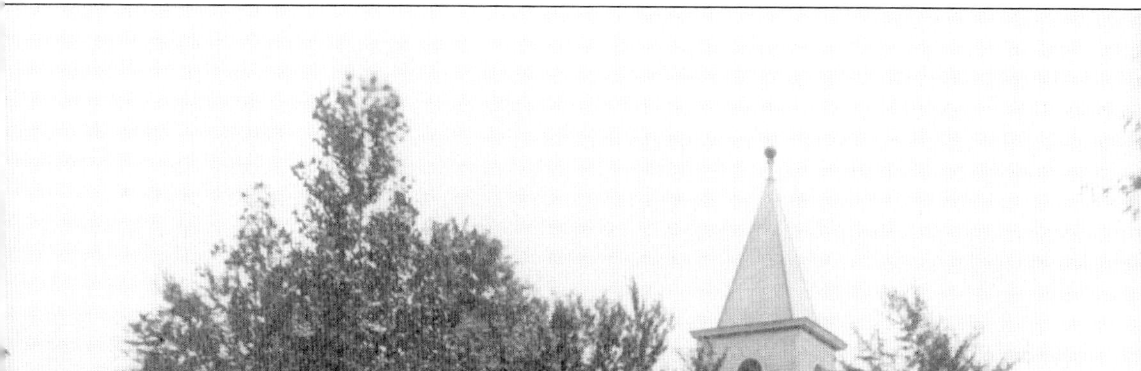

Many of Waunakee's first residents in the 1870s were Presbyterian, including business owner Jacob Buhlman and landowner Ira P. Bacon. Rev. B. Riley, a retired missionary from the Lodi First Presbyterian Church, began services in the old school, which the St. Paul Evangelical Lutherans also desired to use. Then in 1877, the Presbyterian church moved to the second floor of Gussman's carpentry shop. Pictured in 1910 next to the unpaved Fish Street, the new church was built in 1878 with a loan of $500. In addition to the loan, the congregation raised $19 hosting a community "Hard Times Sociable" dinner. Attendees paid 5¢ each to eat only corn out of a bowl with an iron spoon, served by men and women wearing calico. The wooden-plank sidewalks visible in front of the church were the first in the village (the $75 cost paid for by the Presbyterian Ladies Missionary Society), and they extended from the church on Fish Street to the Riley house on Second and South Streets. (WPL.)

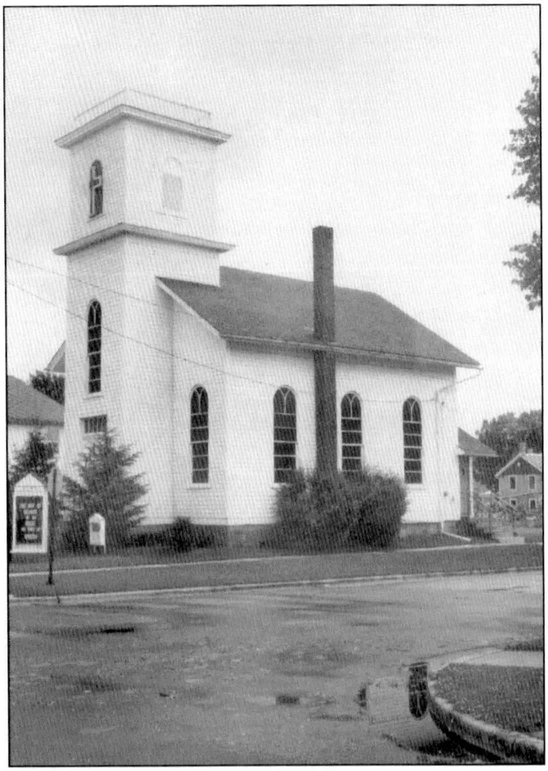

By the time this photograph was taken in the 1960s, the First Presbyterian Church steeple had deteriorated and been removed. Other renovations had taken place in the church, many as a result of C.J. Schmidt's generous donations in the 1950s in addition to his paying off the remainder of the church's $500 mortgage in 1944. Between Schmidt and the Women's Club, the church was able to add a kitchen, furnace room, additional restrooms, and replace the original pews. (WPL.)

For a few months in the early 1900s, Sunday school was the only service provided by the First Presbyterian Church, and it is what kept the church alive. The church community came full circle in 1968 when it contracted Waunakee's Simon Builders to create a Christian education wing for teaching and fellowship. The congregation outgrew its walls 25 years later, sold the historic church, and built a larger space on the south edge of Waunakee. (WPL.)

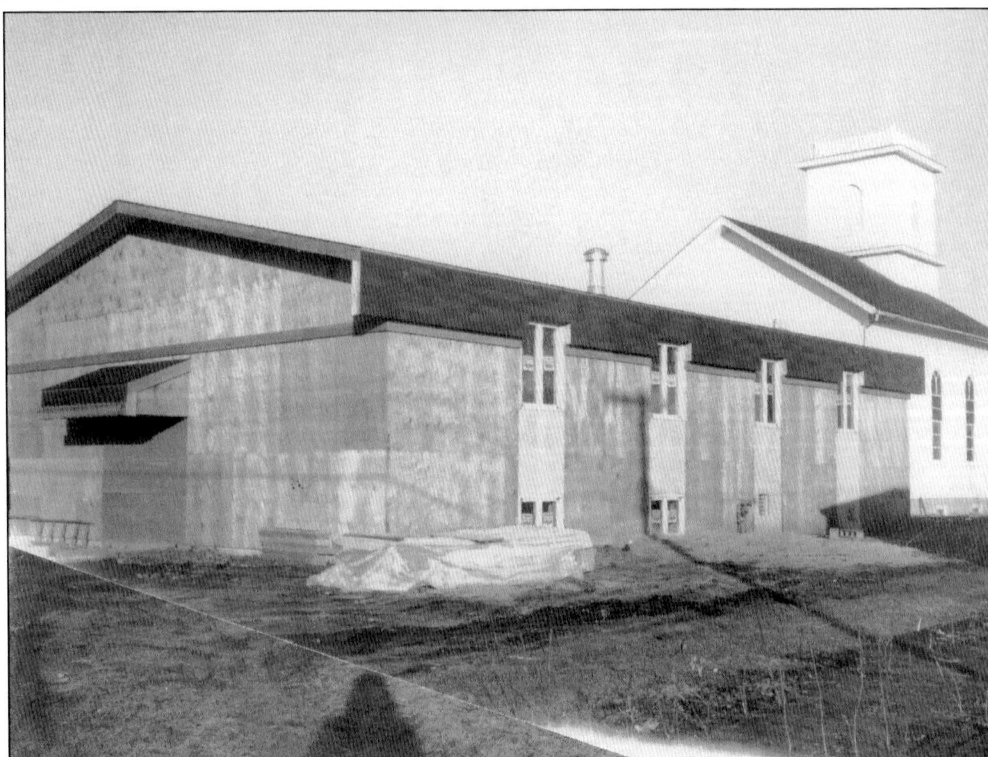

Five

Schools

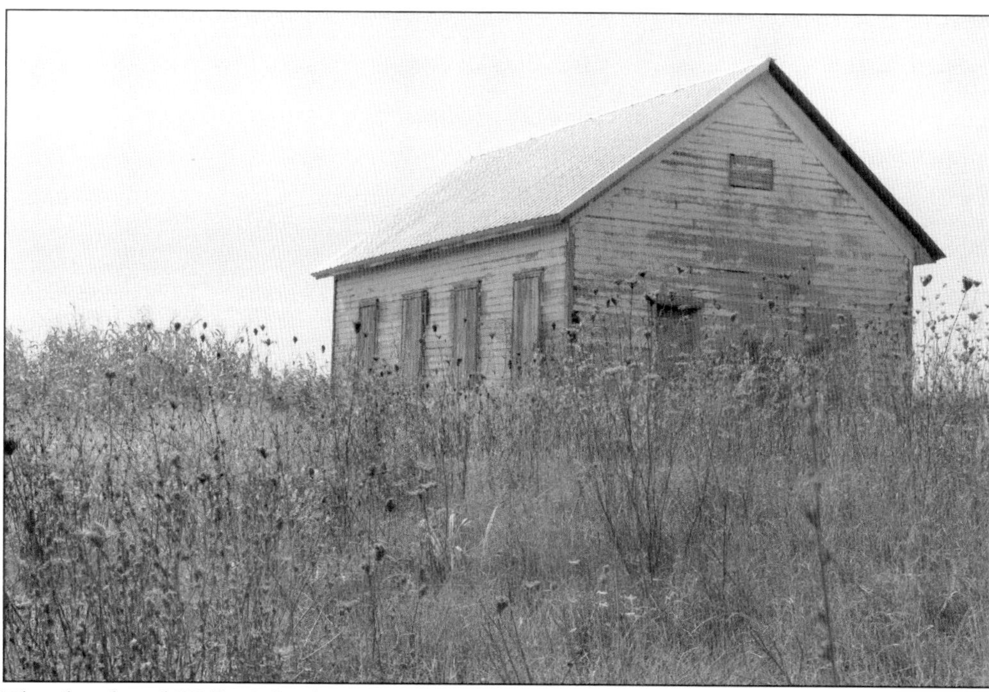

The abandoned Wilke School, Vienna Township's District No. 4 School, stands as a reminder of Wisconsin's past educational system. Soon after the European settlers first arrived, they built one-room structures throughout townships, first of logs and then wood frame. School No. 4 served the families living in and around Leicester, the settlement that gave rise to Waunakee, until the school closed in 1937. Preserved for 75 years in a farmer's field, the former one-room school was demolished in 2012 by the landowner. (Photograph by the author.)

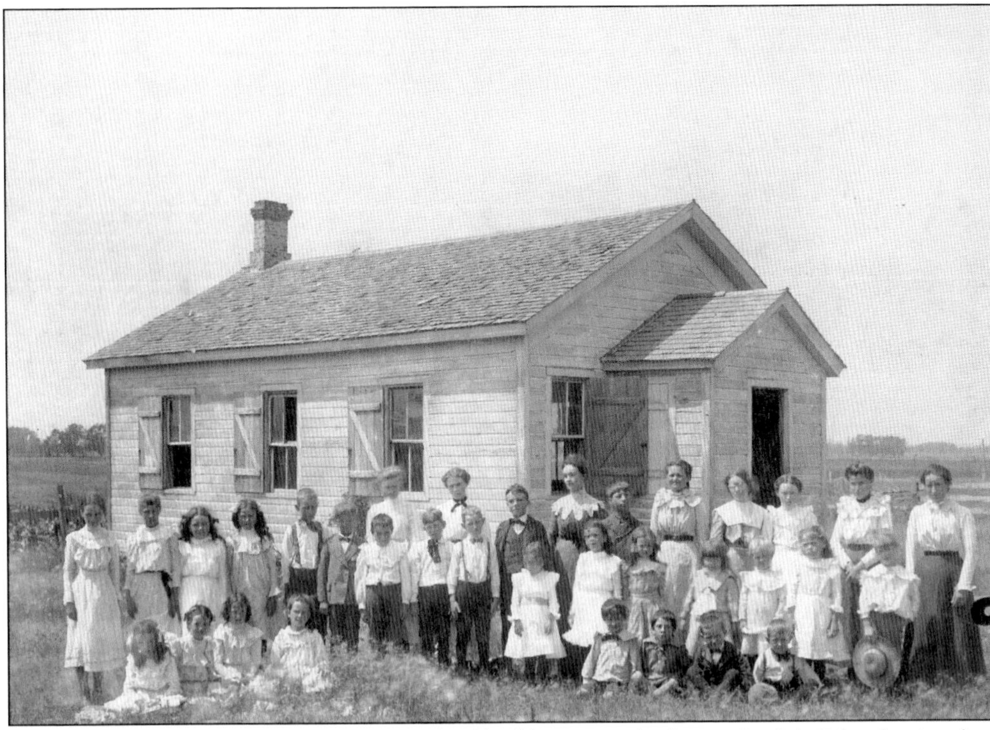

In 1861, before the title of *District No. 5 School* had been attached to it, Catfish School existed on the west end of what would become River Road, north of Catfish Creek. Thomas Shillinglaw's tavern and the Westport Post Office were nearby. The structure in the photograph was later replaced then converted into a residence. (Kennedy family.)

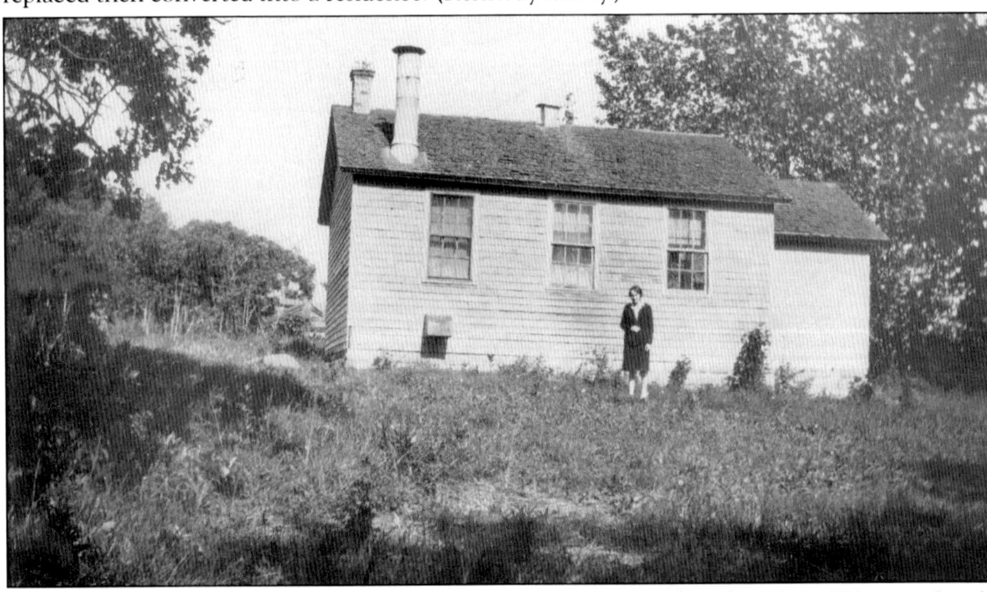

Another Westport school was built before 1873 on Tierney Road at the edge of Tierney family land. Florence Koltes stands in front of the structure, which was known unofficially as Squaw Hill School, or Westport District No. 3 School. Florence's mother, Josephine Tierney Koltes, attended the school. (James P. Koltes.)

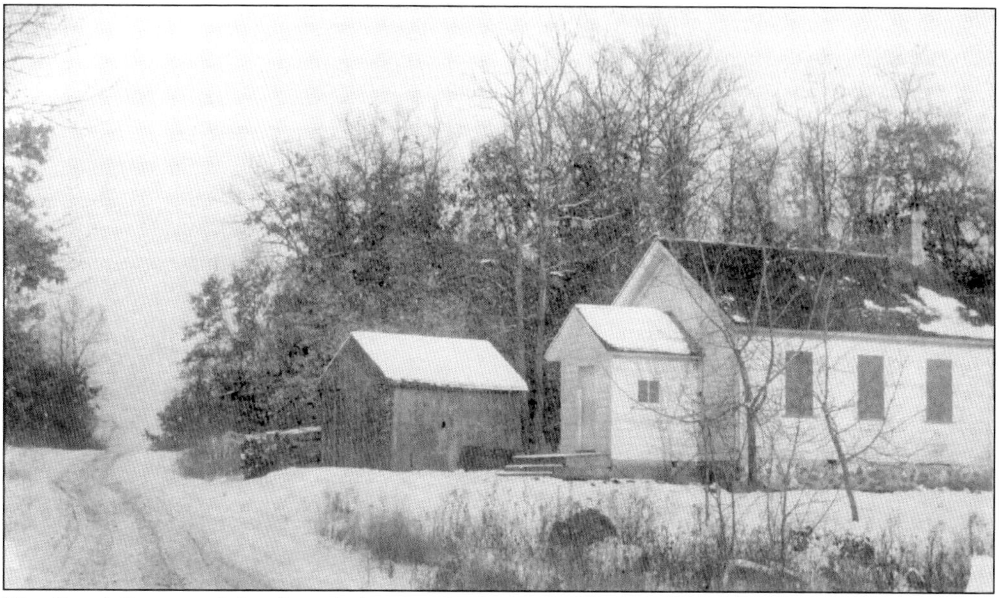

The Rural Crossing School resided at two locations. Marcella Schumacher Pendall wrote about attending District No. 2 School when it was at the junction of Highways 113, 19, and County I then notes that her mother, Eveline Busby Schumacher, attended the same school building when it was a half mile south of the junction. Some of Pendall's classmates in 1918 were Robert Hogan, Dorothy O'Malley, and Joseph Koltes. This building looks very similar to Crossing School and could be the building pictured at its earlier location. (WPL.)

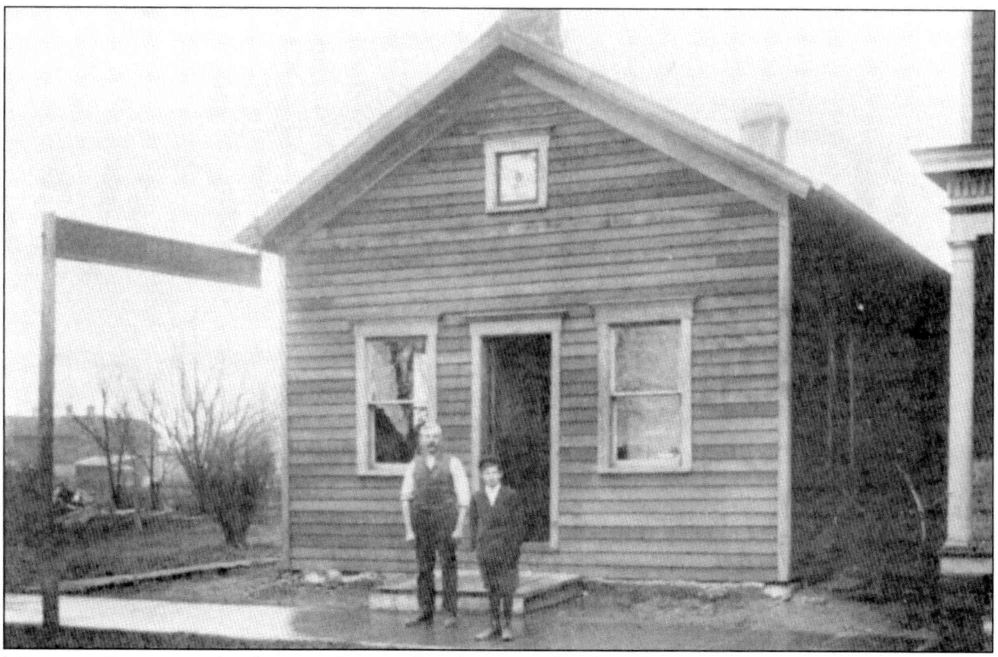

Margaret Jones was the first teacher at this district school in the new village, and she later went on to marry business owner Jacob Buhlman. Standing in front of the school is Simon Kirchesch, Waunakee's town marshal who bought and moved the structure when it was no longer needed for the school. (WPL.)

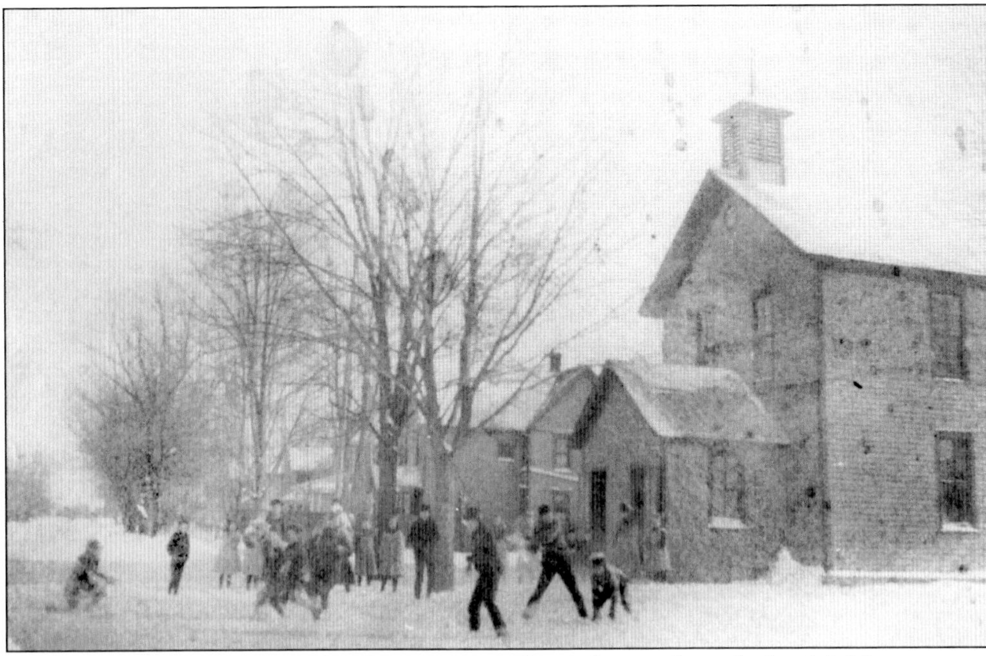

Within seven years of Waunakee becoming a village, the number of schoolchildren outgrew the one-room district school. The village built this two-story school on Second Street in 1878, and Delilah Martin was the first teacher. By 1885, there were 86 students registered. The school building was later converted into apartments. (WPL.)

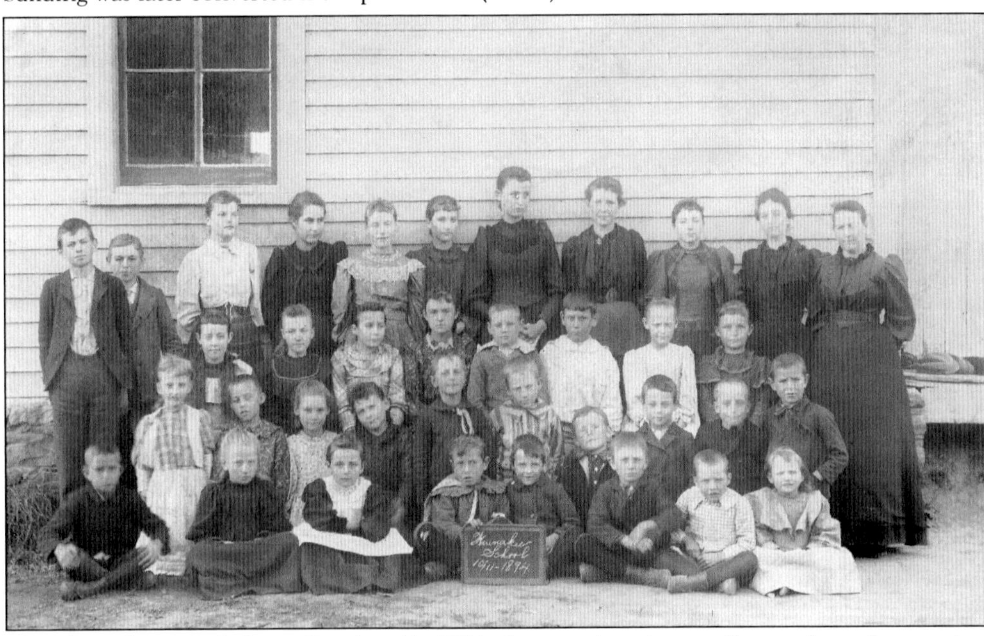

The class photograph from October 11, 1894, shows a drop in enrollment from the previous decade. It is difficult to tell the difference between some of the students and the teacher, as the children who stayed home part of the year to help on the farm might still have been enrolled well over age 18, and the teacher's only requirements were to have graduated from eighth grade and to have passed a written exam. (WPL.)

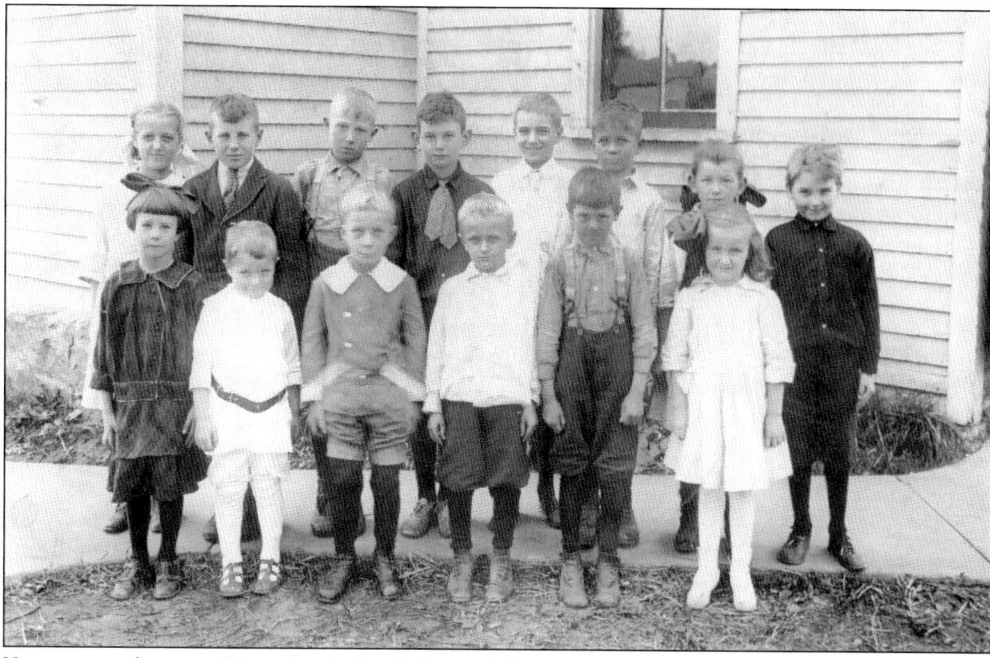

Younger students at Waunakee's Grade School during the 1917–1918 school year are, from left to right, (first row) Fay Wheeler, Norbert Meyer, Lawrence Simpson, Eldridge Shattuck, Charley Deans, and Agnes Struby; (second row) George Taylor, Frank Deans, Maurice Taylor, Thomas Schmidt, Kenneth Shaw, Grace Taylor, and Edward Chambers. (WPL.)

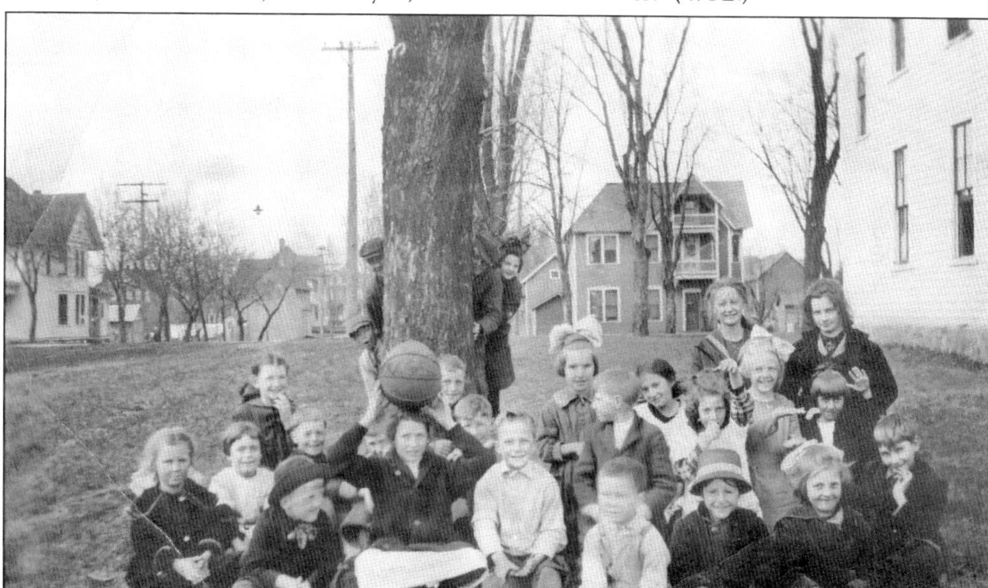

Gathered on the east side of the Waunakee Grade School around 1920 are the following students, from left to right: (first row) Maybelle Wilke, Eldridge Shuttuck, Bernice Stehr, unidentified, Walter Ireland, unidentified, Lucille Simon, and Eddie Chambers; (second row) Helen Hogan, Kenneth Cooper, unidentified, unidentified, Hazel Williamson, unidentified, Daisy Deans, Lucile Wheeler, and Edna Stehr; (third row) Grace Taylor, George Deans, Frances Wilke, Viola Ireland, and Wanda Taylor; (fourth row) Ray Stehr, Harold Wheeler, Ted Taylor, and Dolly Reeve. (WPL.)

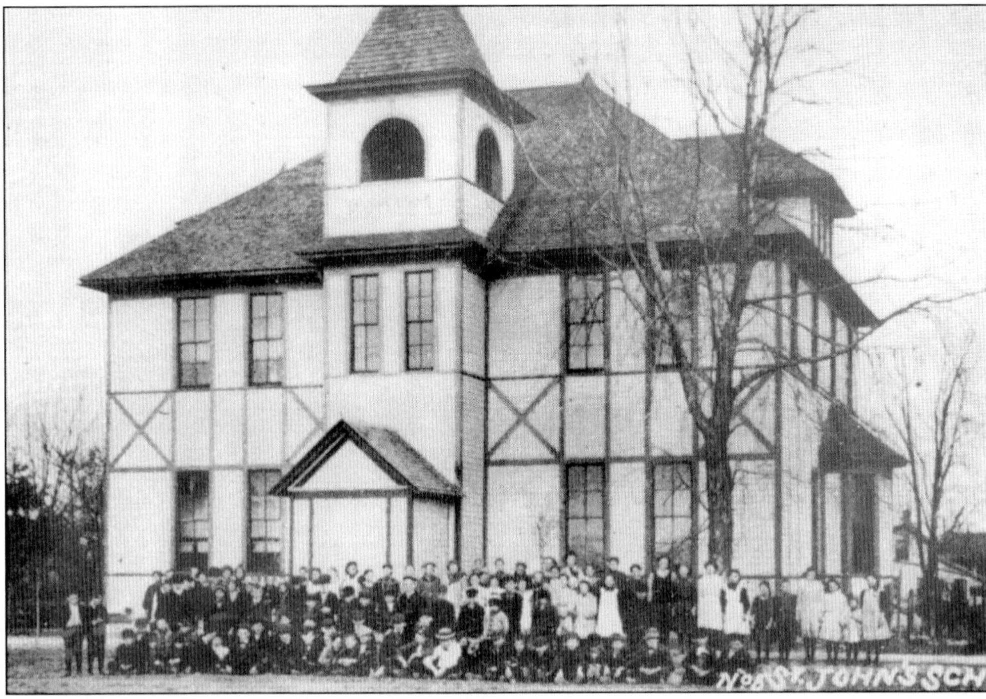

The St. John's Catholic grade school began as a one-room school near the church in 1875; the school met the congregation's needs—even in 1885 when 50 students were enrolled. Pictured in 1908, this four-room schoolhouse was built by St. John's parish in 1895 and was staffed with three nuns from the Sisters of St. Agnes. (St. John the Baptist parish.)

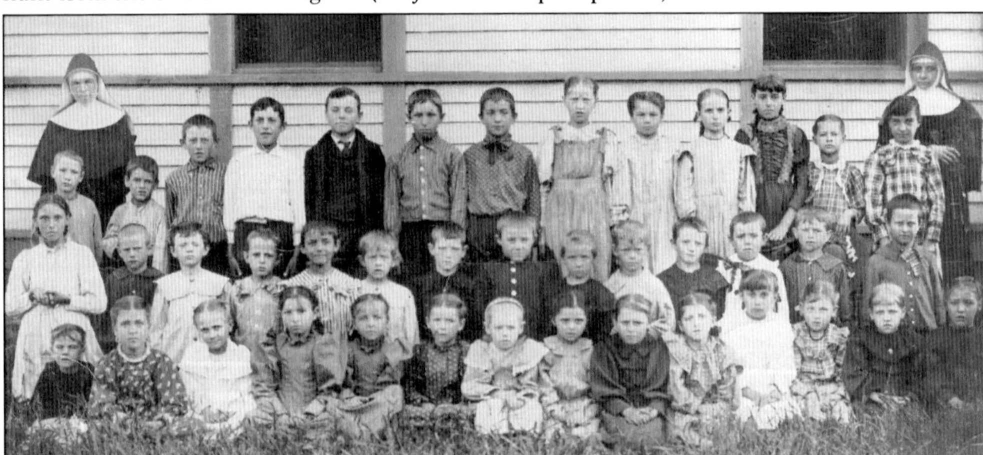

From left to right in this 1898 photograph taken at St. John's grade school are (first row) Lizzie Kirchesch, Theresa Meuer, Agnes Meuer, Maggie Kessenich, Christine Kessenich, Mamie Marks, Marie Schunk, Gertie Kessenich, Ella Rutkers, Christine Brausen, Maggie Romelfanger, Katherine Kessenich, Christine Wipperfurth, and Maggie Helt; (second row) Katie Geiberger, Joseph Kirchesch, Frank Statz, Gabriel Reis, Leo R. Schleck, Joseph Statz, John Brausen, John Wipperfurth, Louis Lester, Paul Esser, Leo Lester, Math Helt, Fred Schunk, and Eddie Dorn; (third row) Sr. M. Amelia, George Geiberger, Frank Adams, Werner Wipperfurth, John Kopp, unidentified, Frank Hauser, Christ Koch, Mary Wipperfurth, Katherine Schunk, Katherine Plendl, Lizzie Koch, Theresa Ripp, Katherine Kopp, and Sr. M. Apolonaris. (WPL.)

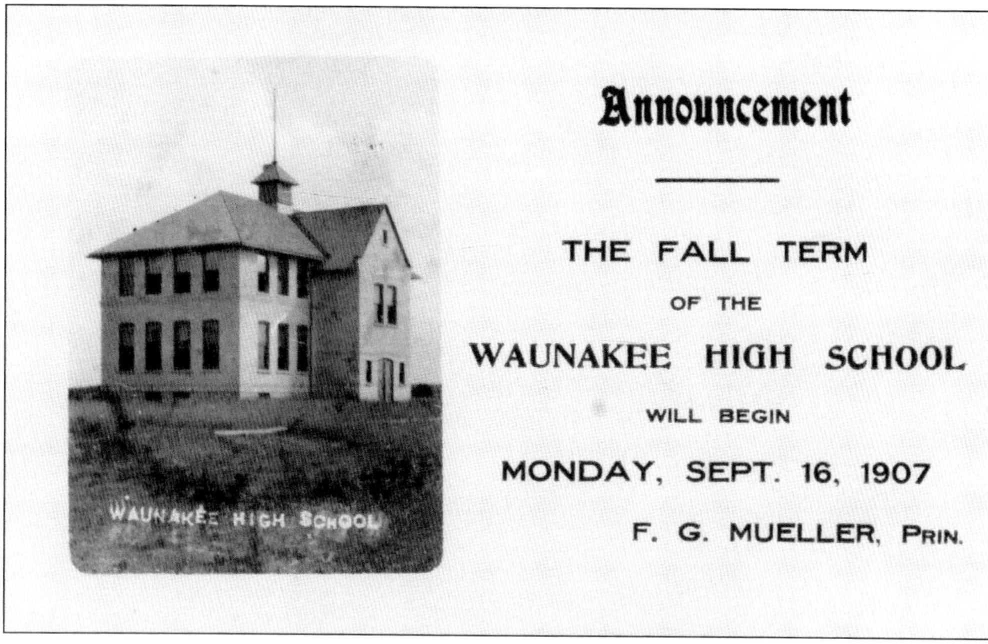

Despite the growth in Waunakee's schools by the turn of the 19th century, the village still had no high school. Students who wished to attend a secondary school had to go to Madison or Lodi high schools, which often meant taking a train for 25¢ each way. Thus, many families could not afford the expense. The cause to build a high school began to gain support, but the motion was turned down in 1902. Just two years later, Waunakee and Westport formed the joint school district and by special election, decided to build a high school. Waunakee High School opened in the fall of 1905. Forty students, including Lillian Oncken and Grace Koltes, are pictured below around 1910. Enrollment grew to 50 by 1920. (Above, James P. Koltes; below, WPL.)

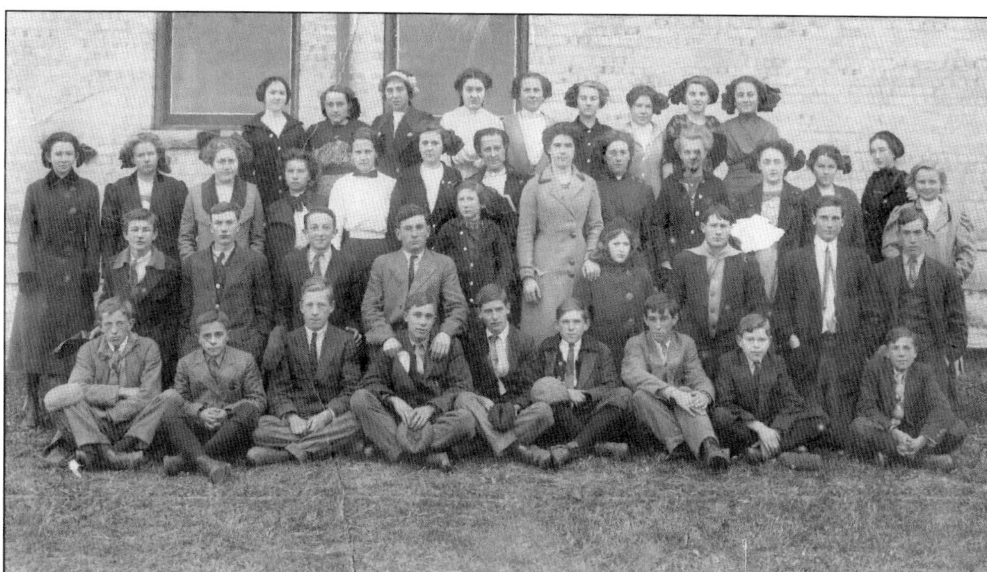

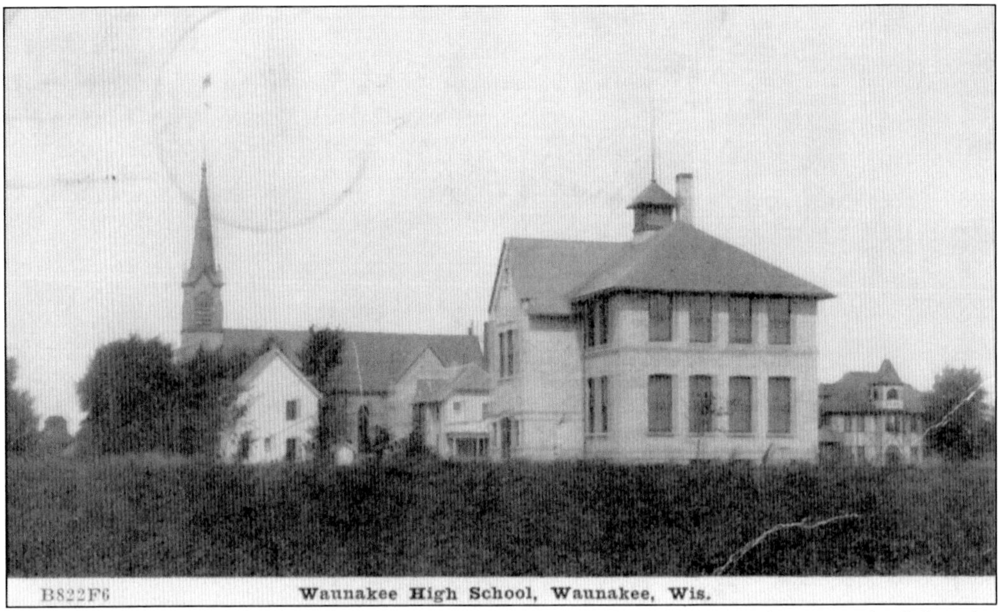

A landscape view of Waunakee High School shows its placement in relation to St. John the Baptist's church, rectory, convent, and grade school. When this photograph was taken in 1905, Third Street continued between the St. John's buildings and the high school, and the streets were not paved. (St. John the Baptist parish.)

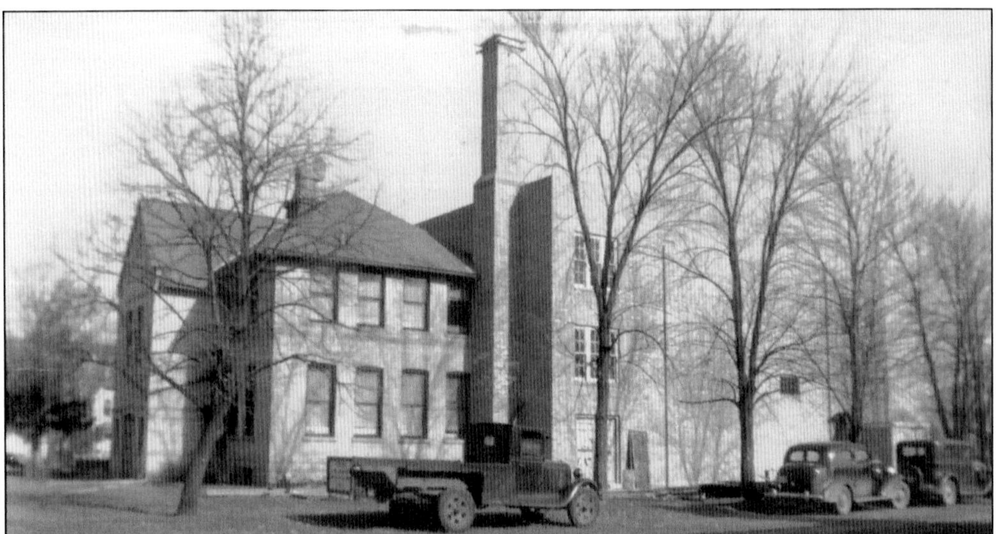

Waunakee High School may have had a gradual start to its enrollment, but there were 25 senior graduates by 1940. The growth necessitated a building addition, which was added in 1936. The original building was completely replaced in 1950. (Kennedy family.)

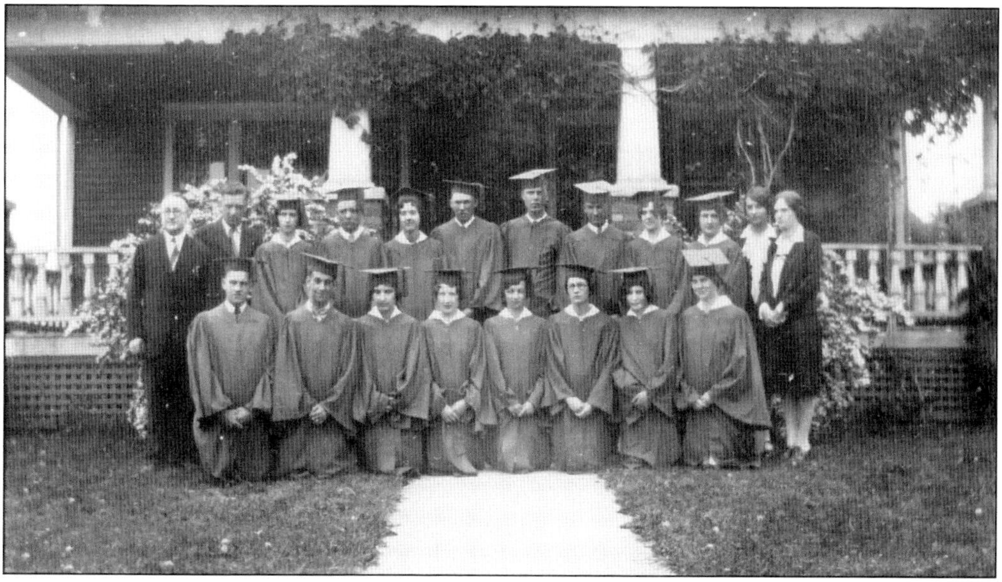

The 16 Waunakee High School graduates in 1929 include Hazel Raemisch, daughter of F.C. Raemisch, on the far front right. The principal that year was B.J. Byrne, who stands at the far left. Hazel Raemisch Roudebush went on to be a nurse for Dr. Austin Blake, and she helped deliver most of the Waunakee babies who were born during her tenure. Roudebush proudly recalled not losing a single baby or mother during her time as a nurse. (Hazel R. Zimbric.)

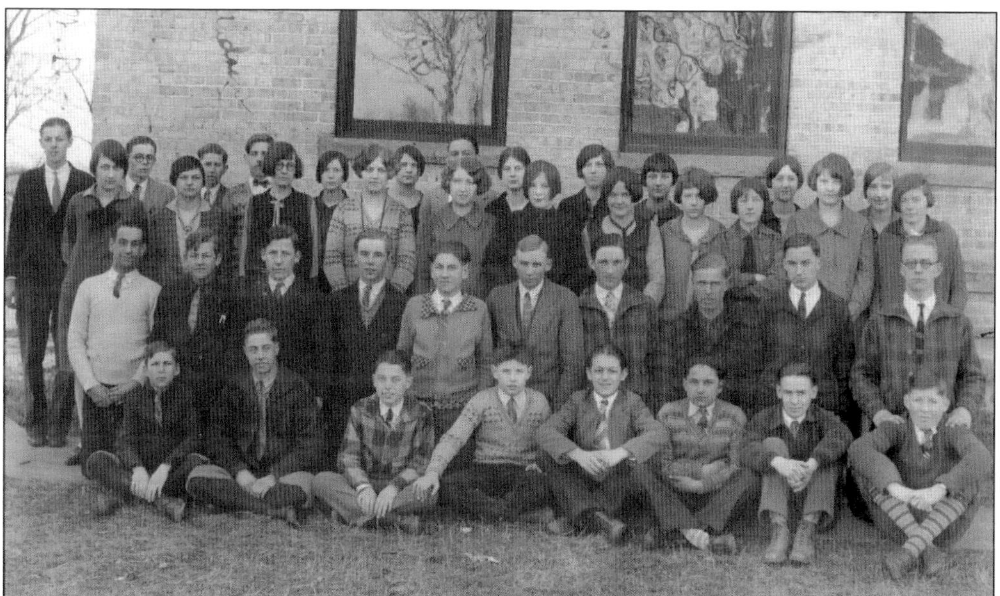

Some of Waunakee's earliest families are represented in the Waunakee High School class of 1930, pictured in front of the school with the class of 1928. The 16 class of 1930 graduates are Bertha Cooper, Ray Deans, Charlotte Doll, Stanley Dulin, Russel Hart, Vincent Hogan, Eleanor Hurst, Catherine Lynch, Joseph Miller, Nicholas Miller, David O'Malley, Herbert Simon (valedictorian), James Tierney (salutatorian), Fay Wheeler, Felix Worringer, and Florence Walsh. (Hazel R. Zimbric.)

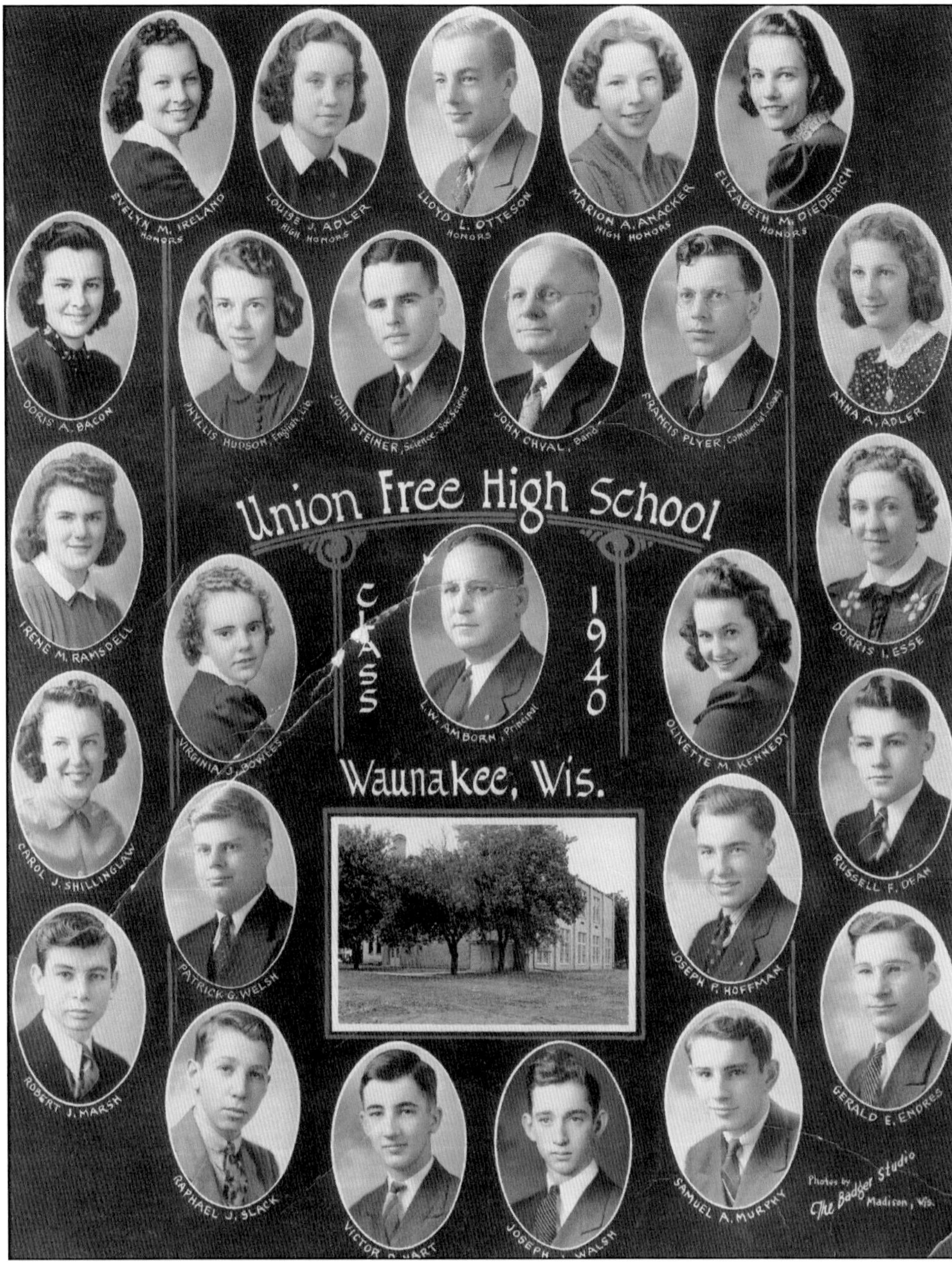

The faculty and graduates of Waunakee High School in 1940 are, from left to right, (top row) Evelyn Ireland, Louise Adler, Lloyd Otteson, Marion Anacker, and Elizabeth Diederich; (second row) Doris Bacon, Phyllis Hudson (faculty), John Steiner (faculty), John Chval (faculty), Francis Plyer (faculty), and Anna Adler; (third row) Irene Ramsdell, Virginia Bowles, L.W. Amborn (principal), Olivette Kennedy, and Doris Esse; (fourth row) Carol Shillinglaw, Patrick Welsh, Joseph Hoffman, and Russel Dean; (fifth row) Robert Marsh, Raphael Slack, Victor Hart, Joseph Walsh, Samuel Murphy, and Gerald Endres. Many of the class of 1940 went on to be valuable members of the Waunakee community, including Lloyd Otteson, who became the town veterinarian. (Kennedy family.)

Sisters of St. Agnes stand watch with the community as the St. John's school building project begins in 1948. Sister Elenore is the second Sister from the right. The construction of a new school was the culmination of a building campaign that started after 1935 when Fr. M.J. Jacobs began leading the parish and continued under Fr. N.B. Schneider's pastorship in 1946. (St. John the Baptist parish.)

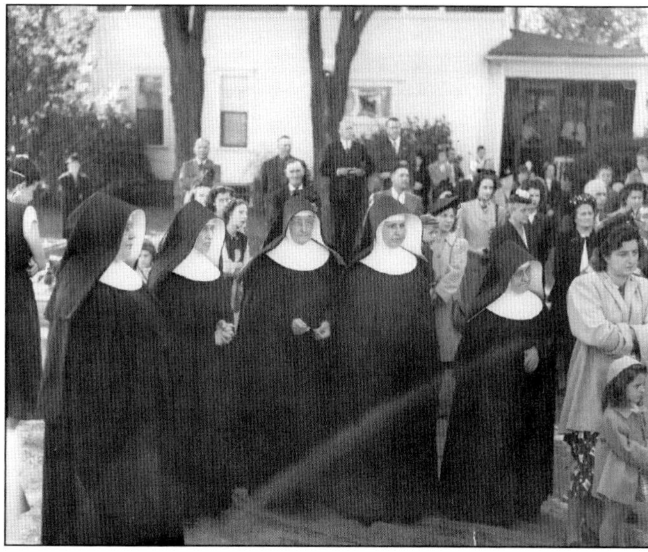

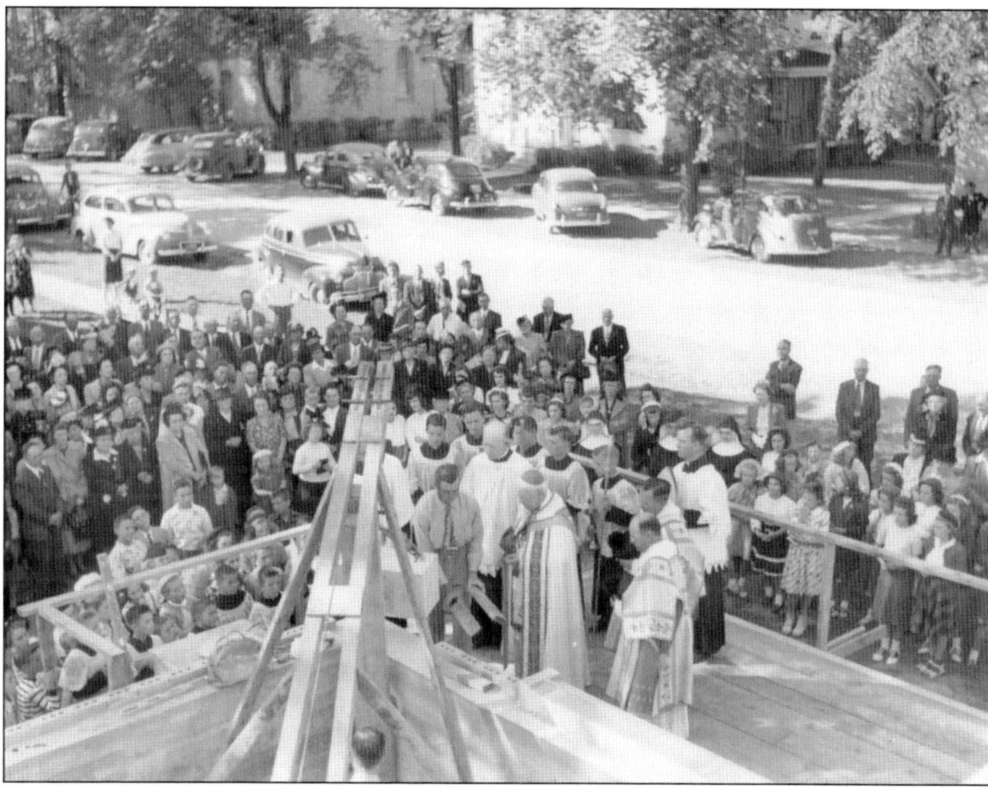

Schoolchildren, parishioners, clergy, and religious line East Third Street in 1948 as Bishop William P. O'Connor of the Madison Diocese readies the cornerstone for St. John's school. The stone contained a metal box with newspapers, church bulletins, information about the schools past and present, and currency. The assisting priests are Fr. Ferdinand A. Mack, Middleton, and Fr. Herbert J. Waldkirch, Roxbury. In the background of the photograph, the rear of the church and rectory are visible; the rectory later was replaced with a parking lot to accommodate the growing parish. (St. John the Baptist parish.)

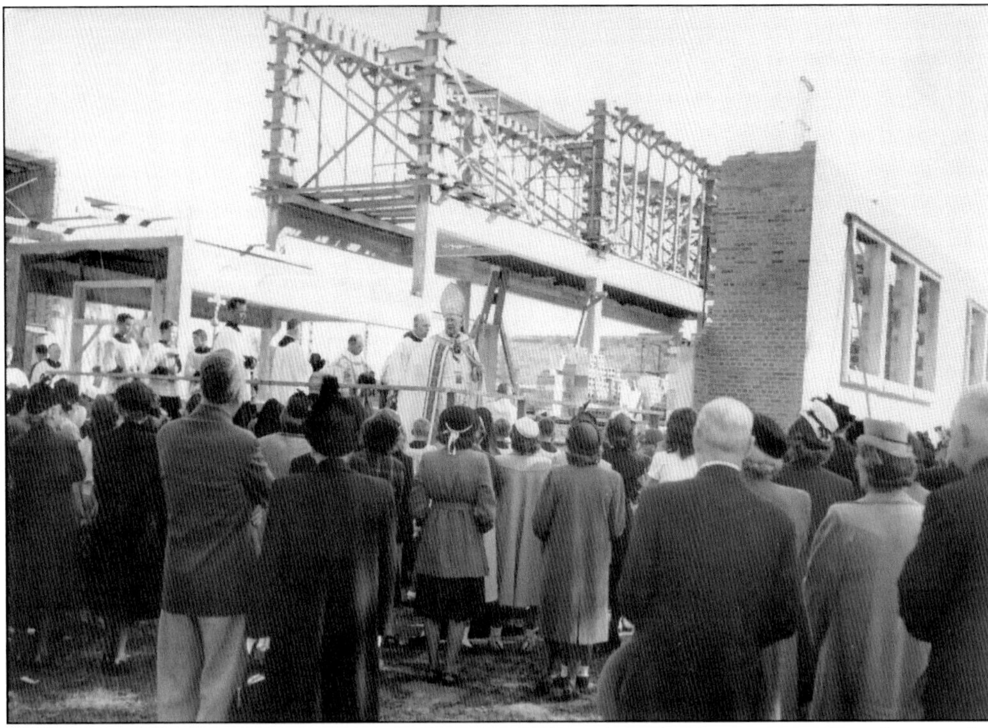

From the time the building campaign was initiated until 1948 when construction began, the cost to build the St. John's school nearly doubled. The school was finished in 1949. (St. John the Baptist parish.)

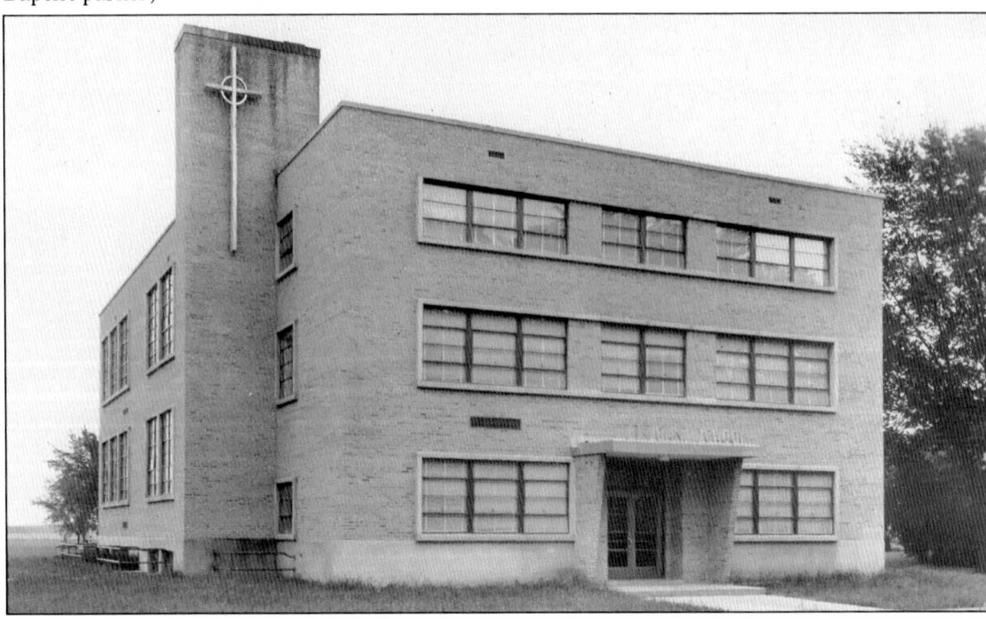

Sr. Rose Marie was principal in the new school space. Within a little more than 10 years, the space was again inadequate for the school population, and a large expansion was begun in 1960. Part of the expansion included a gym in which Fr. Raymond Ziegler initiated a children's roller-skating program. (St. John the Baptist parish.)

Six

HOUSES

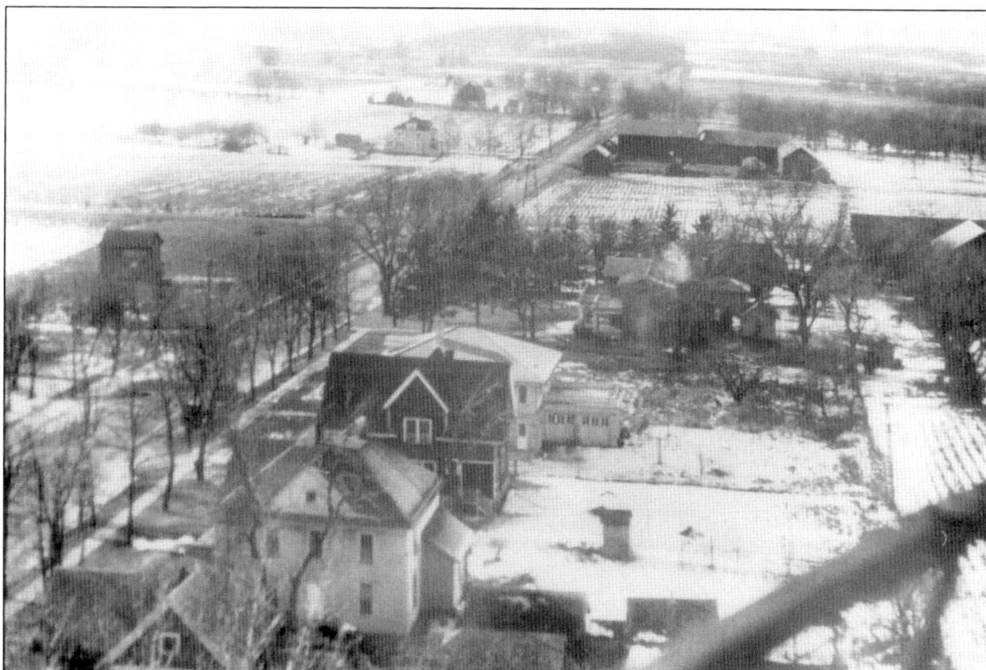

The railing of the water tower in the right corner is evidence of where Kenneth Shaw captured this photograph in 1932. Starting from the lower left, the houses featured belonged to railroad stationmaster H.L. Reeve (305 West Main Street, later moved), the Kalscheur family (307 West Main Street), Joe Hellenbrand (309 West Main Street), Dr. Byron Shaw (311 West Main Street), and the O'Malley family. The Constance Klein farm is in the background, and the south side of Main Street contained a grain storage building. (WPL.)

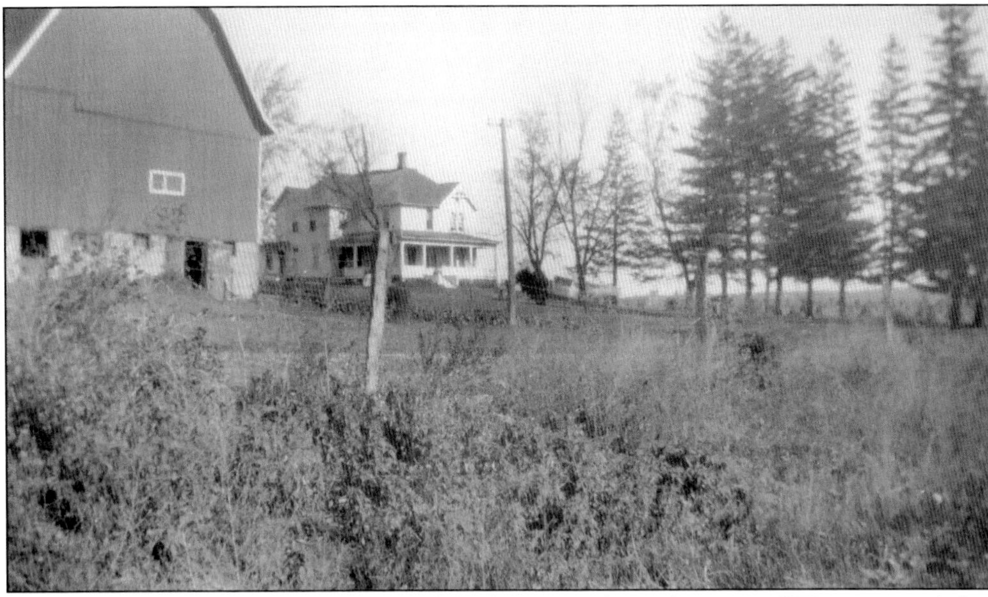

The Michael O'Malley family was one of the first to settle in the town of Westport, and they reportedly played a part in naming the township after their homeland in Ireland. Michael's son Patrick O'Malley went to California with his brother Martin in 1849, made some gold rush money, and then returned to Wisconsin in 1850. Martin owned almost 200 acres along present-day Bong Road along with this farm, which was later purchased by John Bong. (James P. Koltes.)

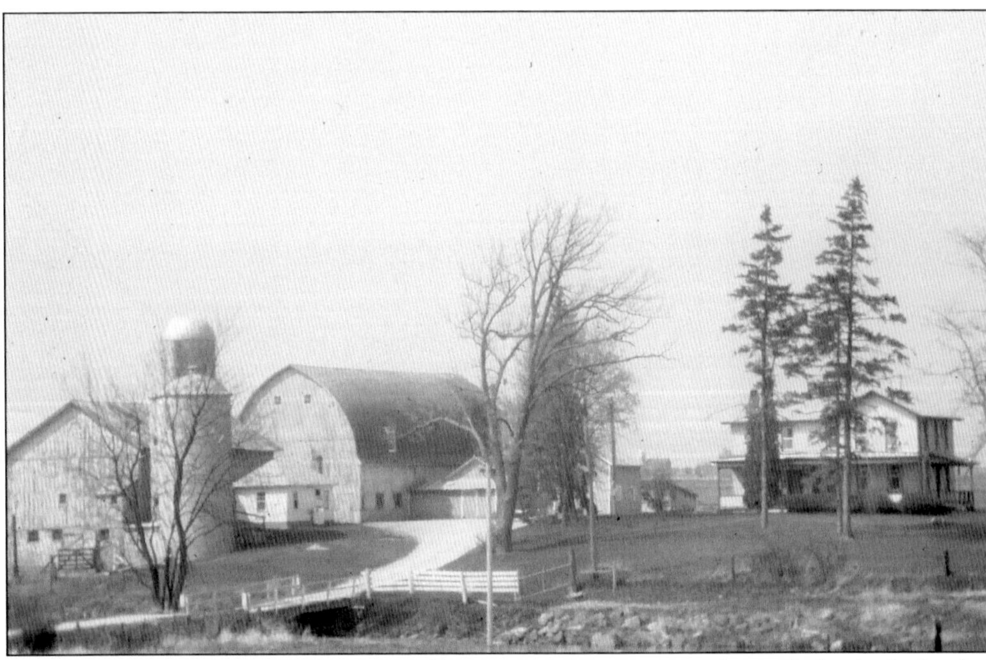

When this photograph was taken, it had been over 100 years since Lewis Baker built the first house on the property and began working the land in 1860. Baker owned much of the land on the north side of the village, including this farm. C.J. Schmidt, owner of the grain elevator, later purchased the farm. (WPL.)

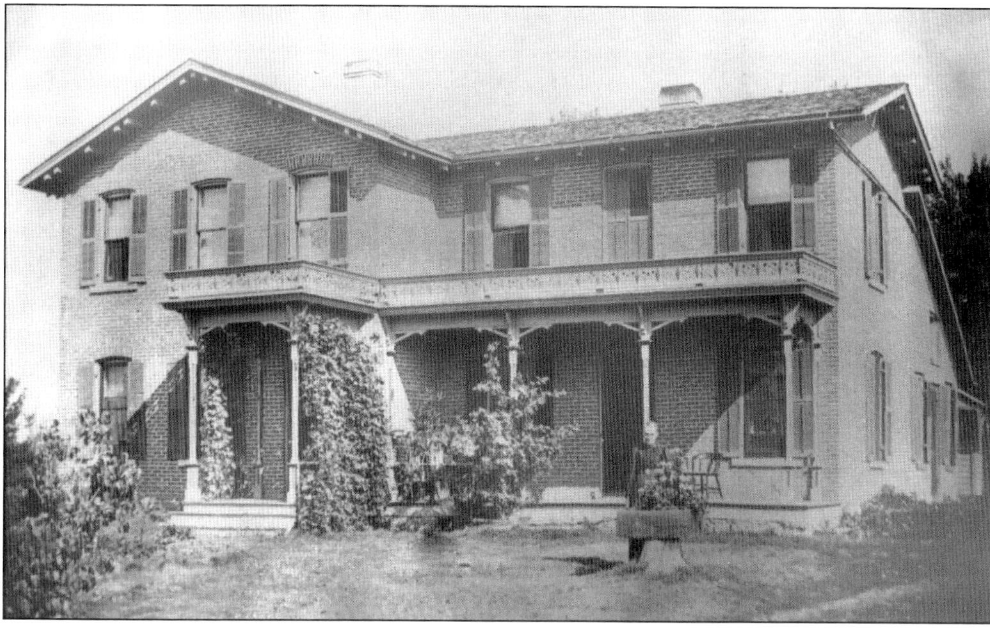

The red brick home at 317 West Main Street was built in 1855 by Daniel Bryant, who brought the brick from Milwaukee by oxcart. Waunakee founder George Fish purchased the house in 1866. Fish farmed 220 acres and is known for bringing the railroad depot to Waunakee along with Lewis Baker. The house was a site of tragedy in 1878 when A.J. Van Tassel was painting the cornice and died from a fall. (WPL.)

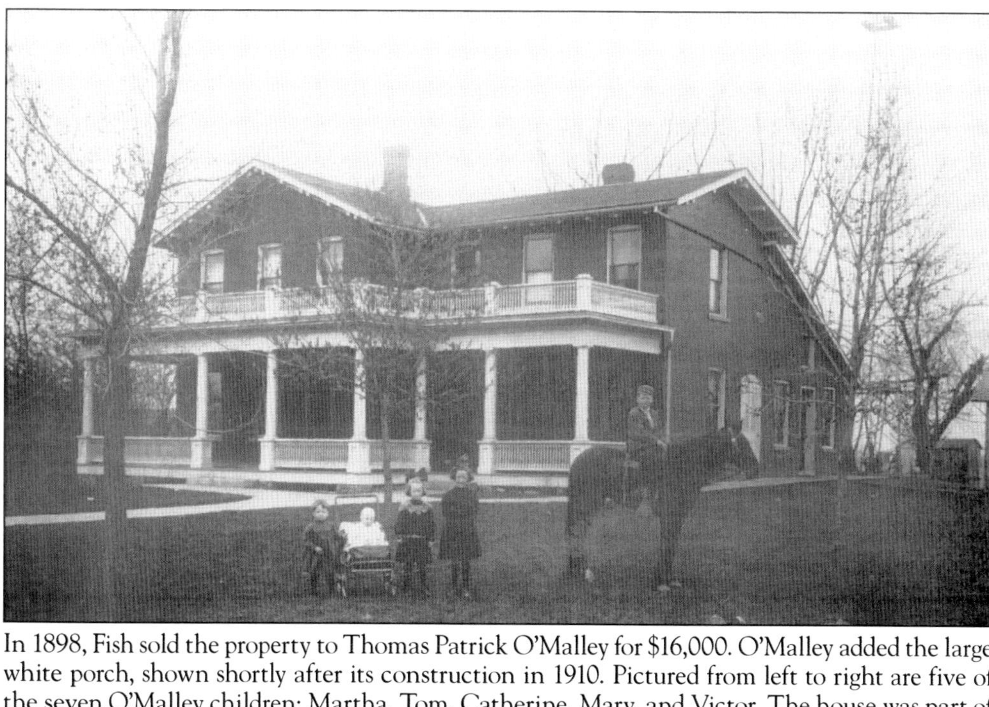

In 1898, Fish sold the property to Thomas Patrick O'Malley for $16,000. O'Malley added the large white porch, shown shortly after its construction in 1910. Pictured from left to right are five of the seven O'Malley children: Martha, Tom, Catherine, Mary, and Victor. The house was part of a farm that O'Malley later divided into parcels south to Third Street, and in their sale he created O'Malley's Addition. (Mary Ellen Kearney.)

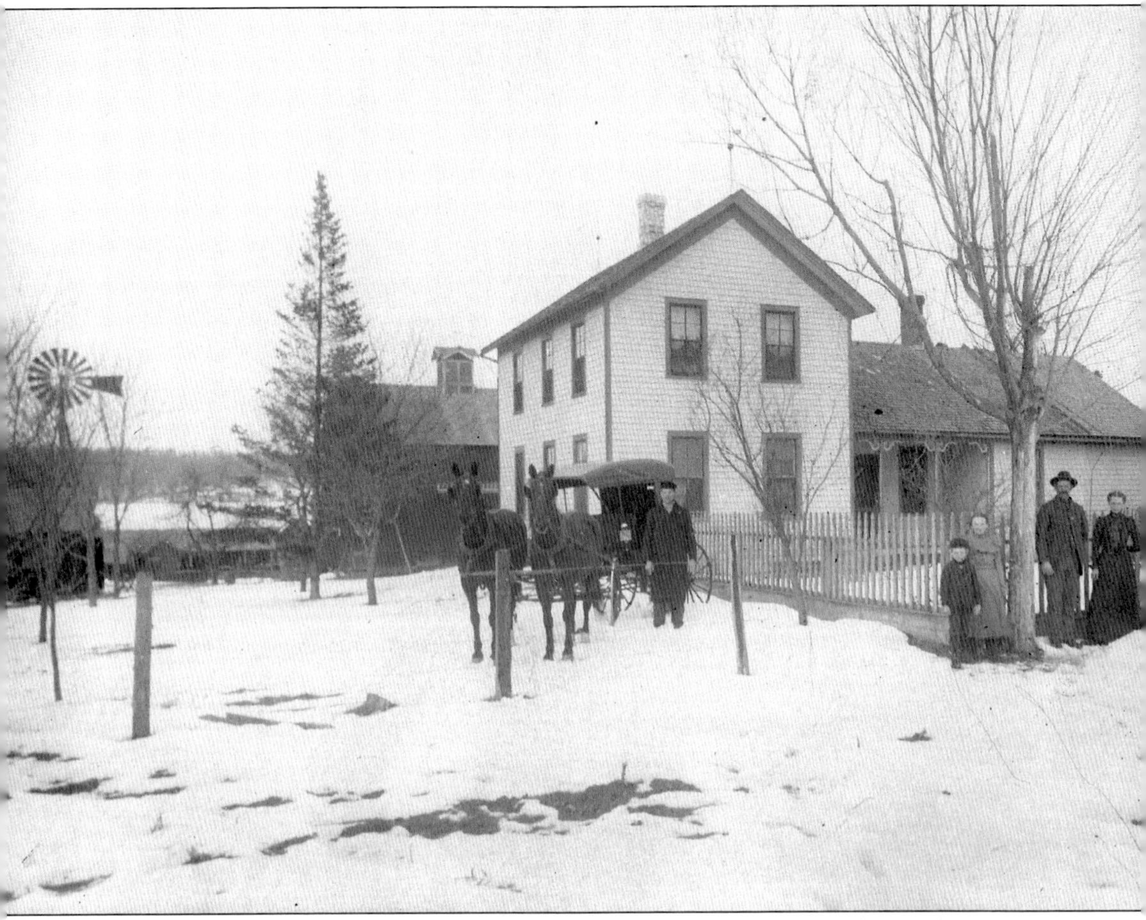

The Bacon house on Main Street at Bacon Street was built by early Waunakee settler Ira P. Bacon. He married Eliza Ikin Flatman in 1877; both had been previously married. Eliza's first marriage was in 1863 to George Flatman, who tragically died at age 35 in Packham's millpond. William Flatman, longtime Waunakee fire chief, was one of Flatman's sons. Eliza and Ira Bacon had one daughter, Agnes, who married Charles McWatty. Pictured in front of the house are, from left to right, Charles McWatty (by buggy), unidentified, unidentified, William Flatman, and Agnes McWatty. (WPL.)

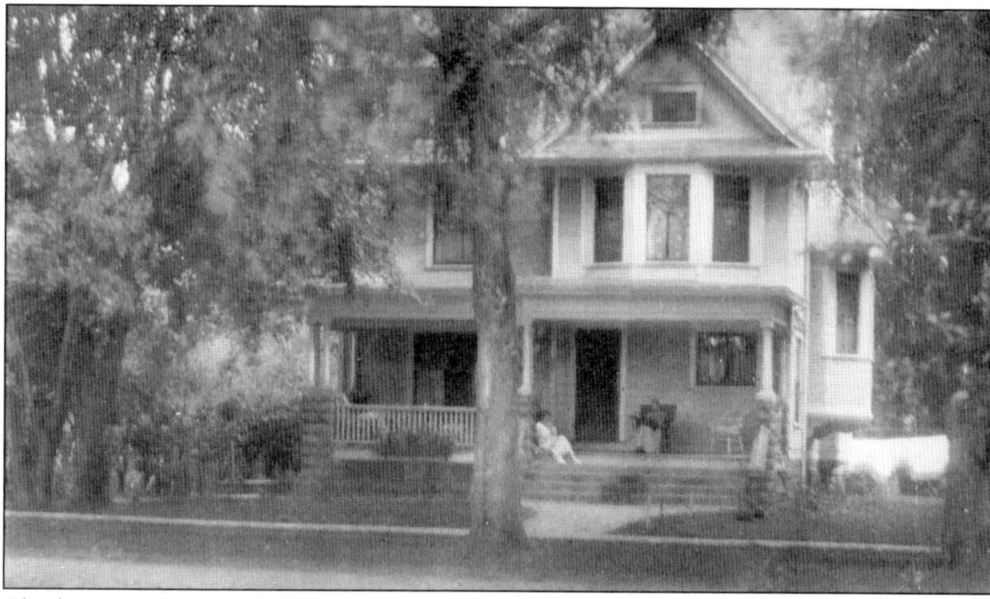

Charles McWatty, one of Waunakee's well-known residents, built this home on East Main Street in the early 1920s at the request of his wife, Agnes Bacon McWatty. During the Great Depression, the McWattys sold the house. It was so expensive to heat that the Smith family, owners from 1936 to 1941, rented the house from the bank for $25 per month. Lounging on the porch in warmer weather are Naomi Smith (left) and Mary Ellen Smith Adler. (WPL.)

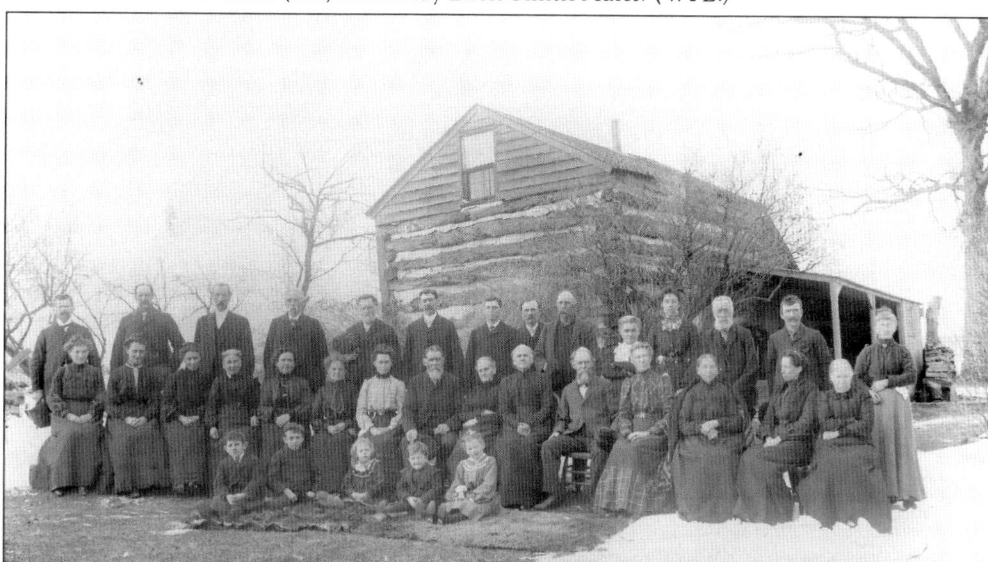

These members of an unidentified family could be descendants of Michael O'Malley. His son Thomas O'Malley arrived before the family in 1843 and built a log cabin much like this one in eastern Westport Township. Described in the *Biographical Review of Dane County* (1893), the cabin was simple, primitive, and inexpensive. "The timbers were hewed by his own hands, and for the remainder of the material he hauled logs ten miles to a mill to be sawed into lumber." (WPL.)

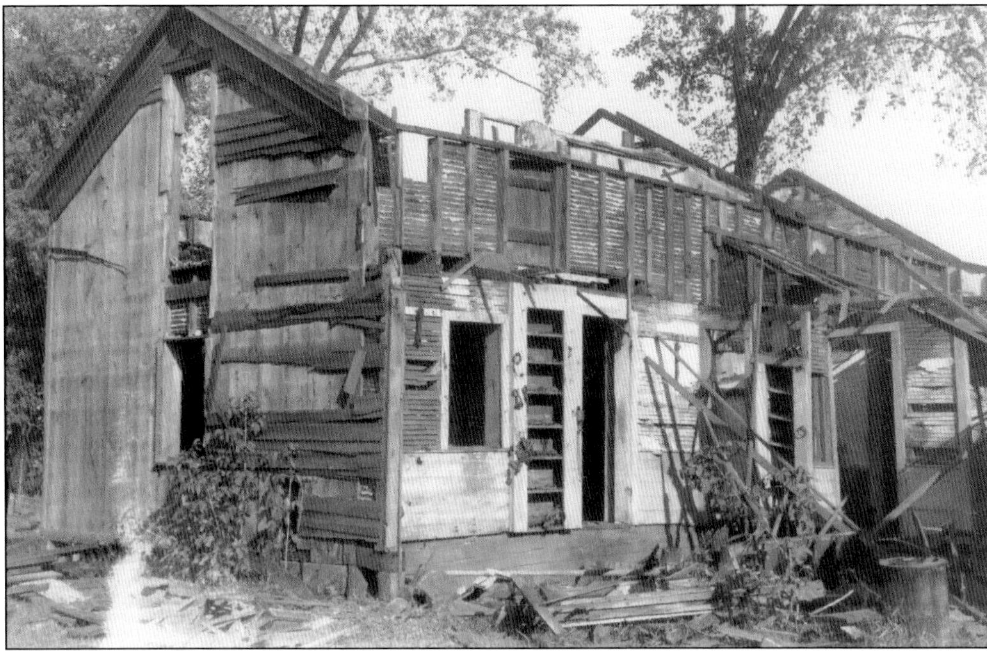

Dr. Nathaniel Wheeler was Waunakee's first physician starting in 1860. The Western Reserve College medical graduate lived in this house, shown in ramshackle condition years after Henry Schumacher turned it into a granary. Schumacher moved the structure north to this area of the property in 1906 when he began to build his two-story house. At that point, he turned Dr. Wheeler's house into a barn for four horses, and he stored grain in the old rooms. (Friends of Schumacher Farm.)

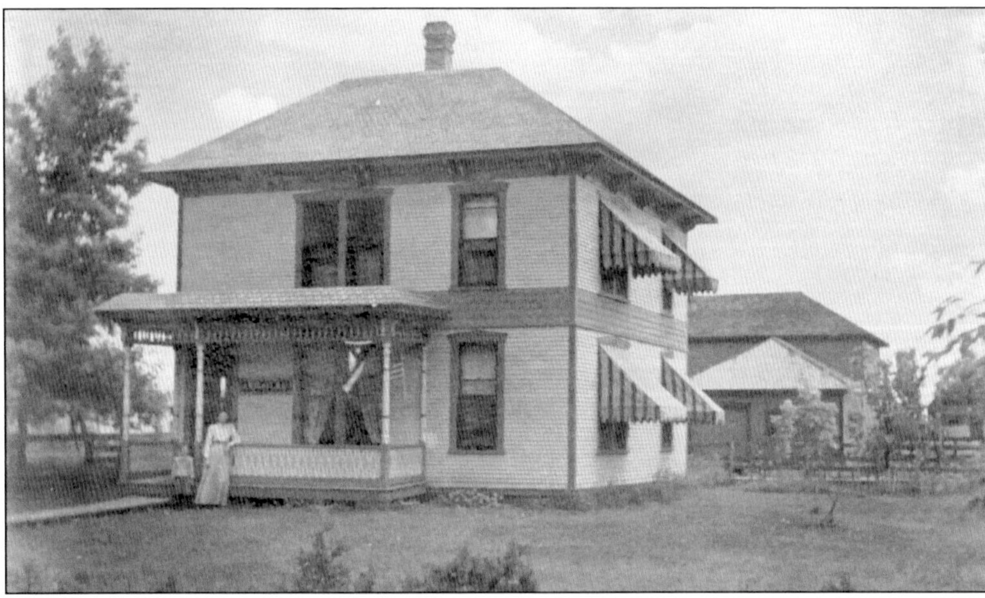

Careful examination of the sign next to the front door of this 1880s house reveals, "A.M. Blake, M.D." Dr. Blake's home office was situated on East Main Street between present-day Madison and Bacon Streets. Behind the home was a carriage house where horses stood harnessed and ready for Dr. Blake to make emergency house calls. (James P. Koltes.)

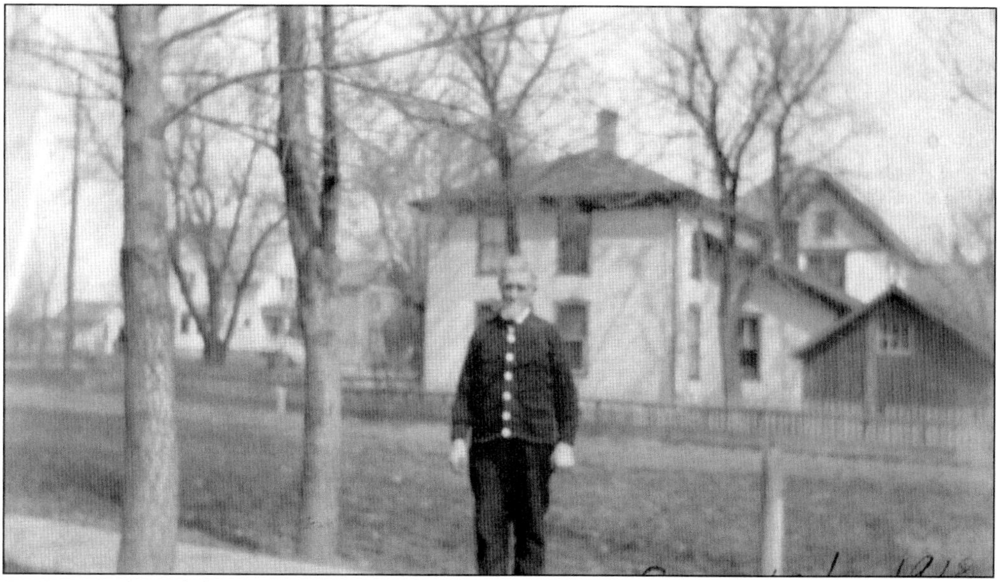

Dr. Byron Shaw (whose first office was in the Brausen Hotel) moved to West Main Street and began his medical practice 10 years after Dr. Blake set up his east-side practice. William Fisher, who posed for this photograph in 1913, lived across West Street from Dr. Shaw's first home office. (Kennedy family.)

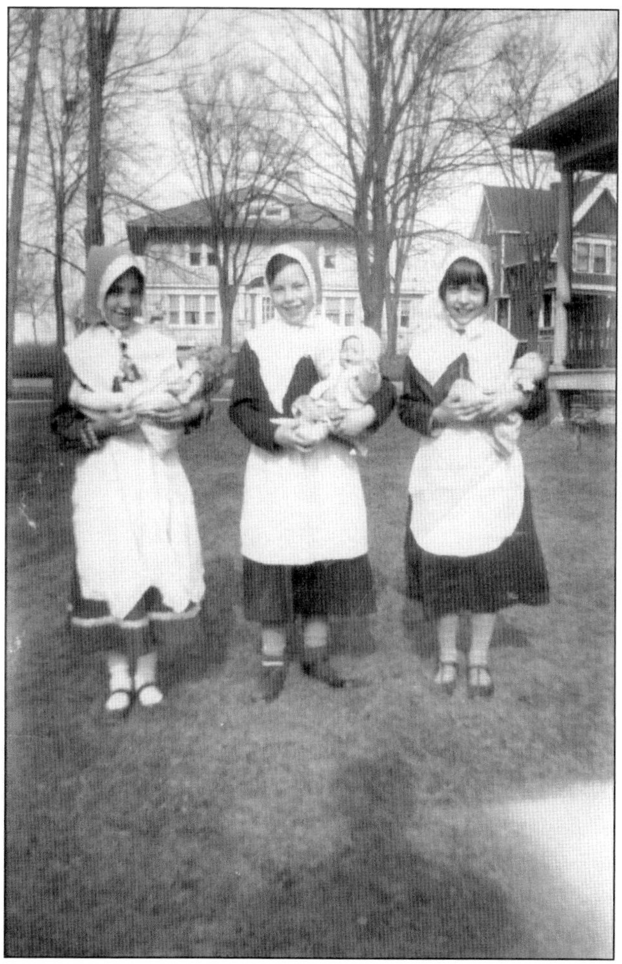

A young Louise Adler (left) gathers with some playmates in her family's side yard around 1930. Behind the girls is the home that Dr. Byron Shaw built for his office in 1928 and used until his death in 1939. (Kennedy family.)

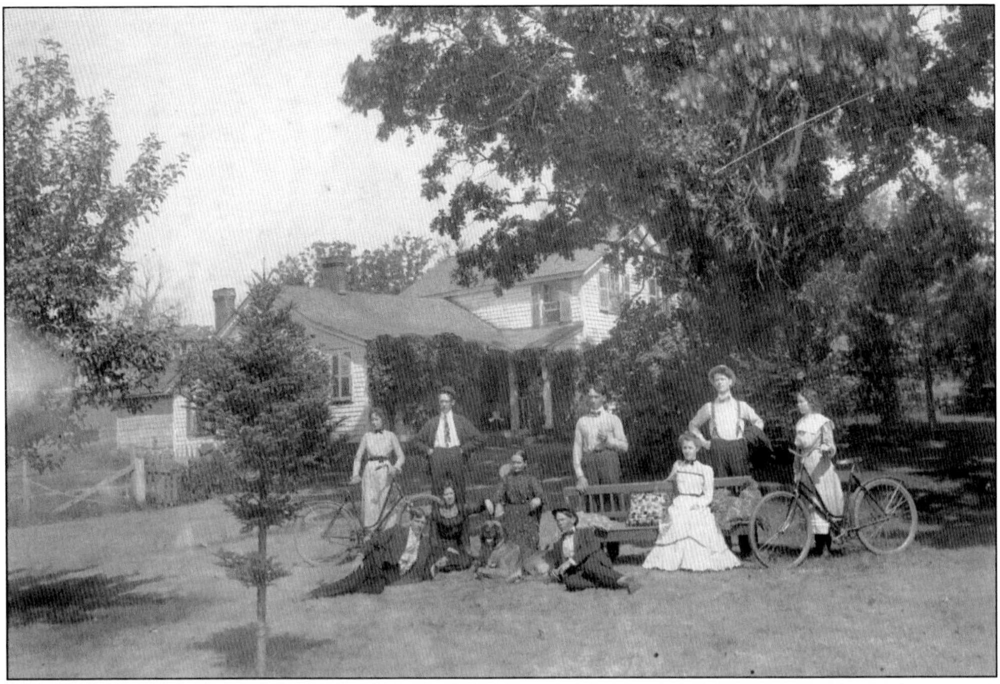

The Kennedy farm was located on Kennedy Drive in Westport. Ellen Hogan Kennedy carried on as landowner and matriarch for 52 years after her husband's death. Relaxing on the farm from left to right are, (first row, seated) Coll Kennedy, Anastasia (Anne) Kennedy Walsh, Nero (dog), Ellen Hogan Kennedy (seated in rocker), James Kennedy, Agnes Lynch (married to Richard), and Mary Kennedy Fisher; (second row) Theresa Borchers, Martin Francis Kennedy, Michael H. Kennedy, and Richard V. Kennedy. (Kennedy family.)

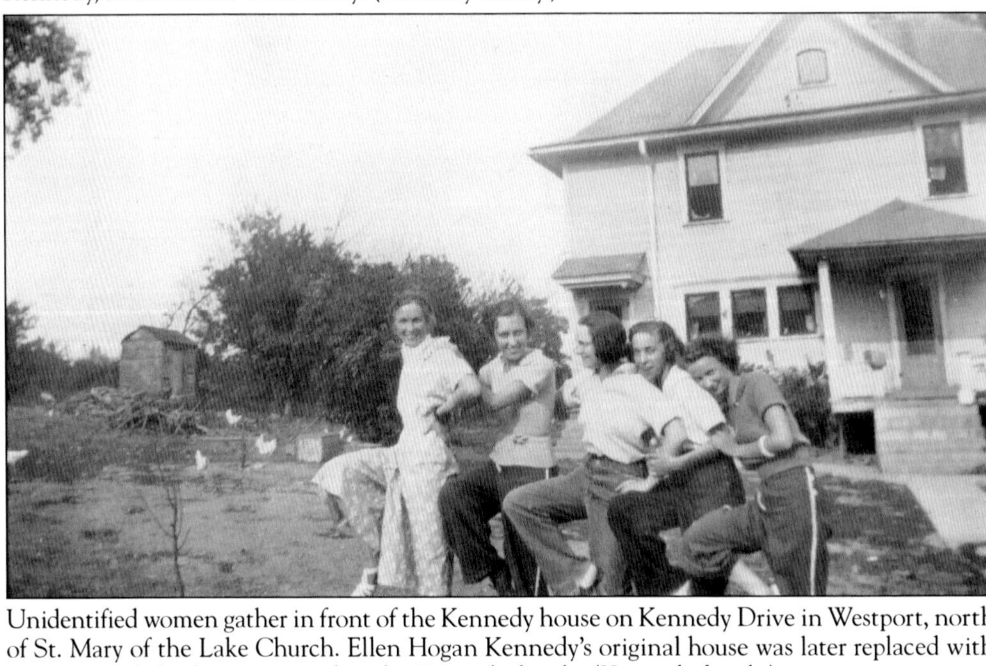

Unidentified women gather in front of the Kennedy house on Kennedy Drive in Westport, north of St. Mary of the Lake Church. Ellen Hogan Kennedy's original house was later replaced with this one, and the farm remained in the Kennedy family. (Kennedy family.)

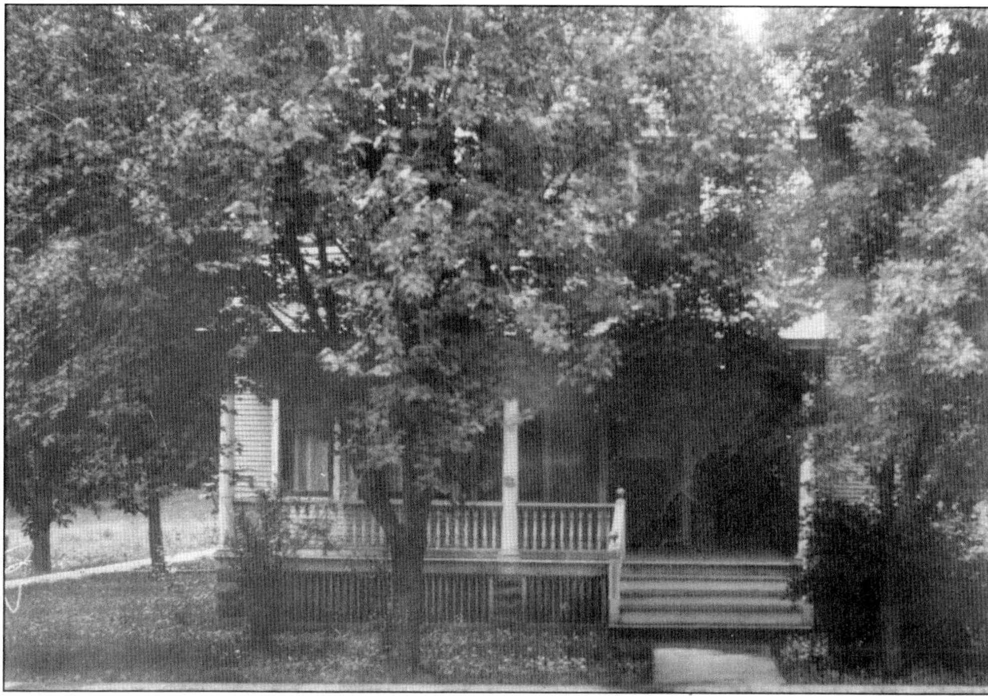

When Henry Heller owned this home at 300 West Main Street, his daughter Anna Heller started the Women's Club meetings there, using the house as a temporary library. William Fisher moved to Waunakee in 1913 and lived in the house on West Main and West Streets for many years before it was purchased by Marcel Schwab and turned into a funeral home. Later, it was converted into the First Baptist Church. (Kennedy family.)

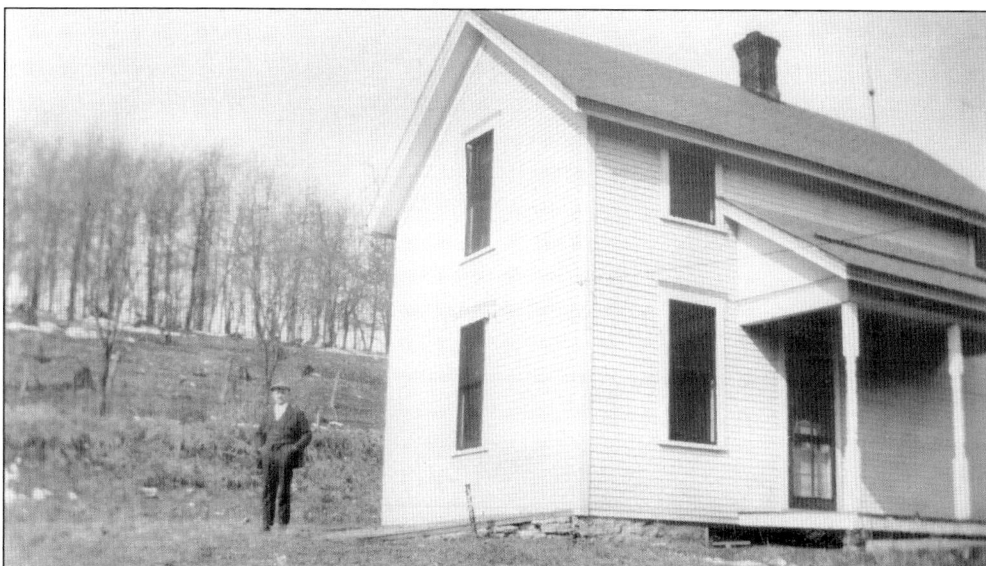

Clear-cut tree stumps mark the progression of the land from Wisconsin's native forests to farmland, as Joseph H. Koltes surveys the farm on present-day Bong Road that belonged to his uncle, also named Joseph Koltes. The elder Joseph Koltes purchased the Westport farm in 1884 and lived there until his death in 1905. His son William Koltes then took over the farm. (James P. Koltes.)

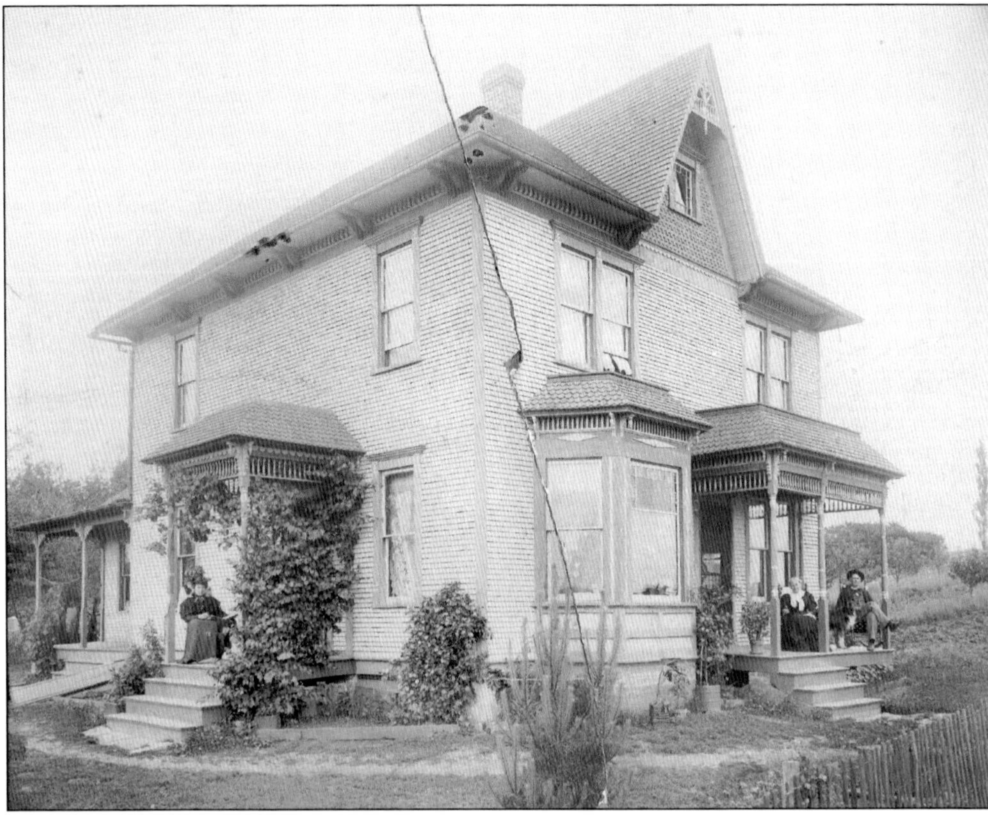

John Hogan Tierney was a prominent landowner south of Waunakee. He lived in this house at the end of present-day Endres Road with his wife, Bridget, who is pictured on the right porch with their son Henry. On the left porch is John and Bridget's daughter Lucy. The curtain billowing out of an open window was a trademark of an unidentified Waunakee photographer. (James P. Koltes.)

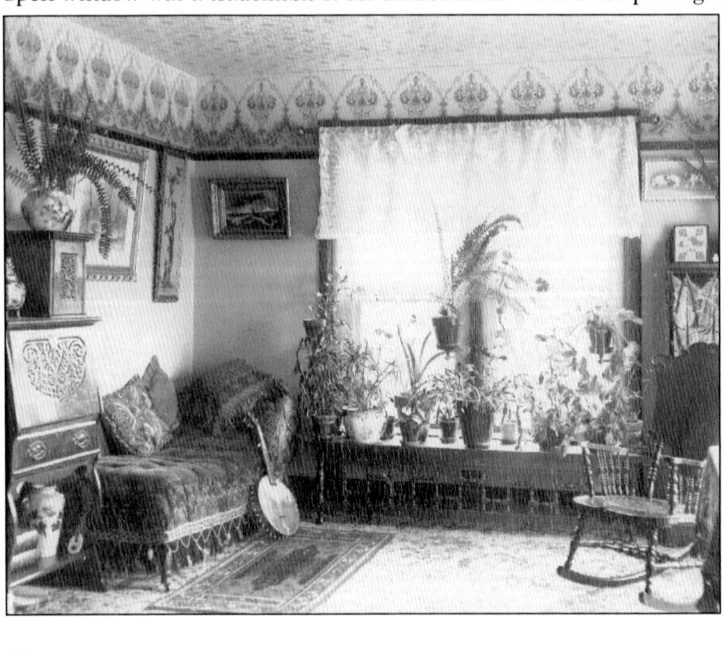

A rare interior view affords a look inside the John Hogan Tierney house. The fine furnishings befit Tierney's run as an assemblyperson and chairman of the township board. Eleven children were born to the family, though two died in early childhood. (James P. Koltes.)

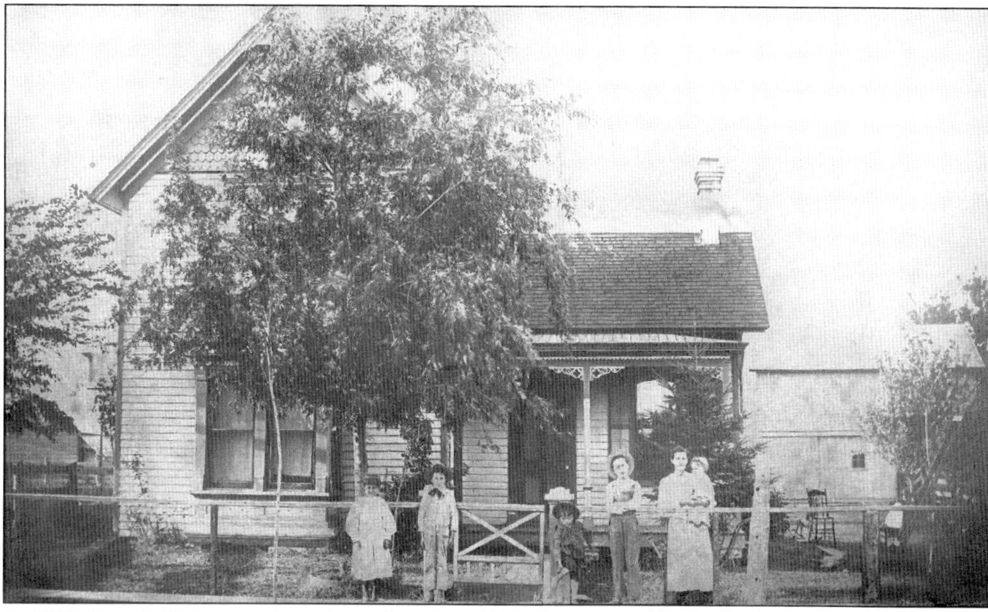

In 1888, Joseph Koltes purchased two lots from E.M. Cooper and built this house, doing half of the work himself. Koltes's children are pictured from left to right as follows: Ida, Harry, Raphael (Gar), Ed, and Grace (held by his wife, Josephine). The original photograph was developed with a blue hue, a trademark of Dr. Austin Blake whose side hobby was photography. (James P. Koltes.)

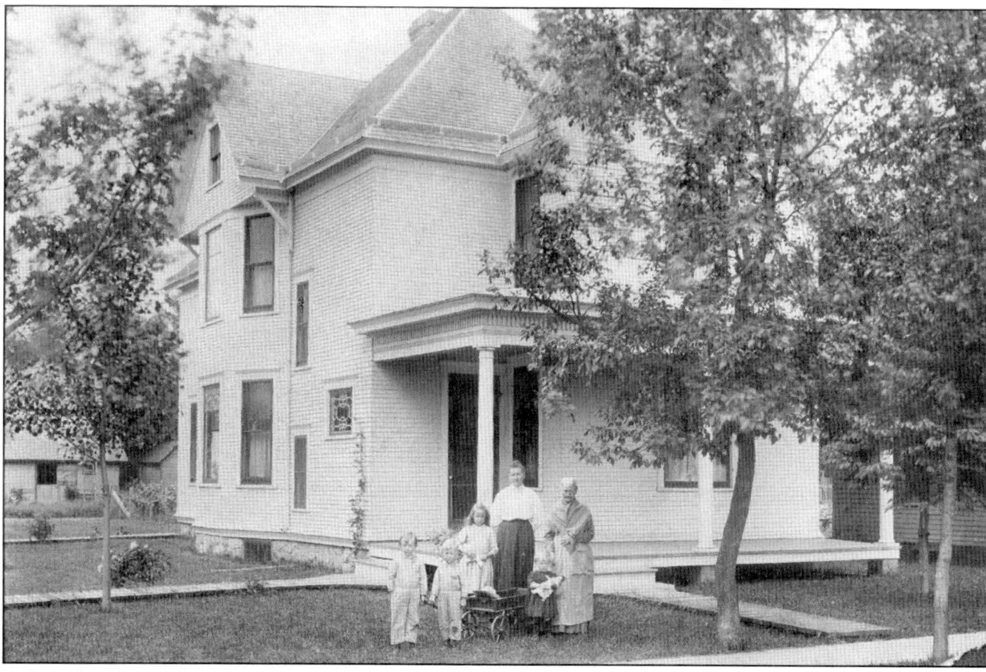

While developing many industries—from shipping animals and supplies to the Dakotas to running his lumber company—Joseph Koltes built this house at 301 Grant Street in 1903. Assembled in front around 1908 are, from left to right, John Cook, Norman Cook, Florence Koltes, Josephine Tierney Koltes, Mabel Cook, and Bridget Tierney. After her daughter Lucy Cook passed away, Tierney took in her grandchildren and lived in the house next door. (James P. Koltes.)

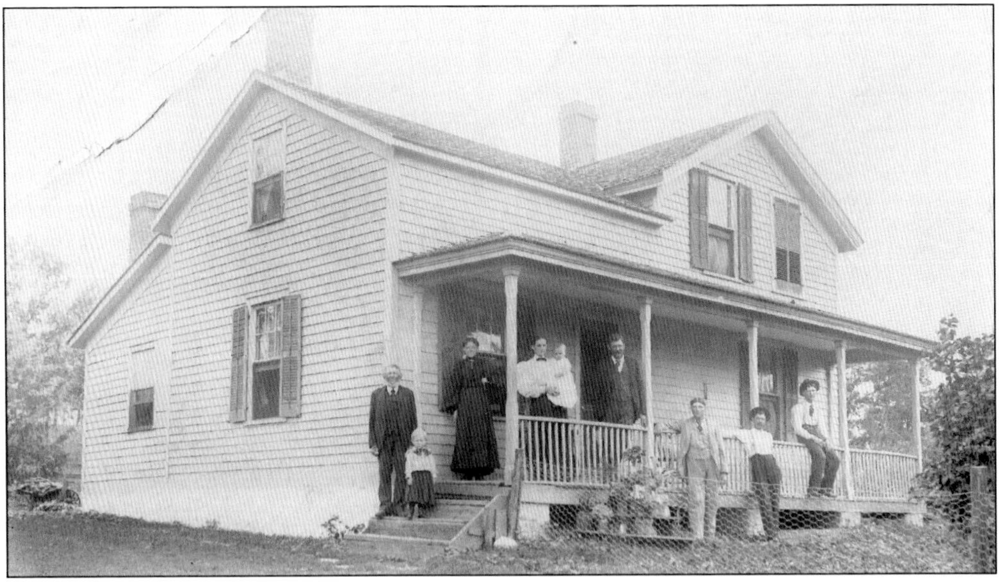

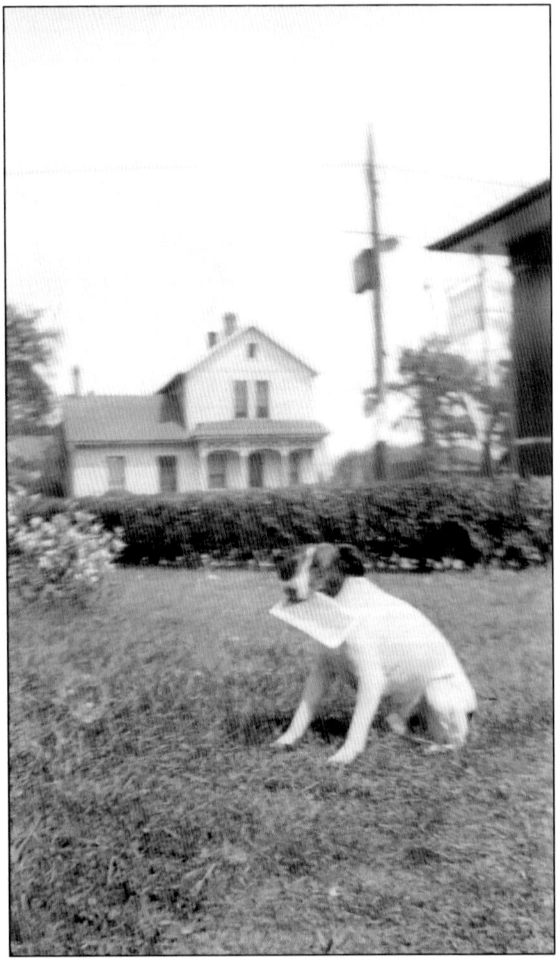

Around 1897, the John Wilken Oncken family occupied this residence on Oncken Road in southwest Westport Township in an area known as the Blackwoods. Noted as they relate to John, the family includes, from left to right, Hajo Harmes Oncken (father), George Henry Oncken (son), Emma Oncken (sister), Ottilie Westphal Oncken (wife) holding Lillian Oncken (daughter), John Wilken Oncken, Henry Oncken (brother), August Junge, and Edward Kupfer (farm laborer). Lillian Oncken later married Harry Koltes, the son of Joseph H. Koltes. (James P. Koltes.)

In the background of this photograph is Julia Bacon Cooper's house. Julia was the widow of Eli Cooper, Waunakee and Westport landowner who expanded the east end of the village, called Cooper's Addition. The dog belonged to Martin "Jinx" and Winnie Ford Corcoran, whose house was behind the photographer. Corcoran's service station, also on East Main Street, is visible on the right. (James P. Koltes.)

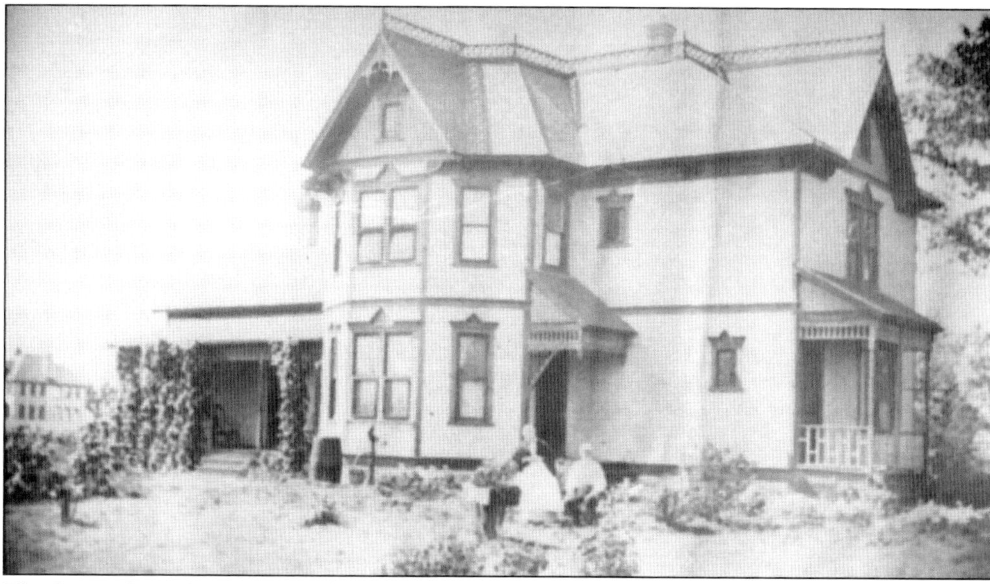

The house Jinx Corcoran and his wife, Winnie, lived in was between the Ford garage and Corcoran's service station. Winnie's father, Al Ford, and Winnie's immediate family occupied the house and all were named in the 1920 census. After Winnie and Jinx were married, Winnie's sisters Myrtle and Florence would also reside there at times. Waunakee High School is visible in the far distance to the left. (WPL.)

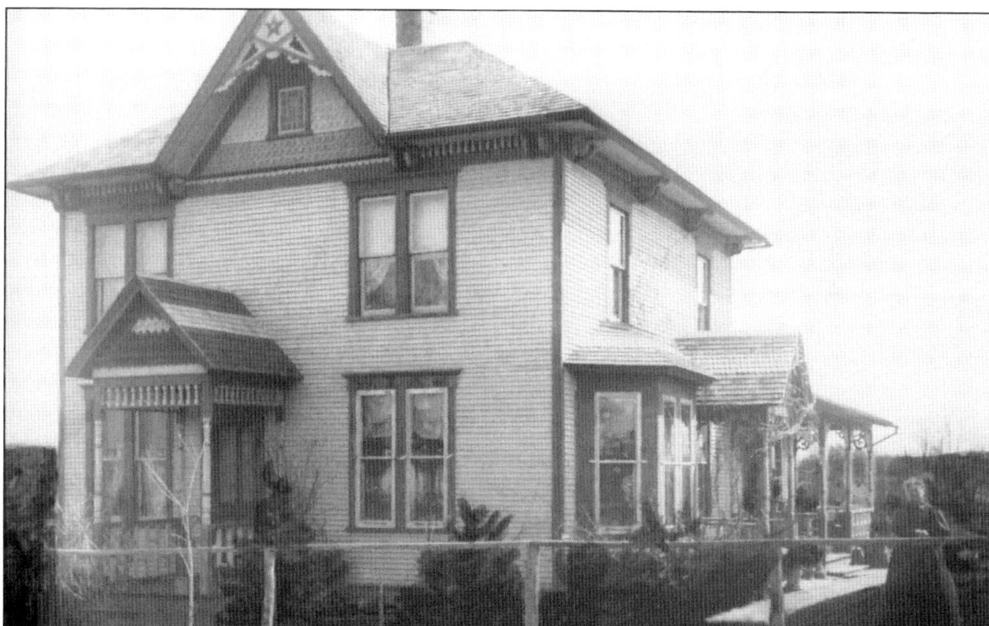

The Truehl house at 105 Bacon Street was occupied by three Raemisch generations at various times. First was Frank C. Raemisch, who lived in the house after his father passed away and his mother, Louise Raemisch, married Robert Truehl, who owned the house. When Truehl died in 1934, the house passed to the late Louise's son F.C. Raemisch. More than a decade later, Raemisch's daughter Hazel Raemisch Roudebush and husband, George Roudebush, moved into the home where they then raised their five girls. (Hazel R. Zimbric.)

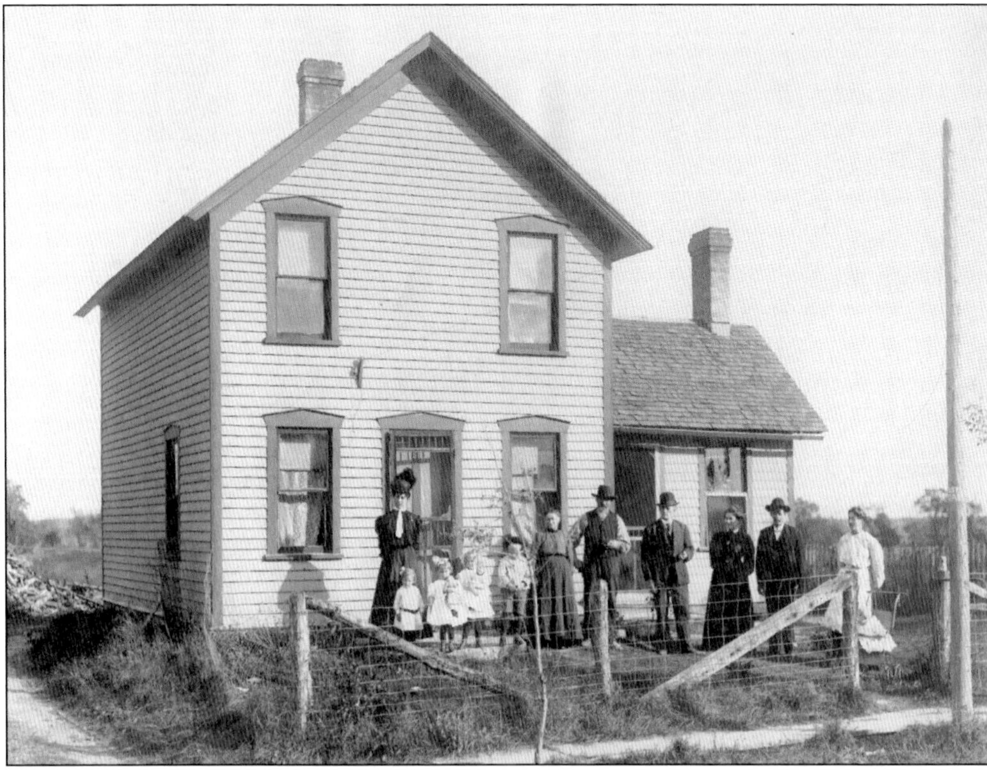

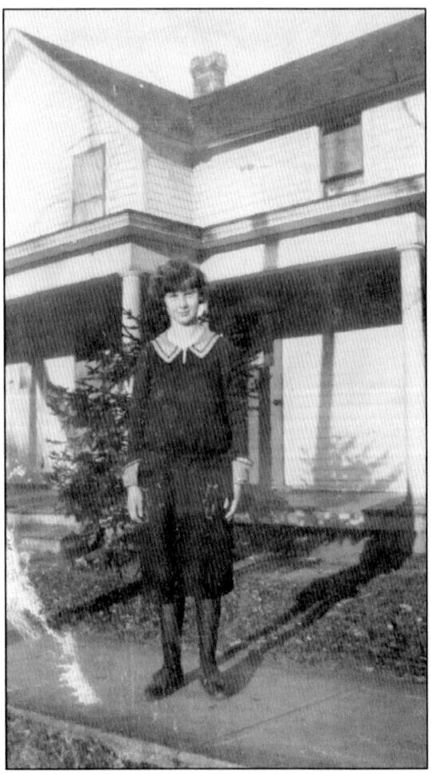

The house on Bacon Street where Frank C. Raemisch and his wife, Mary Miller Raemisch, lived soon after marriage went through many changes over the years. Assembled in front of the original house are, from left to right, Rose Miller Chambers, unidentified children, grandma Mary Miller, John Miller, ? Maulbetch, Bertha Raemisch Cooper, F.C. Raemisch, Mary Miller Raemisch, and baby Louise, born 1903. (Hazel R. Zimbric.)

The F.C. Raemisch house at the edge of Waunakee looked more like a farmhouse at the turn of the century than its remodeled version in the 1920s, accompanied here by 13-year-old Hazel Raemisch. Sister to baby Louise in the previous photograph, Hazel was one of five children raised in the house. (Hazel R. Zimbric.)

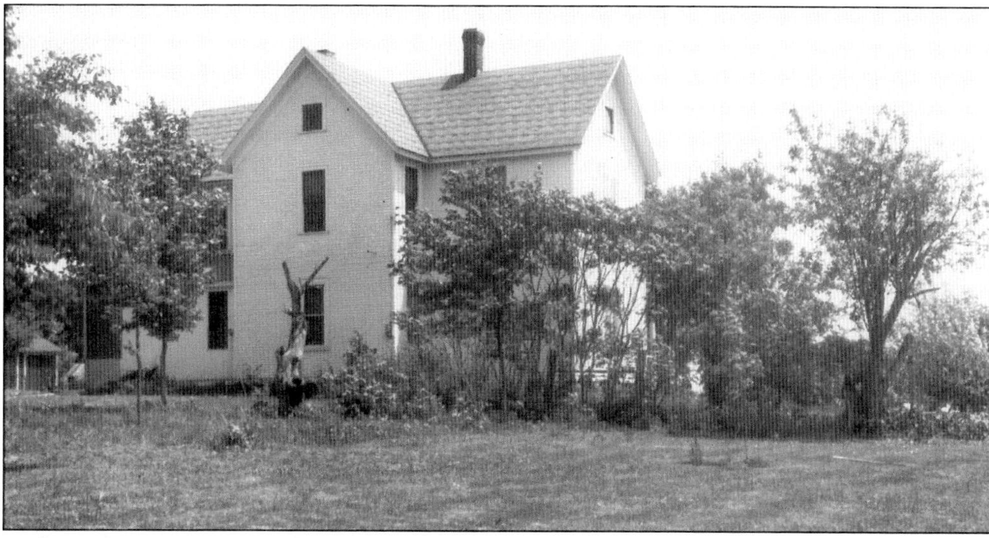

In the early 1890s, Henry Schumacher bought Dr. Nathaniel Wheeler's former home in northern Westport Township. Schumacher moved the structure back 100 feet in 1906 when he hired Frank Schwenn to design and build the new house. Both Henry and Eveline Busby Schumacher's parents' homes were built by Frank Schwenn. The Schumachers moved into the house, shown from the west, during the summer of 1908. (Friends of Schumacher Farm.)

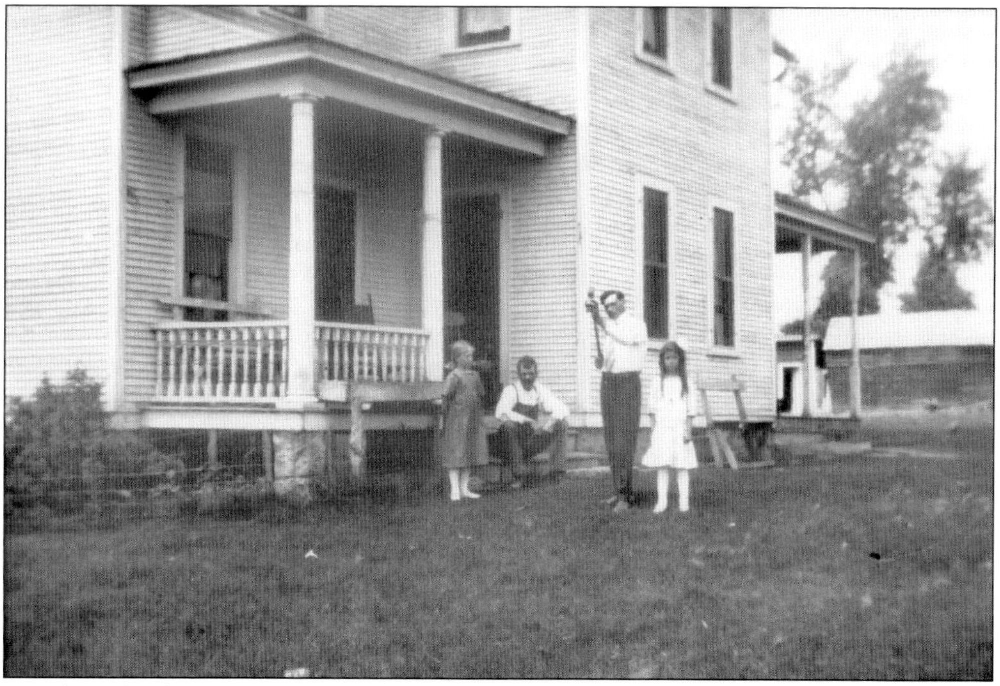

Details in this late-1910s photograph of the Schumacher house, taken from the east, illustrate life in the early 20th century. A wire fence surrounds the decorative plants to protect them from the goats that would roam freely around the yard. The porch leading into the parlor and dining room was fitted with a lathed hand railing in 1915. Henry Schumacher sits on the steps while entertaining guests; his daughter Marcella Schumacher stands on the far right. (Friends of Schumacher Farm.)

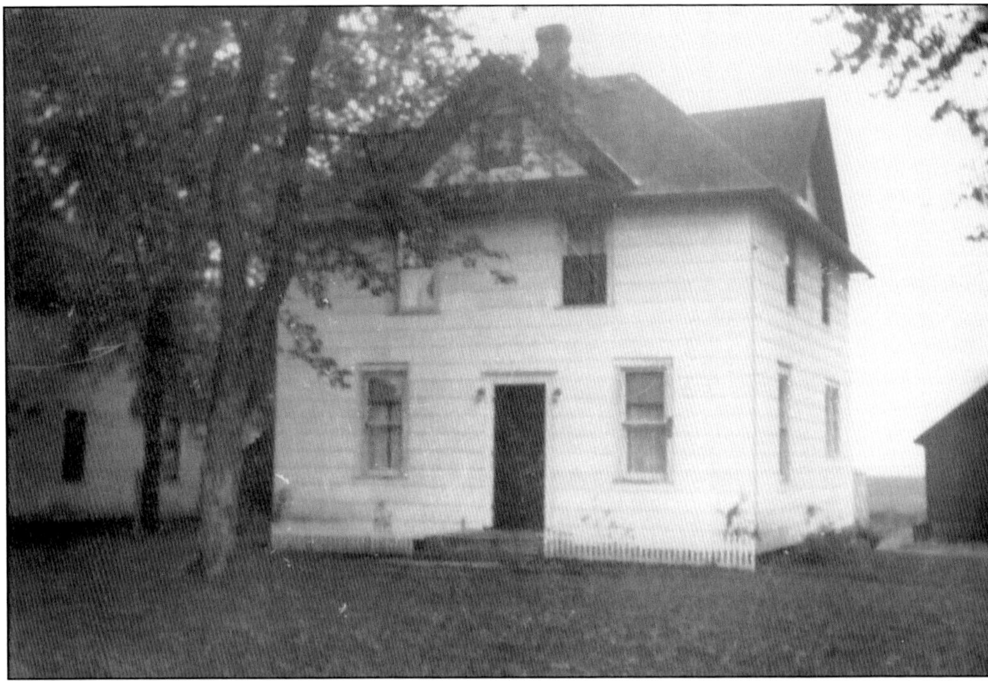

The Kruschek home stood so close to St. John's school that Clara Kruschek took pictures out her window when the new school was built in 1948. However, when the parish needed more room for parking in 1960, homes on Third Street, including Kruschek's, were moved or demolished. This photograph is one last view of the home at its 300 Third Street address. (Kruschek family.)

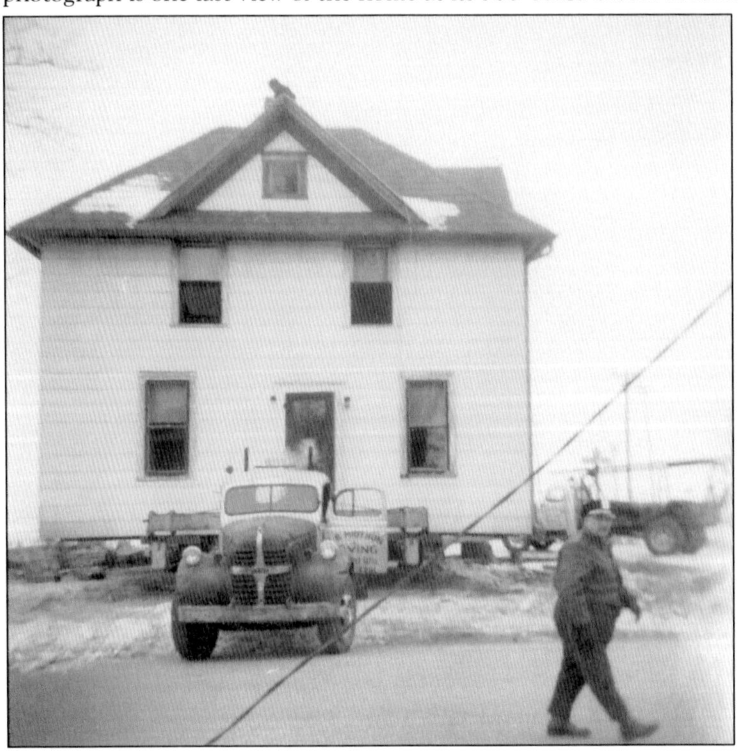

As the Kruschek home is loaded onto trucks, chief of police George Manthey surveys the operation. The truck drove the house east, winding along Third Street until it reached its new corner lot on Grant and Bacon Streets. (Kruschek family.)

Seven

People

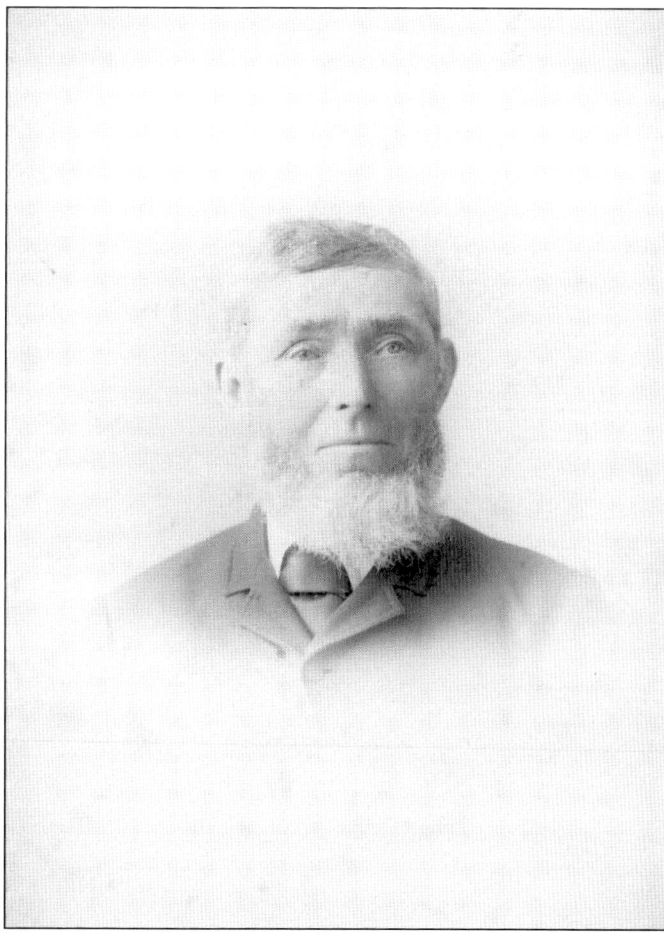

In 1843, Michael O'Malley sent his sons Thomas (pictured) and John from their home in Westport, County Mayo, Ireland, to scope out the new world. Thomas O'Malley traveled to the area later named Westport by his family after their homeland. In the spring of 1843, he built a log cabin on his first 160 acres. O'Malley married Catherine Walsh in 1848, and she moved to eastern Westport Township with him. She was known to visit the Indians whose camps were scattered as near as a half mile from their house. By age 78, Thomas O'Malley owned 400 acres in Westport Township. (Kennedy family.)

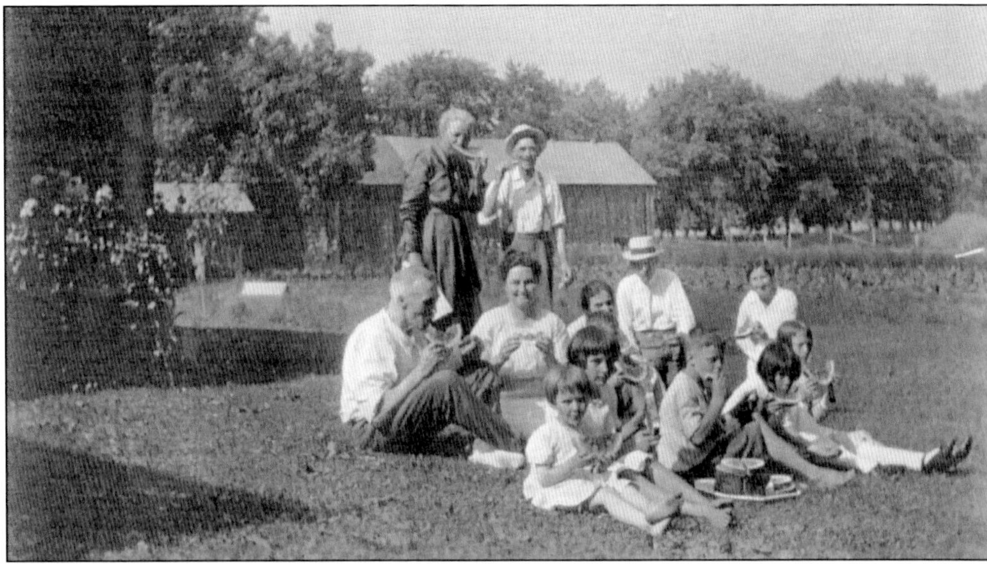

Descendants of Michael O'Malley enjoy watermelon at the Westport farm owned by son Thomas O'Malley, born in 1815. At the time the photograph was taken, Thomas's son Vincent O'Malley owned the farm. He is likely the person standing wearing a straw hat. The farm, located in a hollow east of River Road, was one of 13 Westport farms owned by O'Malley families in 1898. (Mary Ellen Kearney.)

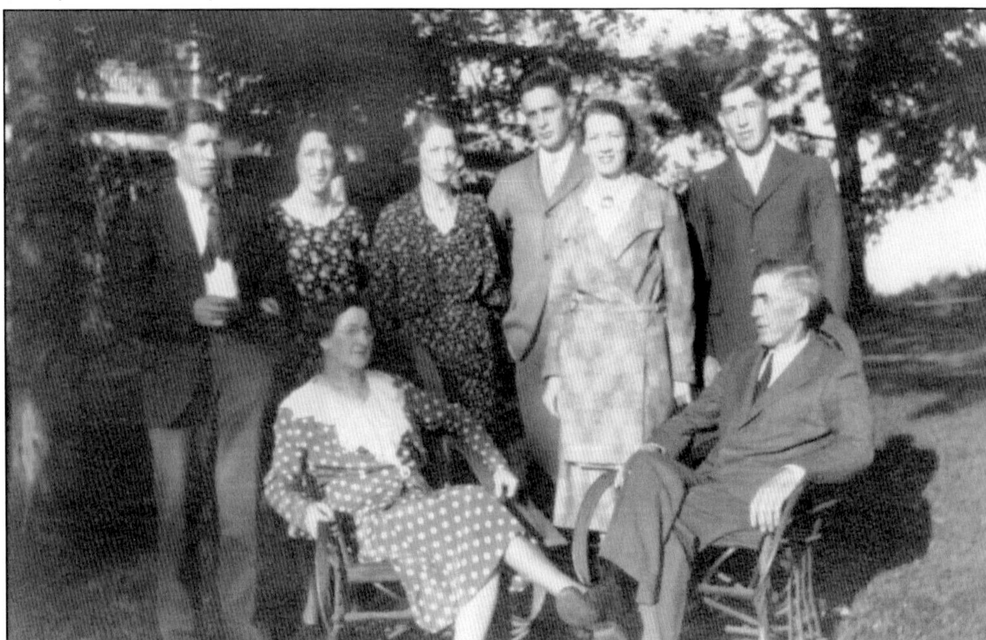

Sitting in front of their West Main Street home in 1940 are Martha Monks O'Malley (left) and Thomas P. O'Malley. One of their children, James—born in 1914, died when he was three. Their remaining six children stand behind them; from left to right are Victor O'Malley, Mary O'Malley Jordan, Catherine O'Malley Homewood, Thomas O'Malley, Martha O'Malley Scanlon, and Dave O'Malley. This was the last family picture taken before Thomas P. O'Malley died in 1941. (Mary Ellen Kearney.)

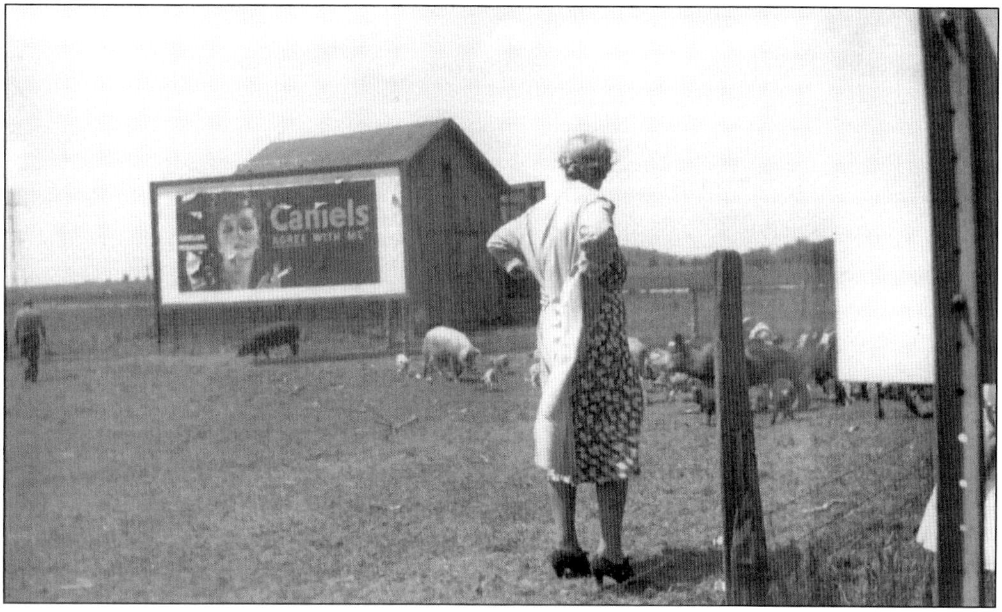

Martha Monks O'Malley (above) looks out across the area that later became the southwest corner of West Main Street and Century Avenue, home to a mini-mall and the village hall. She managed the selling of plots of land from the O'Malley farm as well as the donating of land for the first Waunakee High School. Martha and Thomas P. O'Malley met while he was living at the farm. Martha, who taught at a school north of the village, would ride her bike past the house daily. Thomas followed her to the school one day, and they married in 1901. Martha and Thomas' daughter Catherine O'Malley Homewood, born in 1905, displays the Waunakee sign on the O'Malley property that would greet visitors traveling east into the village. (Both, Mary Ellen Kearney.)

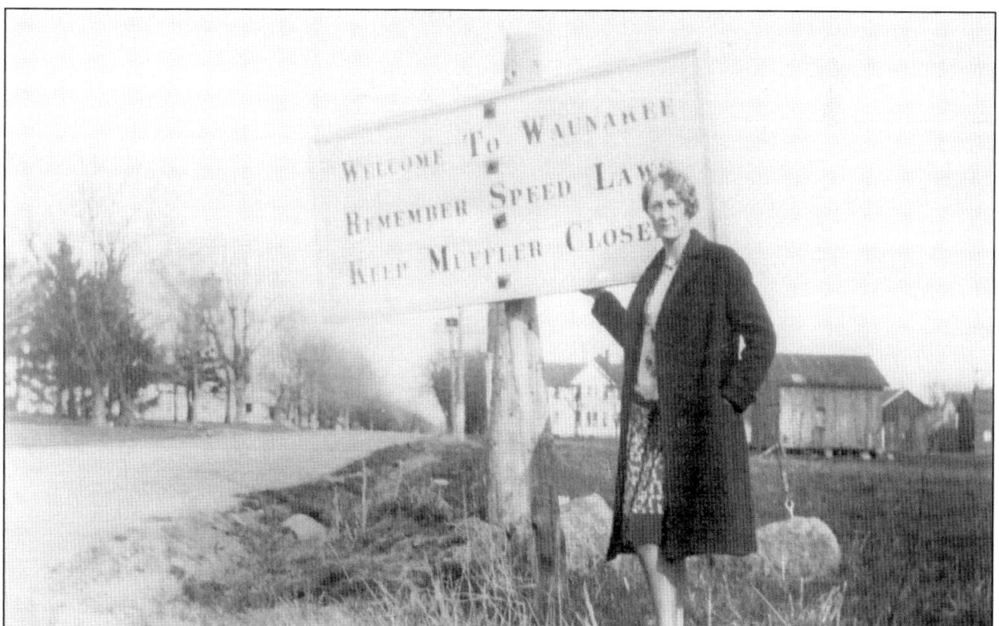

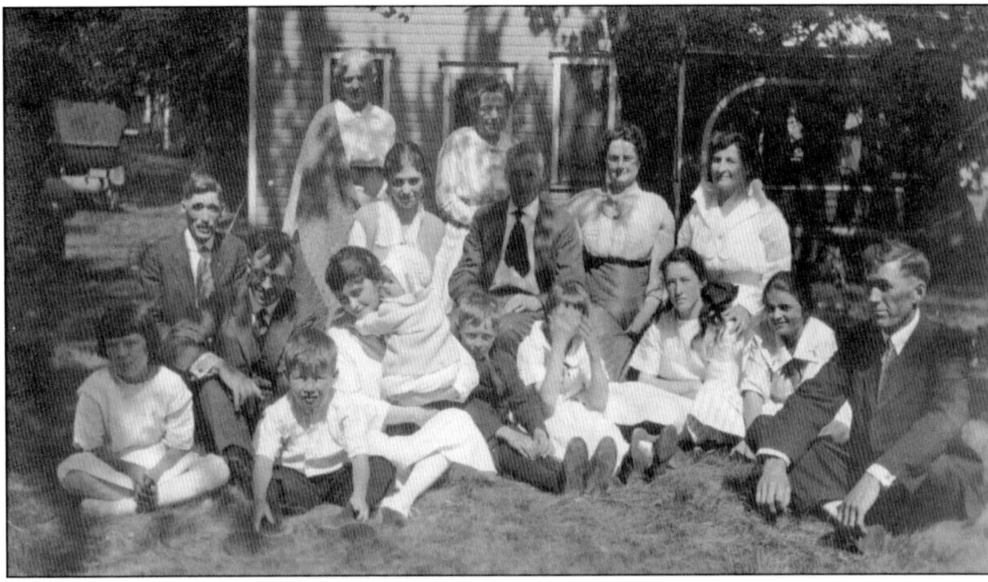

Pictured behind members of three O'Malley families, the Club Cottage was owned by six Westport families. It was located on Borchers Beach Road on the shore of Lake Mendota. The families photographed are the elder Thomas O'Malley's sons Martin (upper left), Vincent (center), and Thomas P. (far right). Others who took part in the share were the Kennedy and Koltes families; each family was allowed two weeks to spend there in the summer. (Mary Ellen Kearney.)

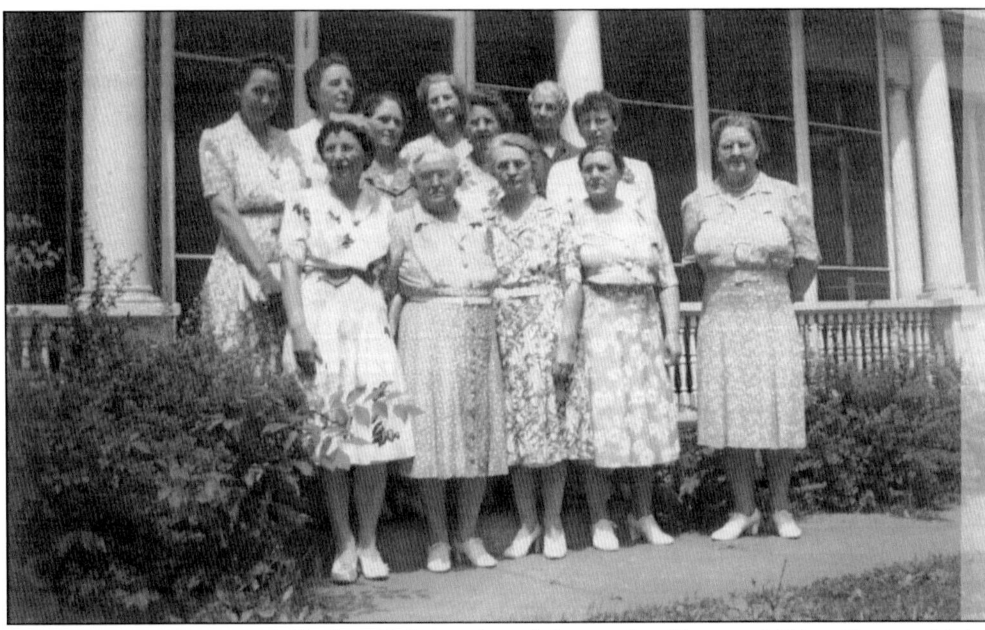

Participants in Waunakee's Bridge Club are, from left to right, (first row) Edna George, Mabel Kenny, ? Clark, Anna Michels, and Kit Weiskirck; (second row) Ada Cameron, Harriet Kuestner, Peg Klingelhofer, Martha O'Malley, Dorothy Koltes, and Carrie Shaw. (Mary Ellen Kearney.)

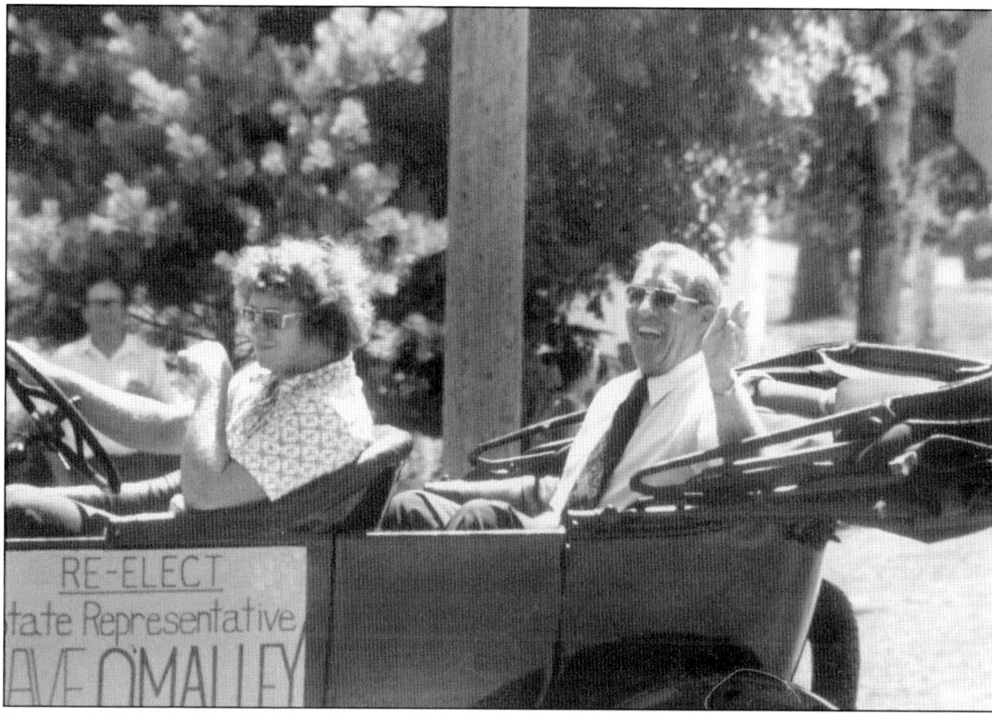

Democrat David O'Malley campaigns for reelection during one of his 18 years as a representative in the state assembly. First elected in 1958, he drew on his experiences living at the Main Street farm to chair the Assembly Agriculture Committee. A year before his death in 1986, O'Malley donated land to the village for building a new library and senior center in Waunakee. (Mary Ellen Kearney.)

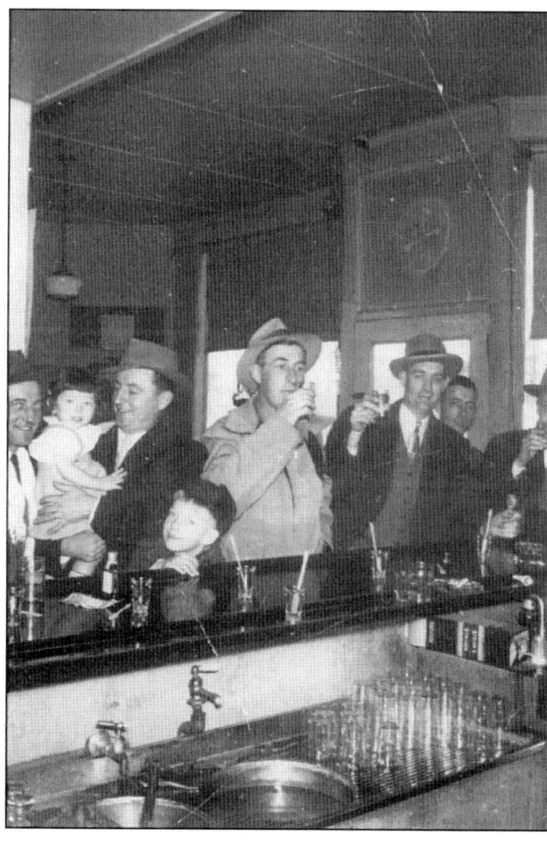

Lenny's tavern on South Street was a popular meeting place in the village. Pictured at the bar from left to right are Ben Uebersetzig, Lenny Adler (owner, holding daughter Lorie), Bernie Uebersetzig (boy in front), Dave O'Malley, Tom O'Malley, ? Adler, and Joe Scanlon. (Mary Ellen Kearney.)

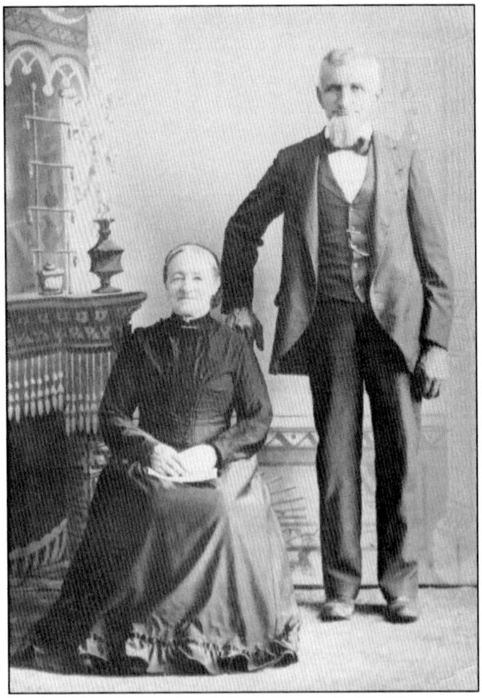

In the 1850s, many German citizens settled in Springfield Township west of Westport. Helena Fischer Koltes (left) and Michael Koltes, one such couple, were married in 1855 at St. Martin's Church in Martinsville. They moved into Westport Township in 1866 and farmed until 1879 when Michael opened a butcher shop in Waunakee. He started Koltes Lumber Company in 1881 and owned 600 acres of land when he retired in 1886. (James P. Koltes.)

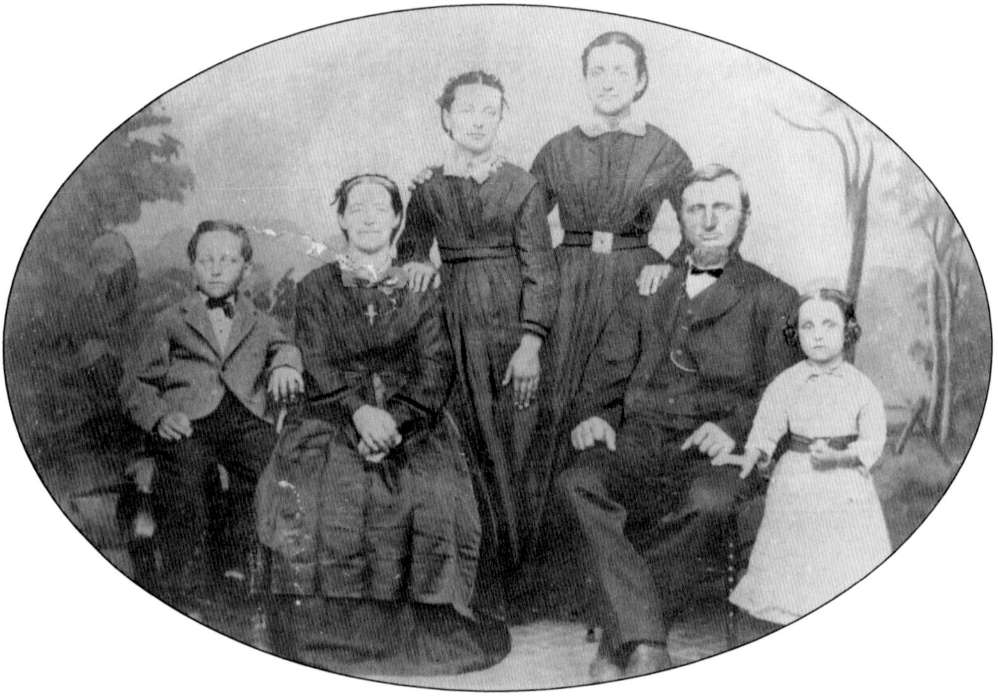

Members of the Michael Koltes family are, from left to right, Joseph H., Helena Fischer Koltes, Susan, Adelaide, Michael Koltes, and Agnes. Helena's mother, Adalhaeide Klosterhalfer Fischer, was born in Prussia, brought her daughters to Wisconsin in 1852, and later lived with the Michael Koltes family. At the time of his death in 1914, Koltes had 19 grandchildren and 41 great-grandchildren. (James P. Koltes.)

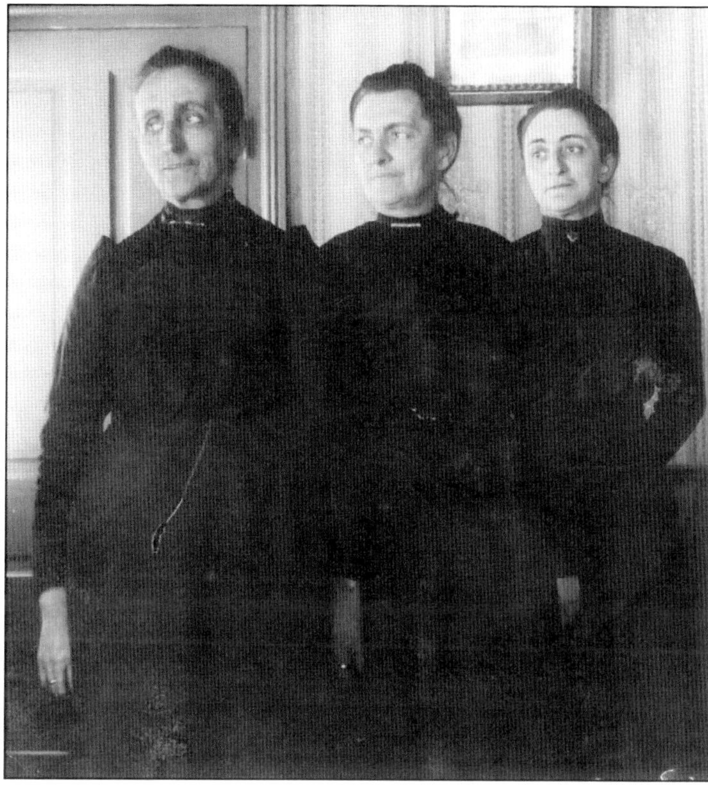

The three sisters of Joseph H. Koltes are, from left to right, Adelaide Koltes Dorn, Susan Koltes Mueller (Miller), and Agnes Koltes Riphahn. Agnes married Joseph Koltes's business partner Peter Riphahn. Behind the women is a framed photograph of Koltes and Riphahn's lumber and hardware store. (James P. Koltes.)

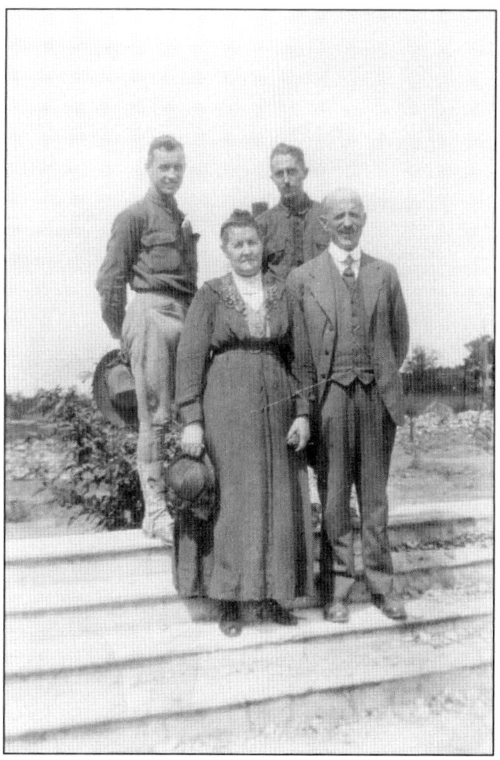

Mary Josephine Tierney Koltes (first row, left) and Joseph H. Koltes (first row, right) were married at St. Mary of the Lake in Westport on February 11, 1885. Josephine's parents were from Ireland, and she was born in Westport in 1862. Josephine and Joseph Koltes were blessed with eight children: Edward, Harry, Ida, Raphael P. (Gar, pictured in second row, right with unidentified friend), Grace, Catherine (lived only a few months), Florence, and Eleanor. (James P. Koltes.)

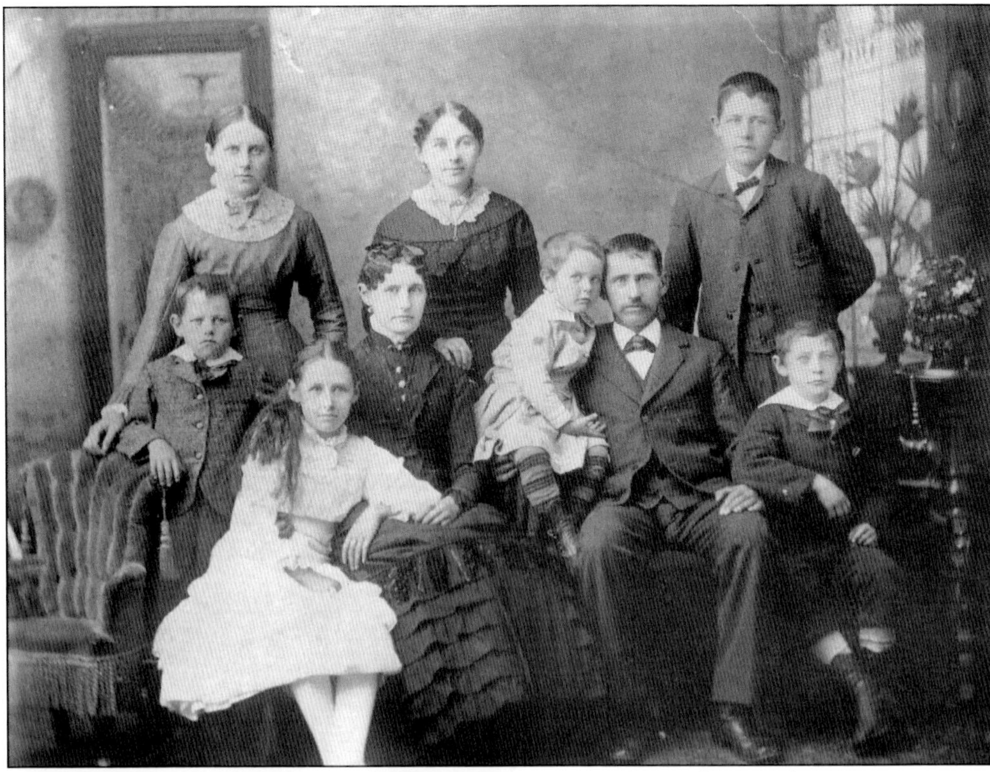

An early couple to settle in Westport Township was Josephine Tierney Koltes' parents, John Hogan Tierney and Bridget Malone Tierney from Ireland. Pictured here around 1880, their children are, from left to right, (first row) James, Lucy, Josephine, Henry, John E., and Robert Emmett; (second row) Catharine, Nellie, and Martin (Bub). Missing are another Martin (John Hogan and Bridget's second boy), who died around age three, and Theresa, who died in 1875 at age five. (James P. Koltes.)

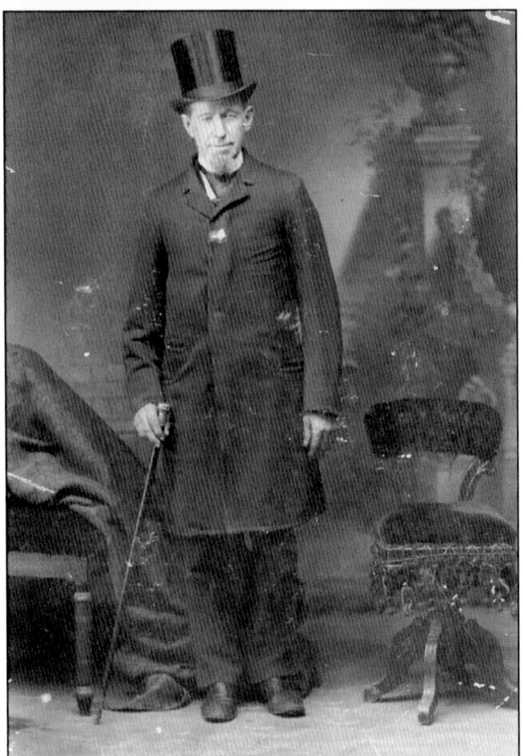

John Hogan Tierney was an Irish immigrant who started out as a landowner and farmer in Westport. He decided to try a run for office, so he campaigned as a Democrat for the state assembly. In that particular election, the votes were split between Republicans and Greenbacks, and Tierney ended up winning by surprise. He served one term. (James P. Koltes.)

In her short 35 years, Lucy Tierney Cook accomplished much. She had three children—John, Norman, and Mabel—who went to live with Lucy's mother, Bridget Malone Tierney, upon Lucy's death in 1907. Cook was involved in the Catholic church, and would go door-to-door asking for subscriptions to fund various church needs. (James P. Koltes.)

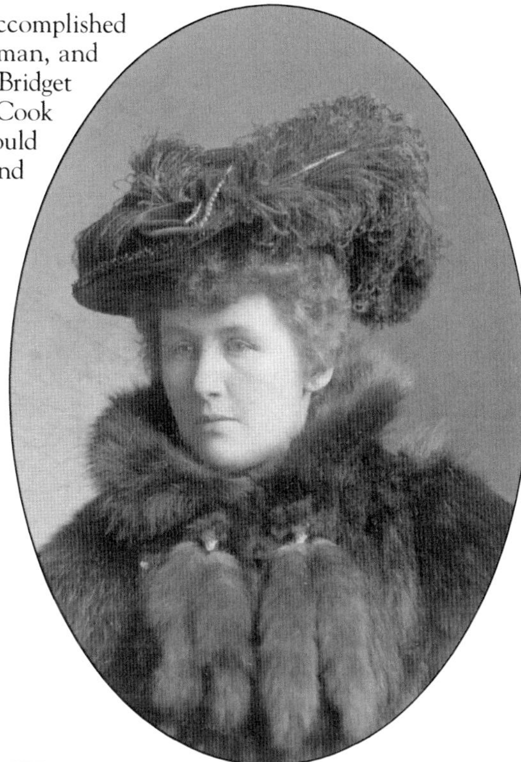

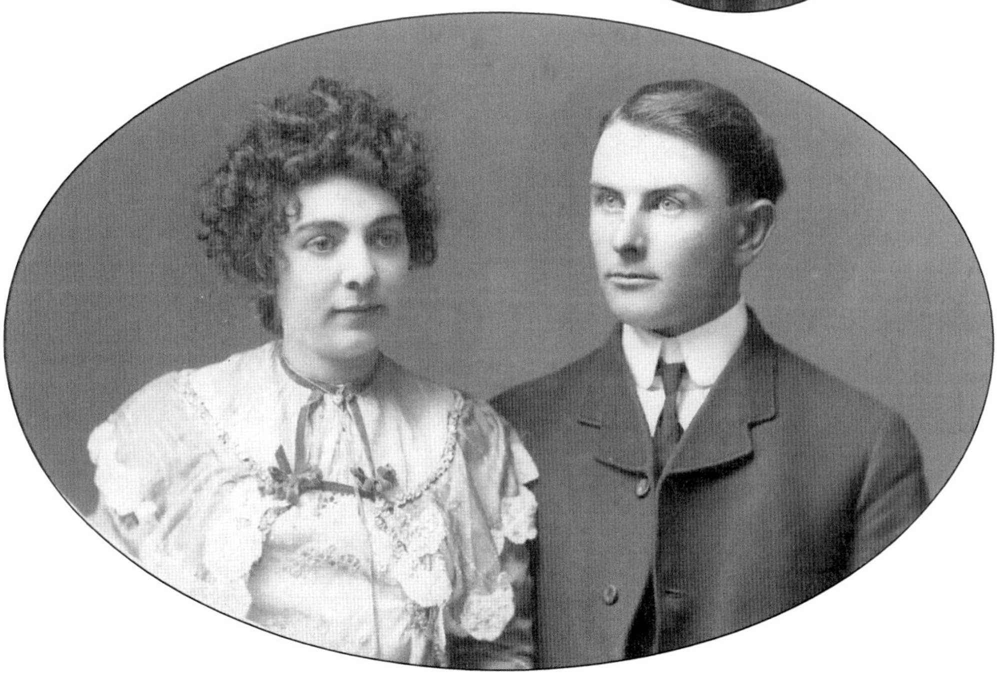

The youngest son of John Hogan Tierney and Bridget Malone Tierney was Henry Tierney, born in 1878. Henry had many adventures with his "boys" in Milwaukee before he married Mamie O'Laughlin and moved to Montana. They had a farm there, and as of 1920 had three children: Elnora C., Laughlin H., and Louise M. (James P. Koltes.)

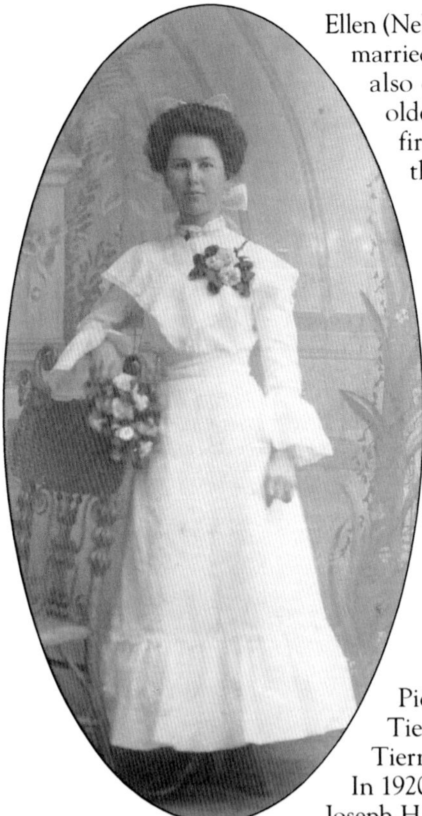

Ellen (Nellie) Tierney, daughter of John Hogan and Bridget Tierney, married Henry Reis and had 11 children. One of their children, also called Nellie (pictured), was born around 1886. Her older sister Gertrude Reis was Waunakee High School's first graduate in 1906; she was more than 20 years old at the time. (James P. Koltes.)

Pictured around 1915 are, from left to right, Josephine Tierney Koltes, her daughter Florence, unidentified, Lucy Tierney Cook's daughter Mabel, and Ida Koltes Shillinglaw. In 1920, Mabel Cook was living with her aunt Josie and uncle Joseph H. Koltes. (James P. Koltes.)

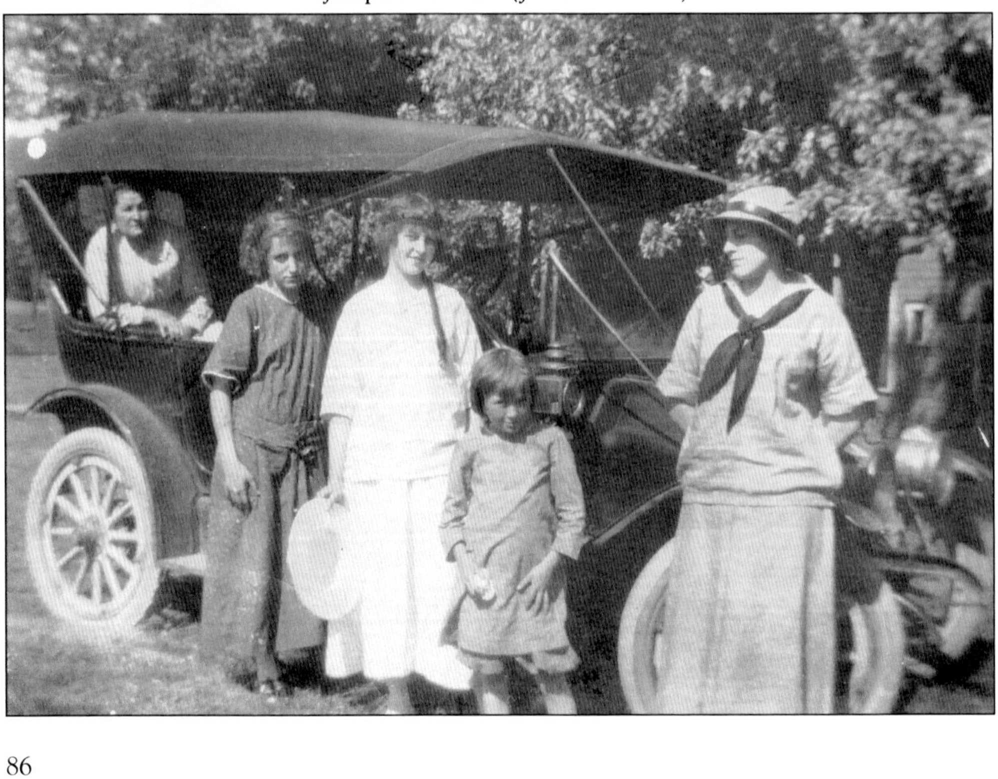

Married around 1893, Ottilia (Tillie) Westphal Oncken and John Oncken pose for their wedding photograph. They lived in a house on Oncken Road with some of John's family members, including his father, brother, and two sisters. In 1900, the Onckens' three children were listed as George (born 1895), Lillian (born 1896), and Myrtle (born 1898). As a farmer, John Oncken hired the neighbor boy as a live-in farm laborer, just as Oncken had done at age 16 for Charles Cooper. (James P. Koltes.)

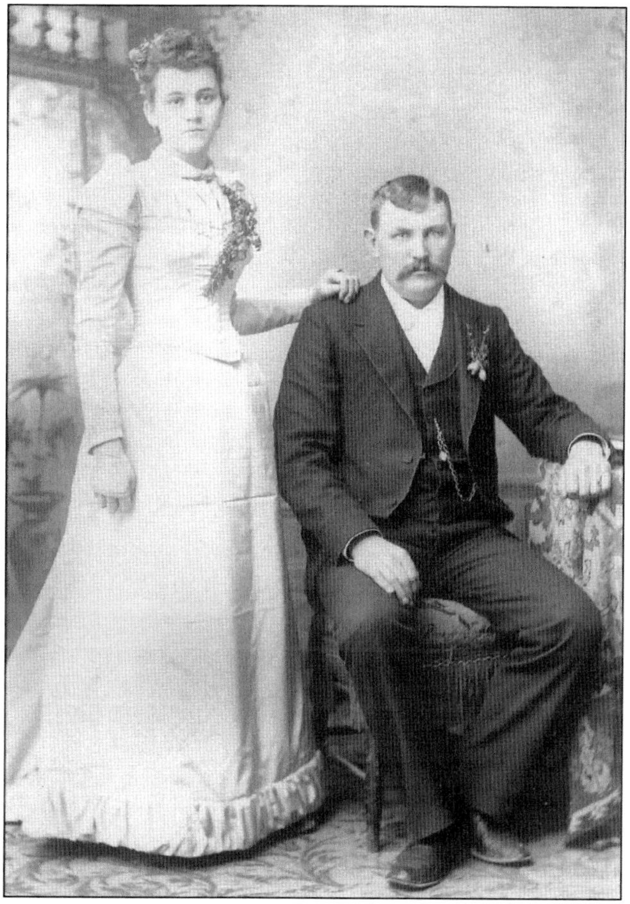

Several Westport families shared ownership of the co-op cottage located on Borchers Beach Road. One such couple was Raphael (Gar) and Dorothy Koltes, pictured submerged in the background of the photograph. Dorothy Koltes was president of the Waunakee Women's Club in 1932. (James P. Koltes.)

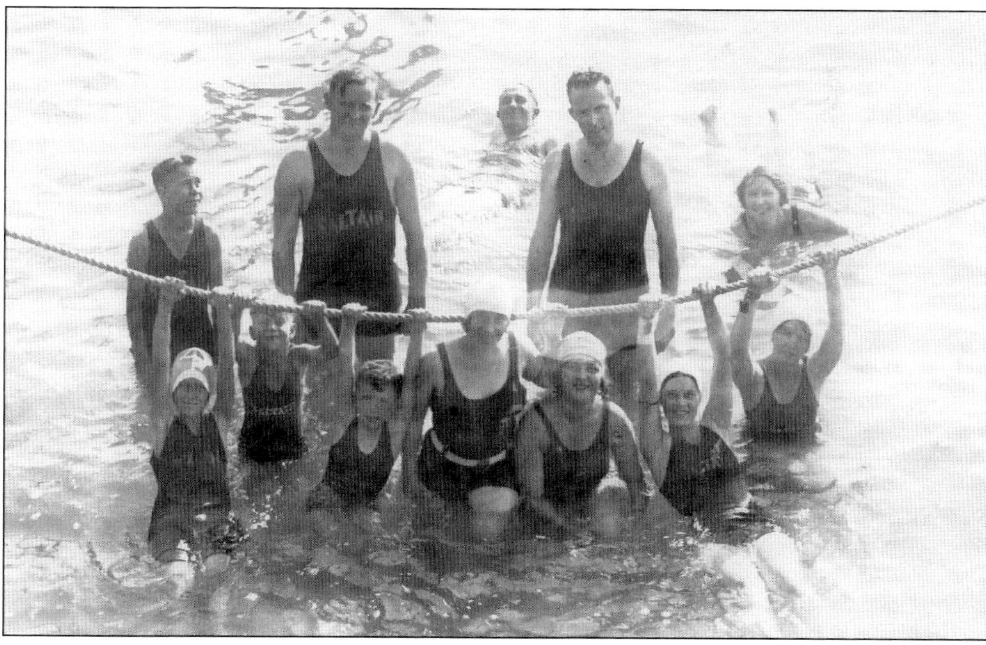

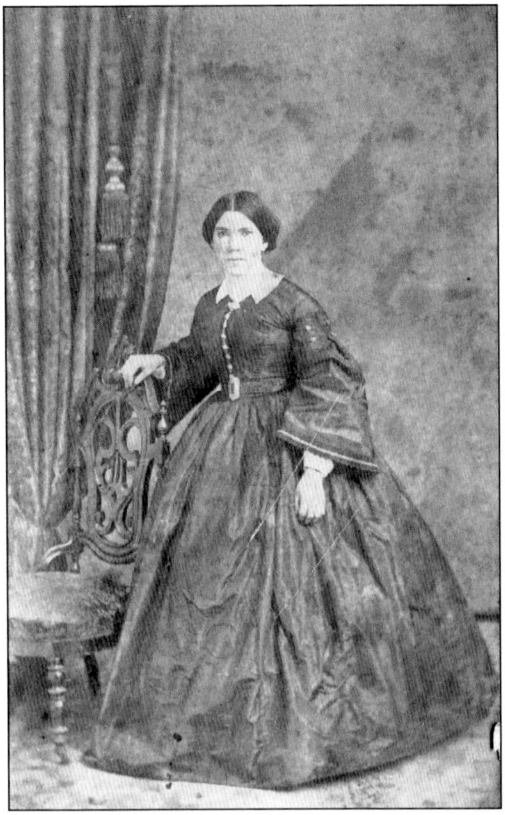

A white marble monument in St. Mary of the Lake Cemetery, Westport, marks the graves of the Duffy family: Patrick, Elizabeth, John E., and a baby. The family lived on a farm in Westport, north of the present Kennedy Drive, with at least one other child named Mary. After Patrick Duffy died in 1876, Elizabeth Duffy, pictured in the 1860s, went on as landowner. She later sold the Westport farm to Ellen Hogan Kennedy. (Kennedy family.)

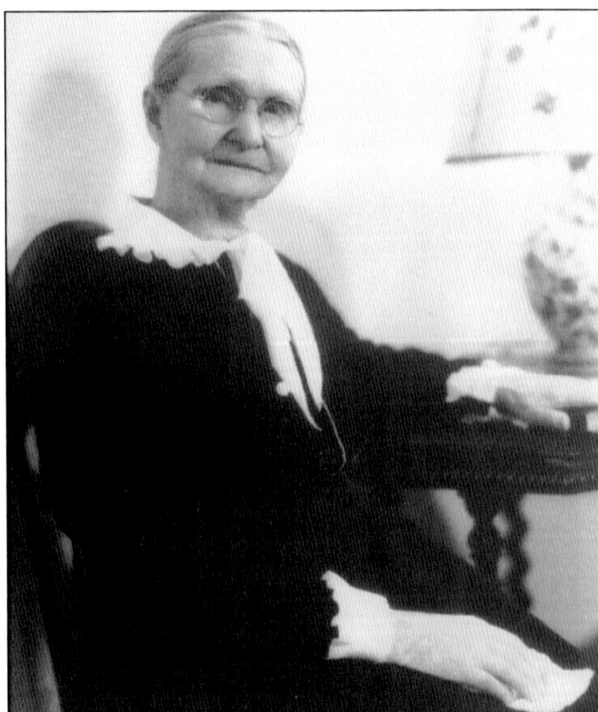

When she died at age 96, Ellen Hogan Kennedy was one of the oldest residents in Dane County. Kennedy emigrated from Ireland when she was 20 years old and lived in Westport for 67 years, 52 of which were after her husband Martin F. Kennedy's death in 1889. The couple married at St. Mary of the Lake Church in 1870, and both are buried there. (Kennedy family.)

Ellen Hogan Kennedy's brother James Hogan arrived from Ireland in 1857 on a ship called the *Underwriter*, which landed at the port of New York. In 1864, the same year he married Honnour "Hannah" O'Malley, James purchased the farm that belonged to Westport Township's famed first settler, Louis Montandon. The farm, which spanned 320 acres, stayed in the Hogan family from that point forward. (Kennedy family.)

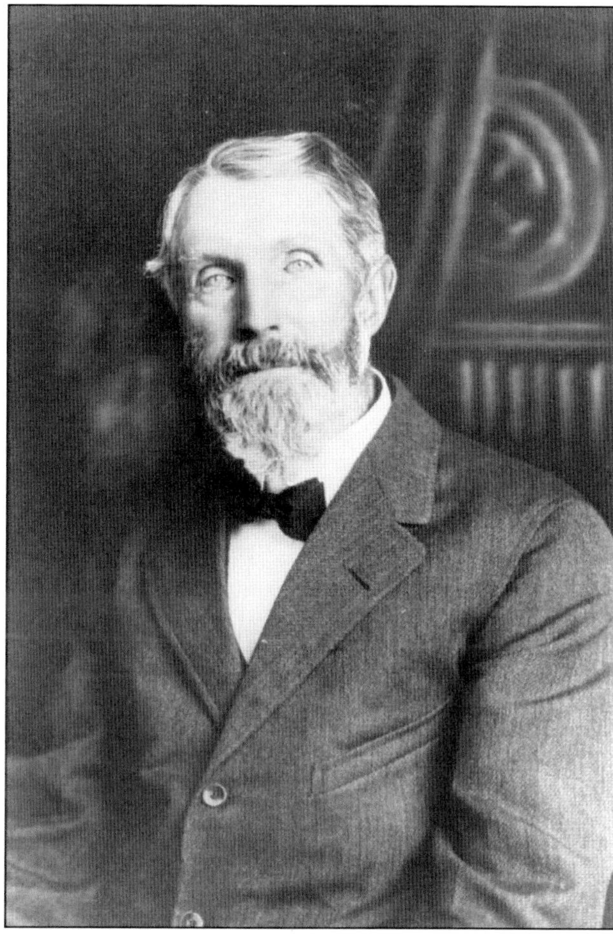

The Kennedy family often got together to celebrate Grandma Ellen Hogan Kennedy's birthday at various parks; this gathering is at Burrows Park on Lake Mendota in Maple Bluff. Grandma Kennedy is in the center of the crowd, which includes many of her nine children, 32 grandchildren, and 16 great-grandchildren. Two of Ellen and Martin Kennedy's children married siblings from the William and Jane Fisher family. (Kennedy family.)

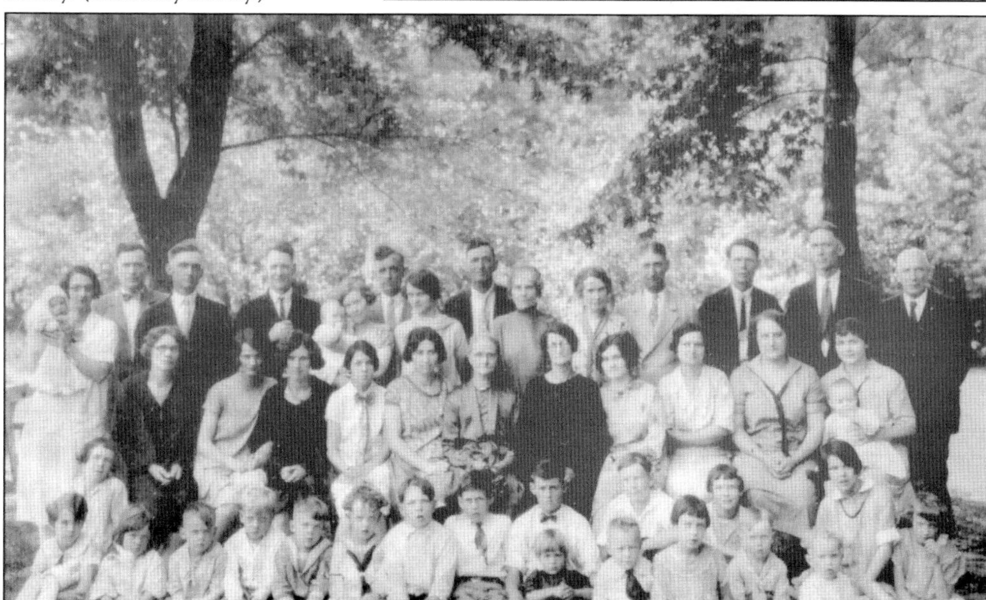

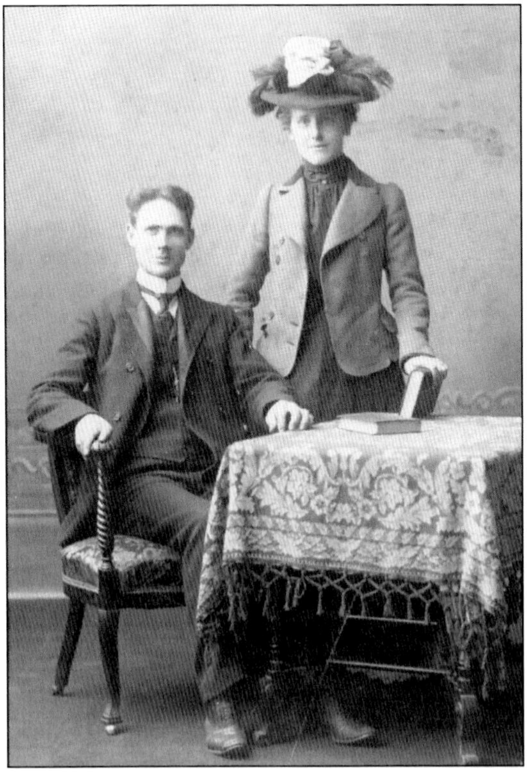

The second child of Ellen and Martin Kennedy was Michael Henry Kennedy, shown here with his wife, Rebecca (Beck) Jones Kennedy. His older brother John died at age 23. In 1904, Mike and Beck Kennedy purchased their Westport Township farm where they grew tobacco and raised eight children. Besides farming, Mike Kennedy served many years as chairman of the board in Westport and was a member of the school board. (Kennedy family.)

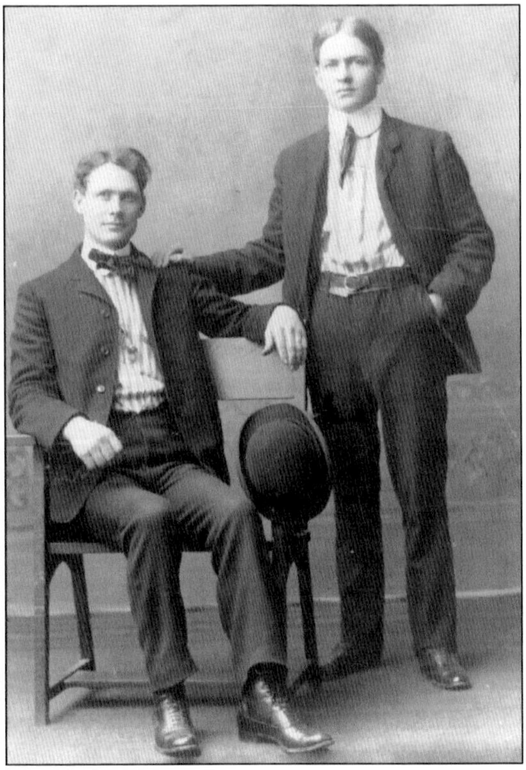

Richard V. Kennedy, born 1875, sits beside his friend Eddie Foye (standing). Kennedy married Agnes Lynch in 1900; she is pictured with the Ellen Hogan Kennedy family at the farm in chapter six. In 1902, Agnes died of tuberculosis. (Kennedy family.)

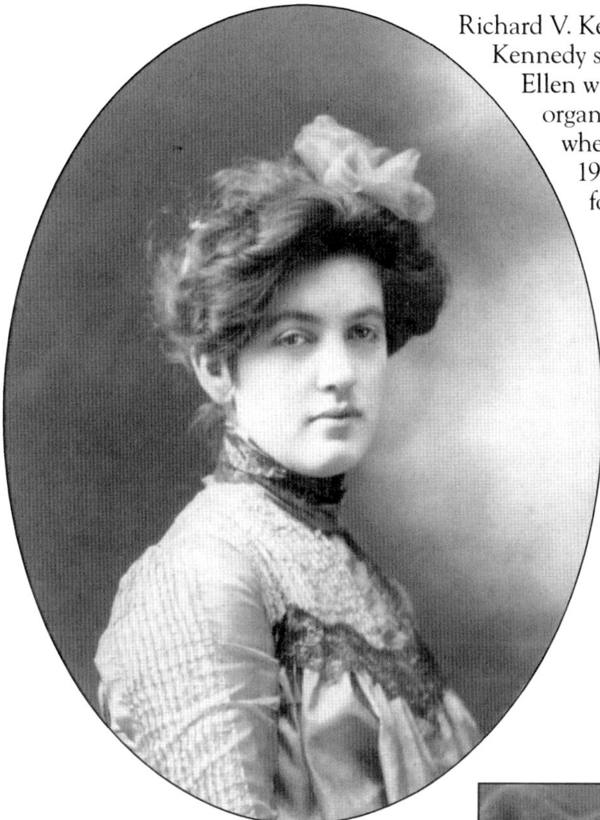

Richard V. Kennedy married Ellen Shillinglaw Kennedy six years after his first wife died. Ellen was active as a choir member and organist at St. Mary of the Lake Church where the couple was married. Around 1910, they moved to Madison and had four children. (Kennedy family.)

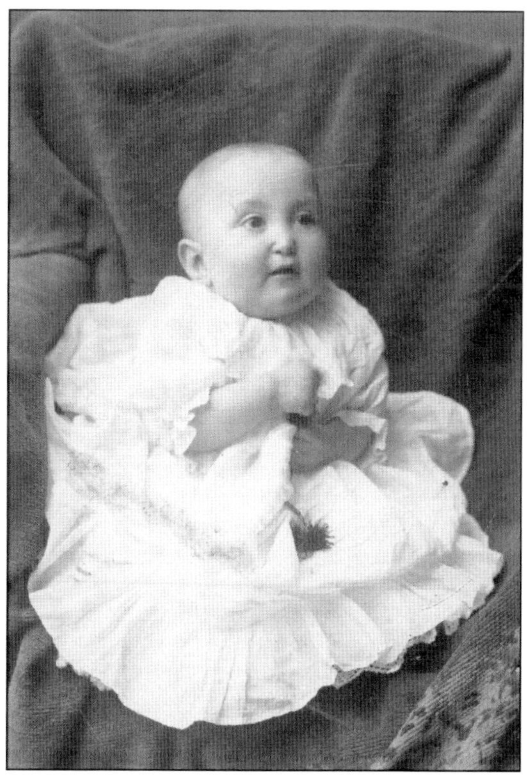

Pearl Borchers Kessenich, daughter of Theresa Kennedy Borchers and William Borchers, was one of Ellen Hogan Kennedy's 32 grandchildren. Pearl married Gerald Kessenich in November 1926, and they lived with the Borchers at the family farm in Vienna Township. They had two children, Romain and Lou Ann. (Kennedy family.)

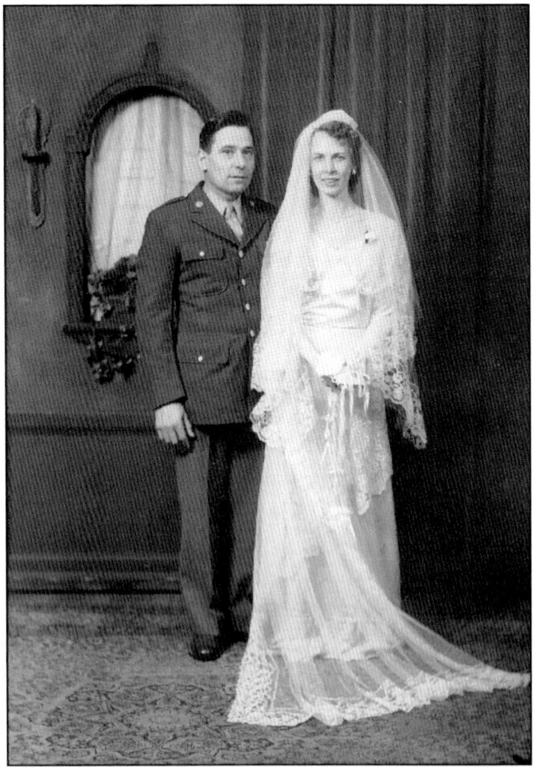

Rosellen Theresa Kennedy married Frederick F. Poster on December 26, 1942, at St. Mary of the Lake Church. Her parents, Frances Fisher and James J. Kennedy, met at the church when Fisher was singing in the choir and Kennedy came to join it. Frances' sister Rose made the dress that both Frances and Rosellen wore at their weddings. (Kennedy family.)

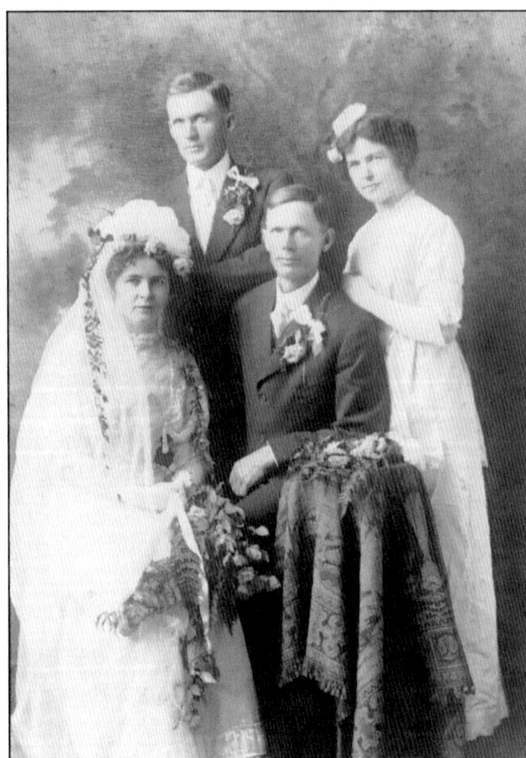

It was a beautiful day in September 1914 when James J. Kennedy and Frances Fisher were married. The day was the culmination of a six-year wait, required by their parents who thought them too young to get married at age 18. Despite the nice weather, the unpaved roads were so muddy that it took them two hours to drive from Waunakee to St. Mary's in Westport. After the wedding, the couple moved to the Westport farm occupied by James Kennedy's mother, Ellen Hogan Kennedy. The farm later passed to the couple's son, Bernard Kennedy. By 1976, their extended family included 42 grandchildren and 43 great-grandchildren. (Kennedy family.)

Before William P. Fisher died in the 1930s, he was the only surviving Civil War veteran living in the village. When Fisher was 20 years old, he enlisted in the 49th Regiment Infantry, Company G. He spent much of his nine-month service in St. Louis guarding government property and prisoners, and he had the opportunity to shake hands with Generals Grant and Sherman. Fisher was mustered out at Madison in November 1865. A total of 54 men in his unit died, all from disease. (Kennedy family.)

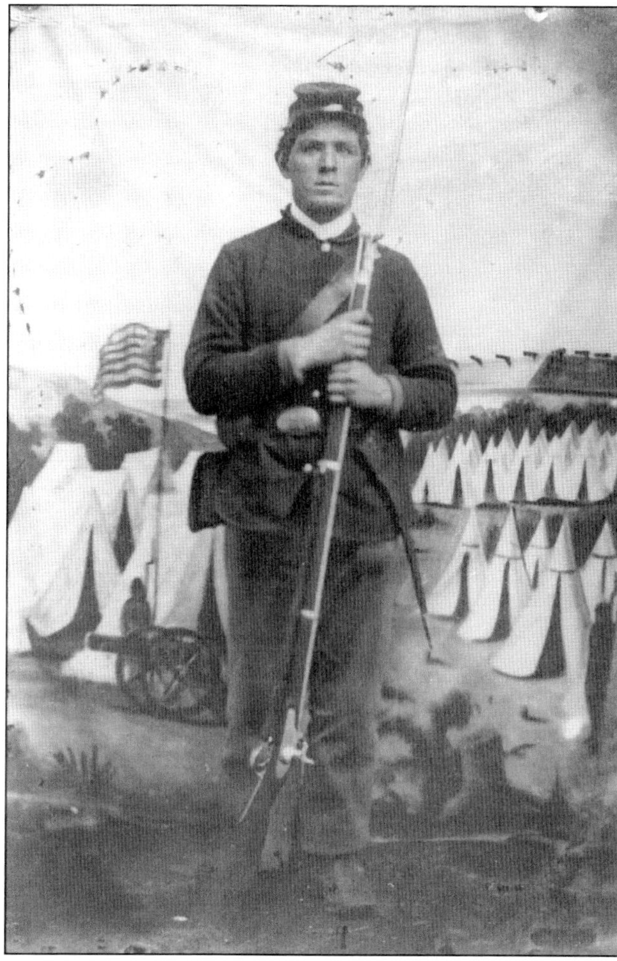

Waunakee was proud of all its veterans, many shown here in the early 1900s at the Decoration Day parade marching to the east on Main Street. Civil War veteran William P. Fisher is third from the right. The buildings are, from left to right, the IOOF hall, Hilgers & Bernards Bar and Meat Market, the village hall and fire station, Lawrence Freney's machinery shop, and a saloon. (WPL.)

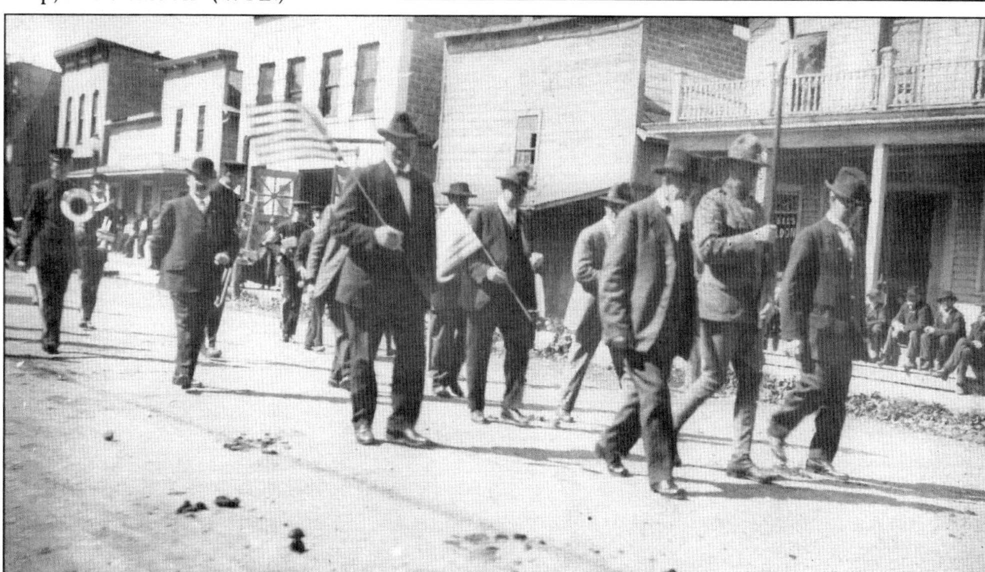

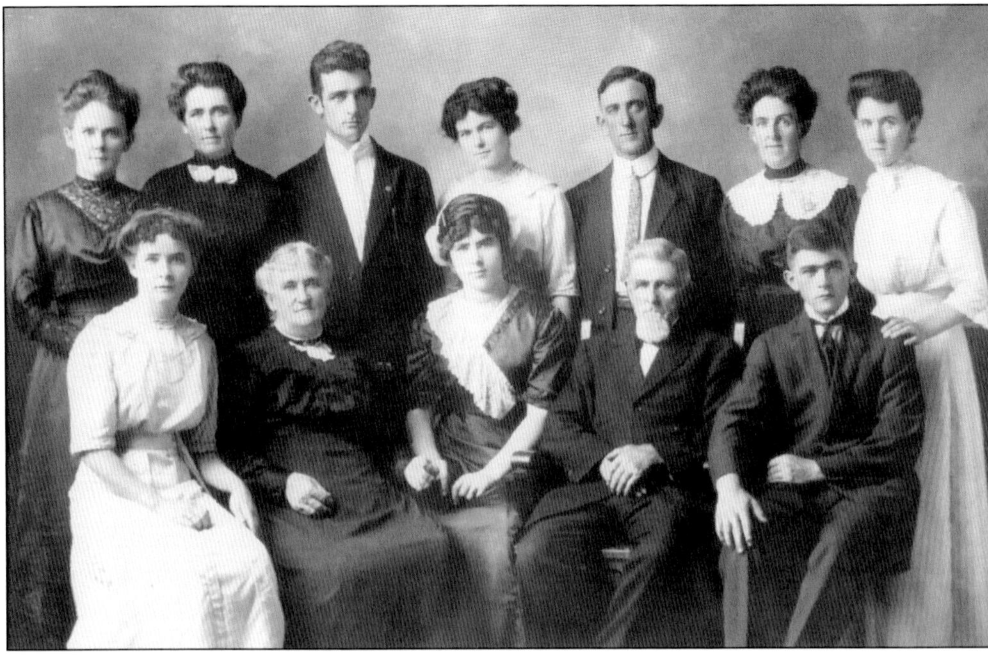

William P. Fisher and Jane Glennan married in 1872. They are pictured from left to right with their 10 grown children as follows: (first row) Frances Fisher Kennedy, Jane Glennan Fisher (mother), Ellen "Nell" Fisher Endres, William P. Fisher (father), and Daniel Fisher; (second row) Maud(e) Fisher, Mary Ann Fisher McCloskey, William G. Fisher, Rose Fisher (became Sr. Jane William), John Fisher, Jane Fisher Watzke, and Kathryn "Kate" Fisher Walsh. (Kennedy family.)

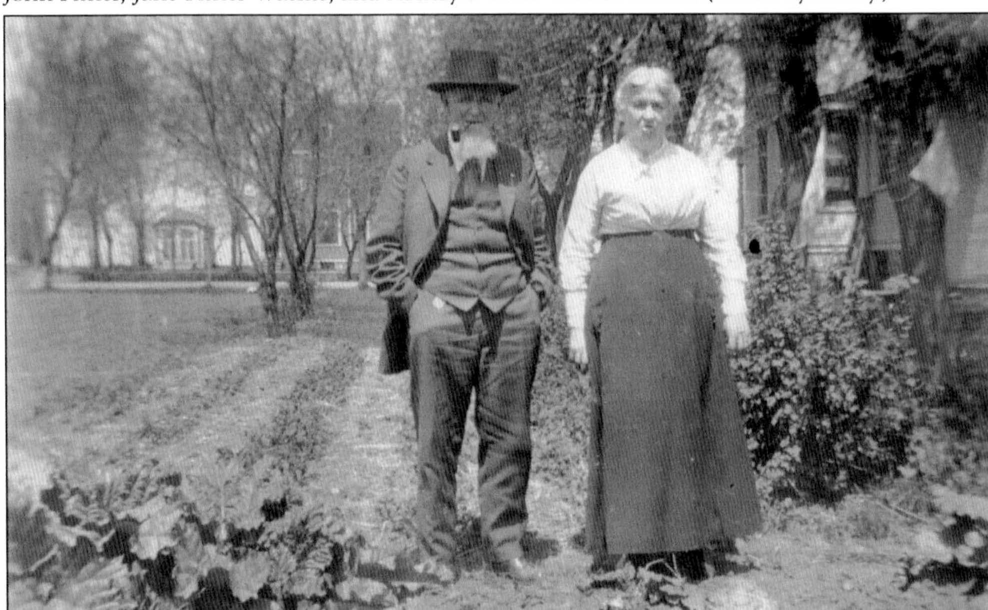

The lots on Main Street were spacious in the early 1900s, and William and Jane Fisher had plenty of room for a garden. William P. Fisher learned through his work converting Wisconsin wilderness to farms, including first his parents' farm in Berry, then the one he owned in Springfield for 16 years. The Fishers moved to the Main Street house in 1913. (Kennedy family.)

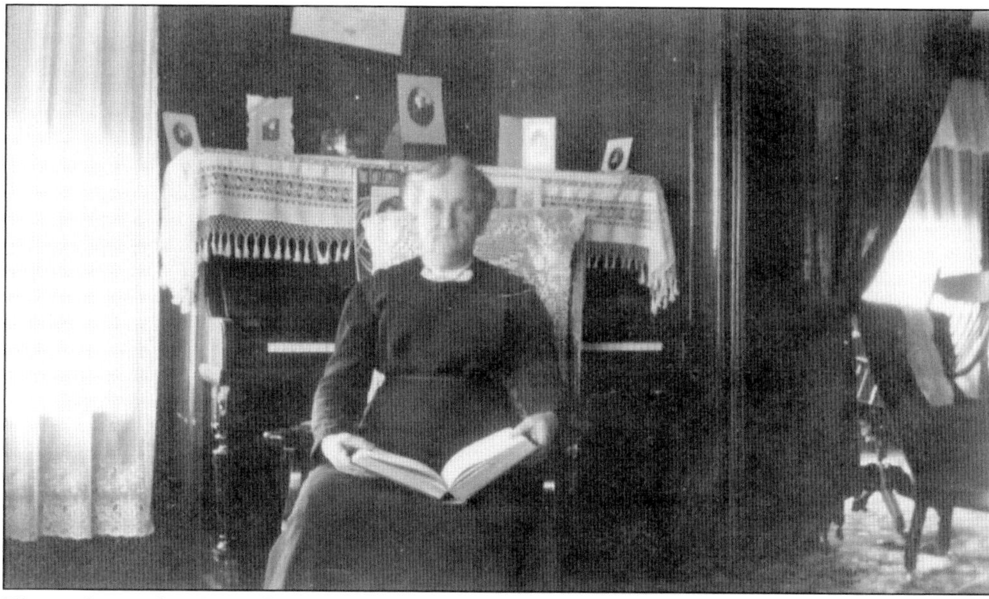

The parlor in the Waunakee Fisher house shows popular design features of the time, including the dark, striped wall covering, large draperies between the rooms, and the upright piano where Jane Glennan Fisher sits. The sheet music behind Fisher is Carita Day's "You Can't Expect Kisses From Me," published in 1911. (Kennedy family.)

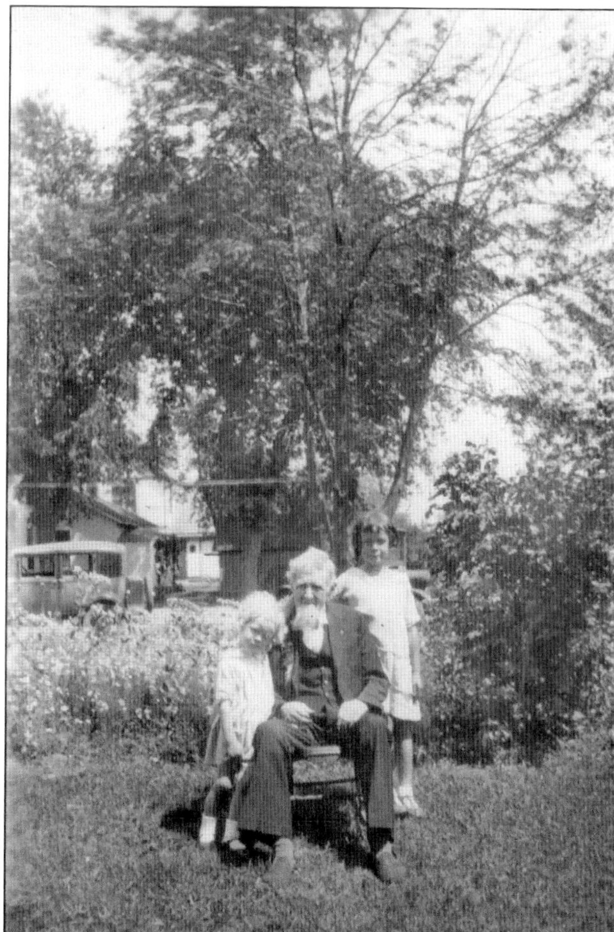

William P. Fisher enjoys some time with his granddaughters Patricia Kennedy (left) and Ruth Ann Kennedy. Both girls are children of Fisher's daughter Frances Fisher Kennedy and her husband, James Kennedy. The photograph was taken around 1935. Later, Patricia Fisher married William Vilbrandt, and Ruth Ann married Robert Kaether. (Kennedy family.)

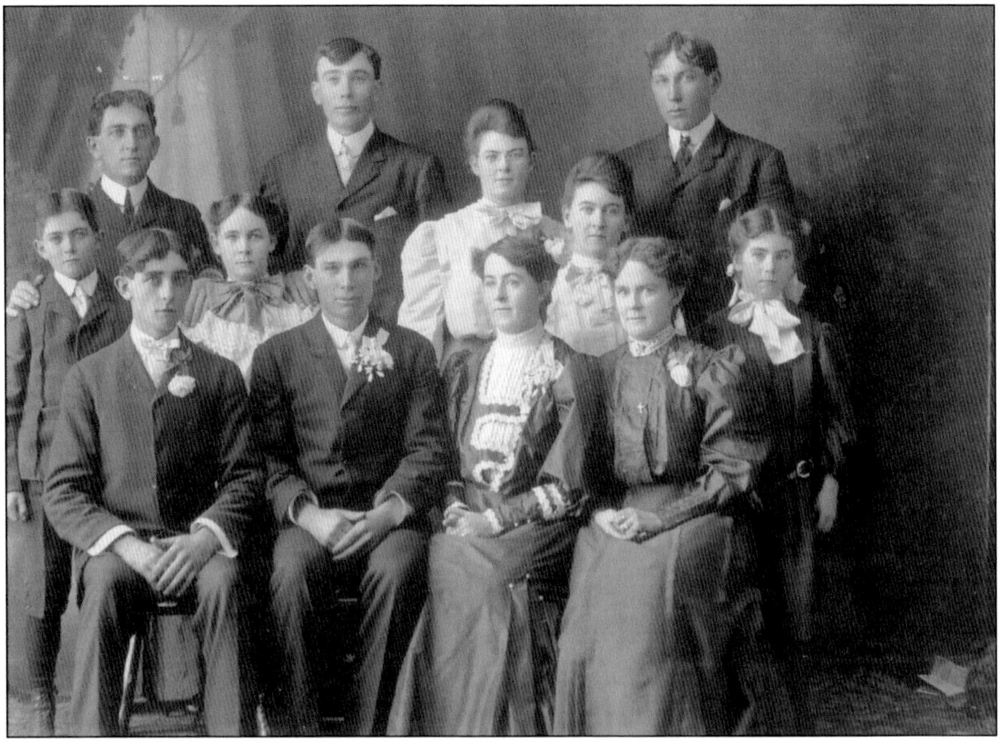

Young people gather from both sides of a Fisher-Watzke wedding in January 1906. Pictured from left to right are (first row) William G. Fisher, Edward Watzke (groom), Jane Fisher Watzke (bride), and Maude Fisher; (second row) Daniel Fisher, Frances Fisher, Rose Fisher, Kate Fisher, and Ellen (Nell) Fisher; (third row) John Edward Fisher, Robert Watzke, and Walter Watzke. (Kennedy family.)

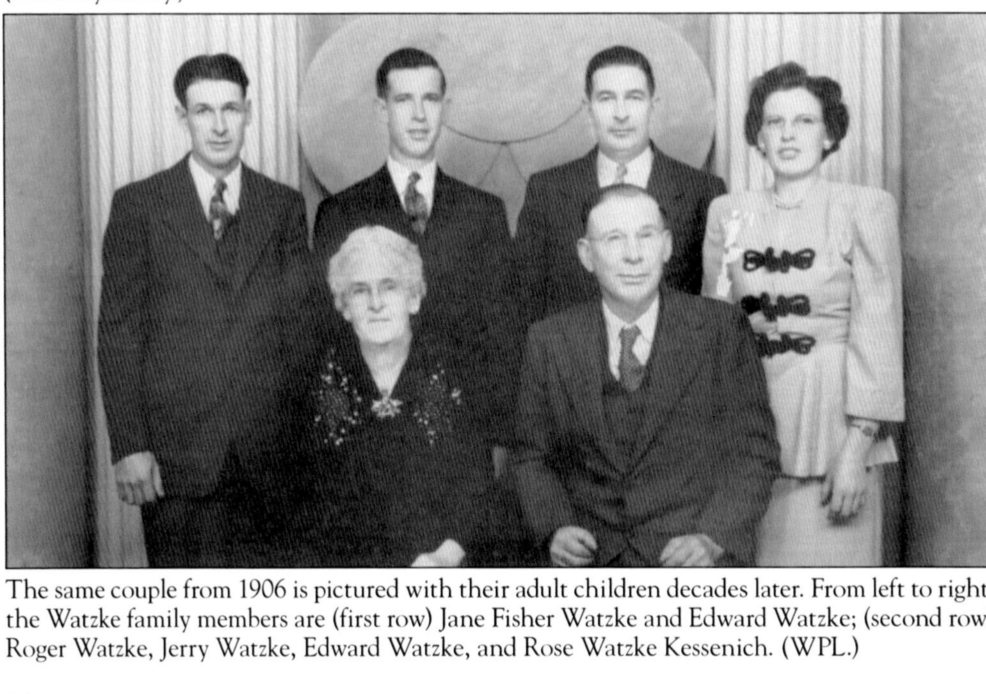

The same couple from 1906 is pictured with their adult children decades later. From left to right, the Watzke family members are (first row) Jane Fisher Watzke and Edward Watzke; (second row) Roger Watzke, Jerry Watzke, Edward Watzke, and Rose Watzke Kessenich. (WPL.)

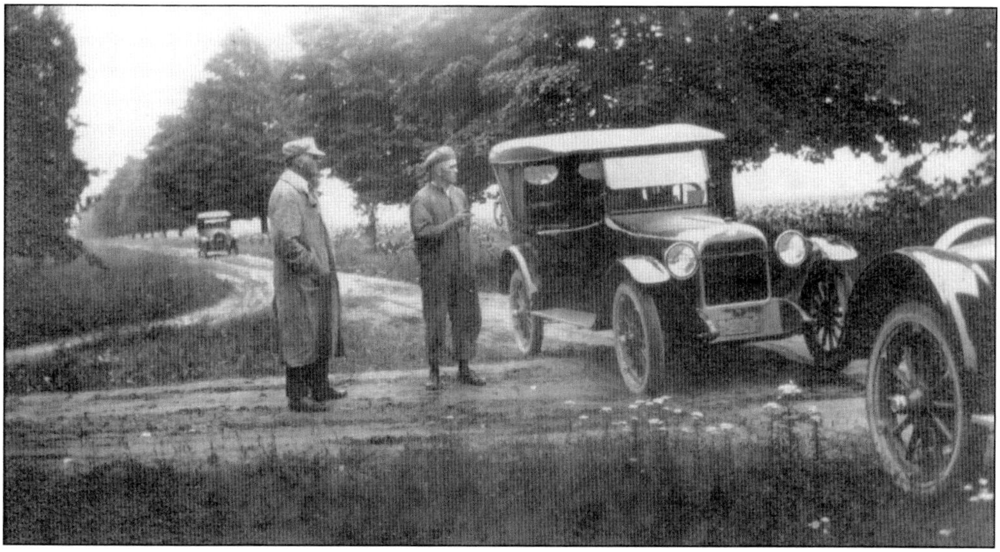

Rows of trees along muddy dirt roads guide a shipment of vehicles to Waunakee while Charles McWatty and Daniel Fisher oversee the operation. Charles McWatty started his Chevrolet dealership in 1924, and these automobiles were most likely the first stock he brought in to be sold there. Daniel Fisher was a pilot and served 18 months with the 354th Aero Squadron. (WPL.)

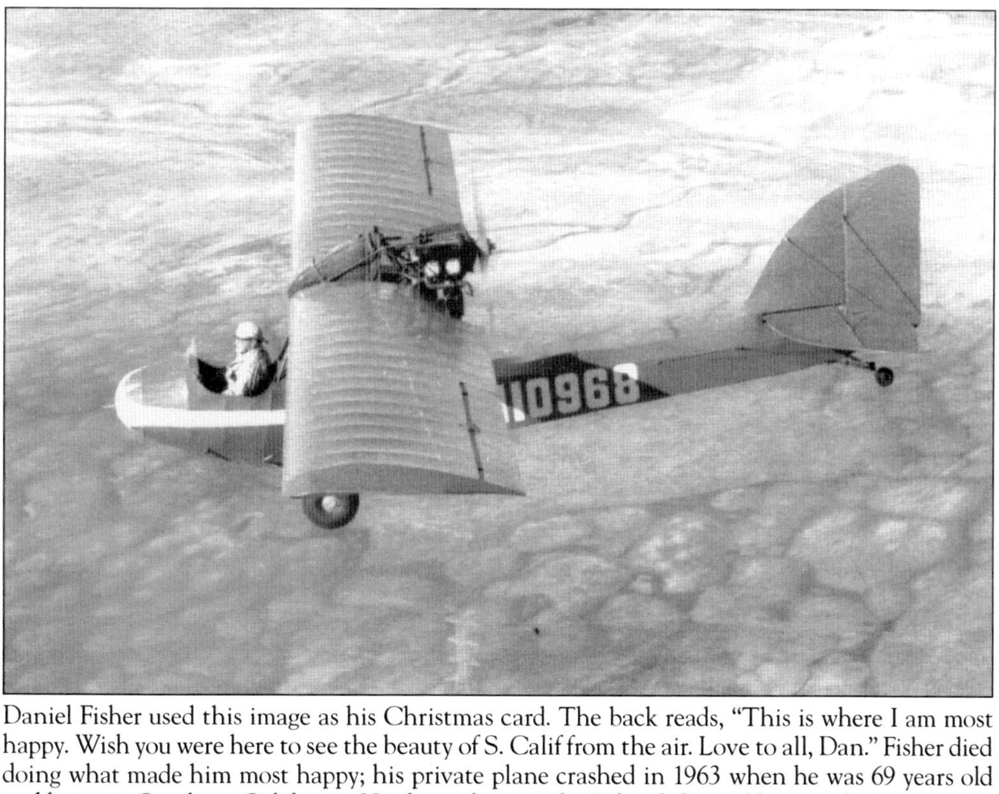

Daniel Fisher used this image as his Christmas card. The back reads, "This is where I am most happy. Wish you were here to see the beauty of S. Calif from the air. Love to all, Dan." Fisher died doing what made him most happy; his private plane crashed in 1963 when he was 69 years old and living in Southern California. His funeral was at the Schwab funeral home, which originally was the house of his parents, William and Jane Fisher. (Kennedy family.)

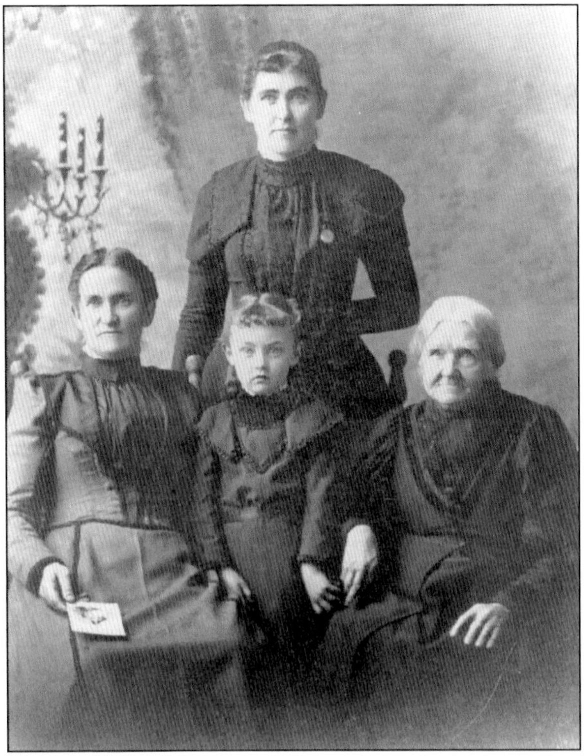

Four generations are represented in this c. 1900 photograph featuring, from left to right, (first row) Jane Glennan Fisher (grandmother), Nellie McCloskey (daughter), and Ellen Madden Glennan (great-grandmother); (second row) Mary Ann Fisher McCloskey (mother). Nellie McCloskey was born January 1894 and her aunt (Mary Ann's sister) Nellie Fisher was born two years after her. Great-grandmother Ellen Glennan was the oldest woman in Dane County when she died at age 105. Two of her six daughters married the two Fisher brothers, William P. and Bernard J. (Kennedy family.)

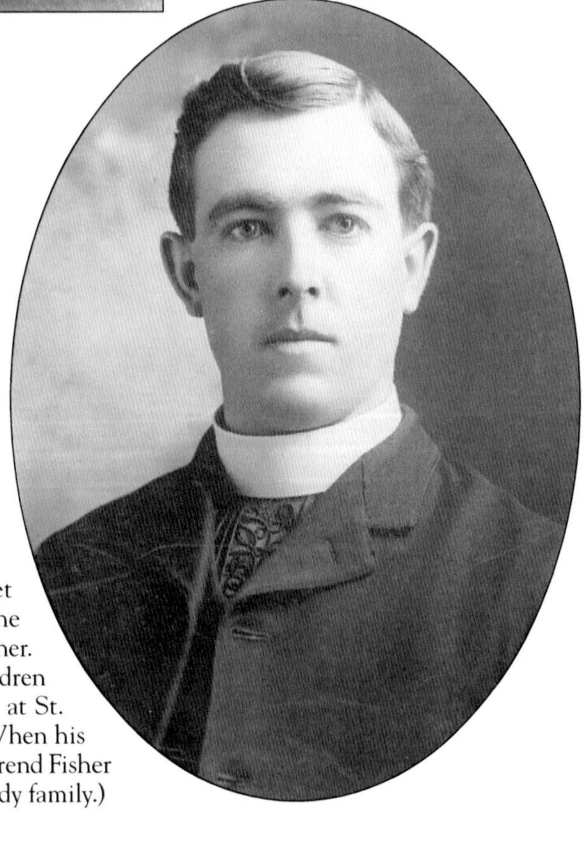

Jane Glennan Fisher's sister Margaret Glennan married Bernard J. Fisher, the brother of Jane's husband, William P. Fisher. One of Margaret and Bernard's five children was Rev. John Fisher, who was located at St. Bernard's parish in Madison in 1900. When his grandmother Ellen Glennan died, Reverend Fisher conducted the funeral services. (Kennedy family.)

Like her cousin John Fisher, Rose Fisher chose the religious life. Fisher became Sr. Jane William and in 1930 was living in St. Louis and attending the newly established School of Nursing with the Franciscan Sisters of St. Mary. Prior to that, Fisher was a public school teacher in the Waunakee and Westport public schools for more than 10 years. (Kennedy family.)

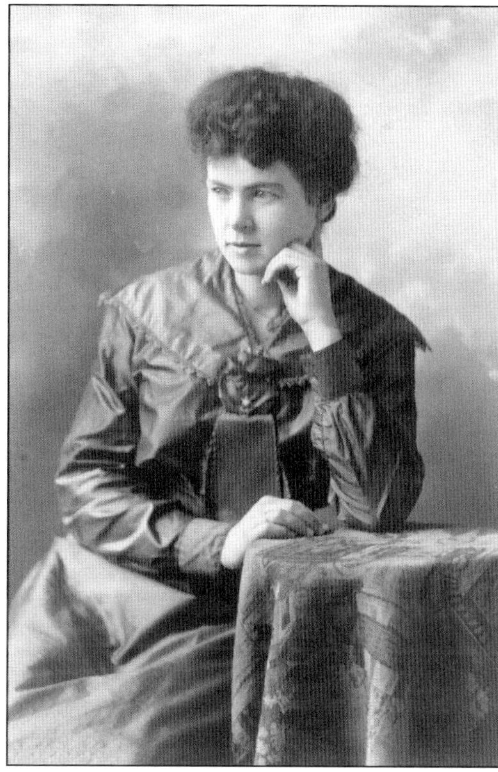

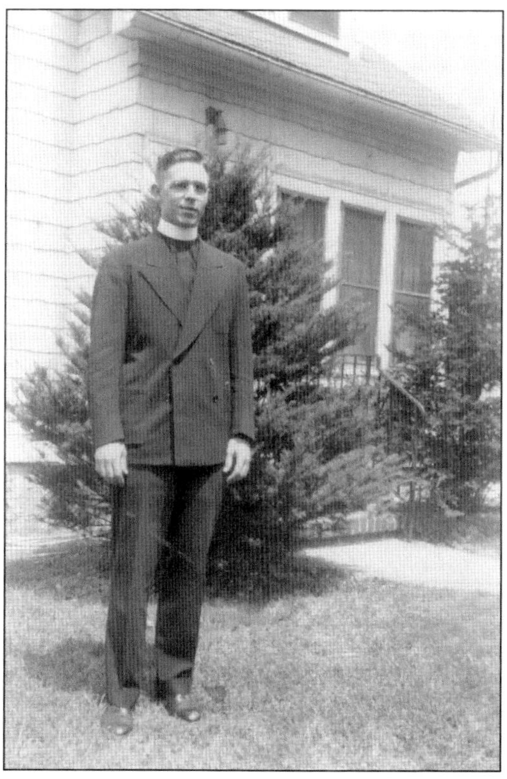

Rev. Leroy Endres, the son of Henry Endres and Nell Fisher Endres, was a Jesuit priest who studied law. He accomplished much, including making newspaper headlines as a "top lawyer in the United States." In 1971, Father Endres was professor of law at Creighton University in Omaha, Nebraska. (Kennedy family.)

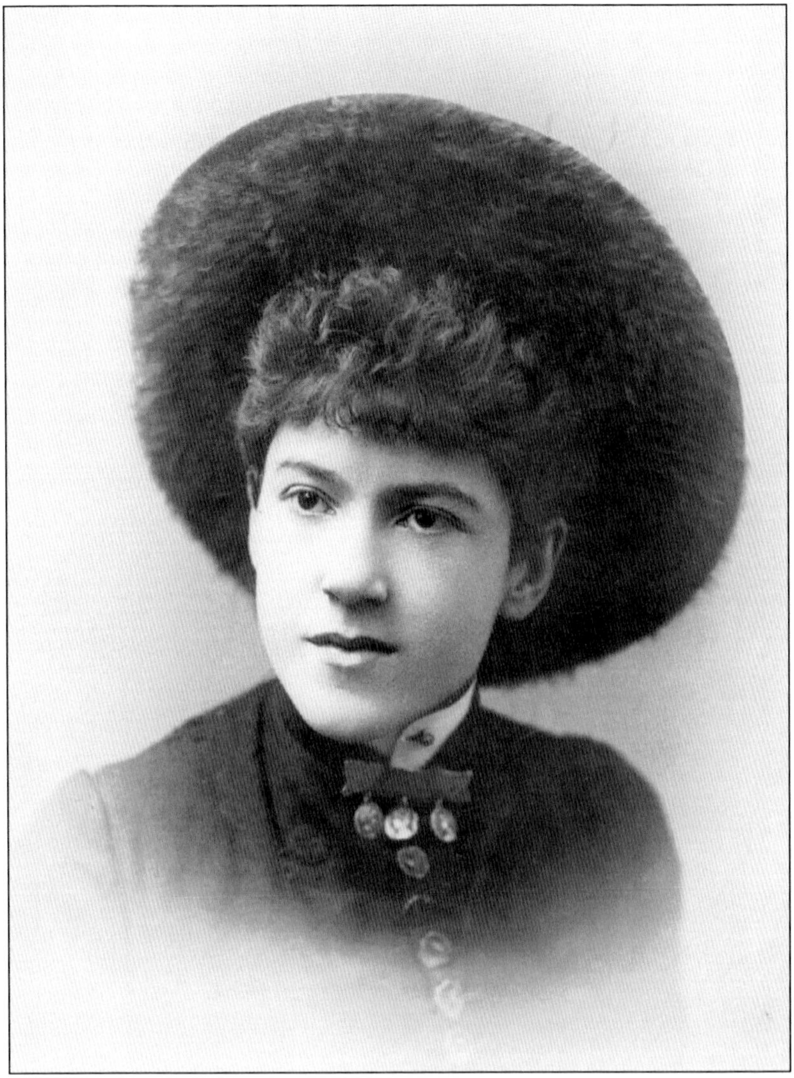

The poet Ella Wheeler was born November 5, 1850. She attended one-room schools and spent her days exploring the glaciated areas surrounding her family's Westport farm where they had moved in 1852. Ella Wheeler's early literary influences were magazines to which her Aunt Abigail subscribed, until one day the subscriptions ended with no money to continue. There were two choices in Wheeler's 14-year-old mind: sell subscriptions or write articles to be published. So she sent the publishers her essays, and they sent back-issues of the magazine. In February 1883, after riding a train from Windsor to Madison, Ella Wheeler wrote her most famous lines: "Laugh and the world laughs with you, / Weep and you weep alone. / For the sad old earth must borrow its mirth, / It has trouble enough of its own." She had witnessed a woman on the train, described as "the bride of a year, the widow of a week," sobbing with grief. Wheeler later was surprised how soon after she arrived at a party she had forgotten about the woman. The poem was called "Solitude" and was published first in the *New York Sun*, then in her book *Poems of Passion*, May 1883. She married Robert Wilcox in 1884 and became Ella Wheeler Wilcox. Their one child, Robert M. Wilcox Jr., died in New York in 1887 after living only 12 hours. His father was in Tennessee on business and never got to meet him. Ella Wheeler Wilcox, shown as photographed by J.F. Green, had no other children. (WPL.)

When Ella Wheeler Wilcox wrote of her family's meager home and resources, she noted that in addition, her brother Edward G. Wheeler lived at the old Westport farmhouse with "an ever-increasing family." They are, from left to right, (first row) Armine and Ella; (second row) Delphia (mother), Edward G. (father), and Archie; (third row) Maurine, Edith, Clytie, and Ralph. The name *Maurine* was one Ella Wheeler Wilcox invented; after reading Nora Perry's poem "Norine," Wilcox published a story in verse called "Maurine." (WPL.)

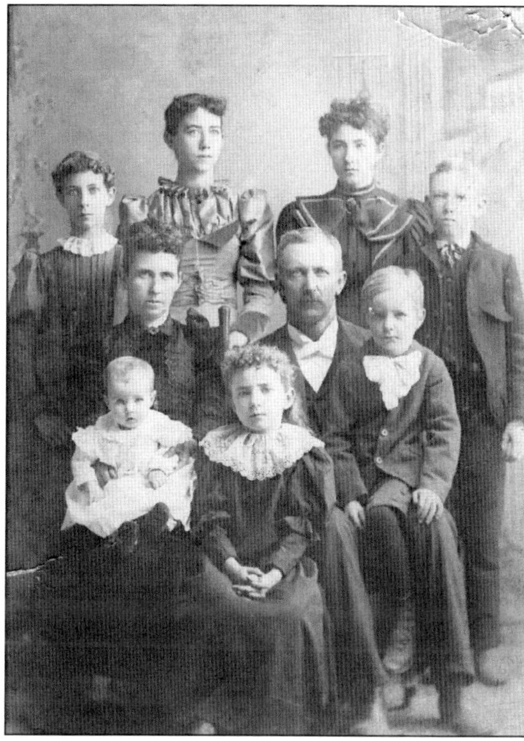

Ella Wheeler Wilcox's three siblings are, from left to right, Edward Wheeler, Sarah Wheeler Bond, and Marcus Wheeler. Sarah and Marcus were named after their parents. Sarah was a teacher and musician and moved to Illinois with her husband who worked as a physician. Marcus moved his family to the Dakotas to work as a ranchman. (WPL.)

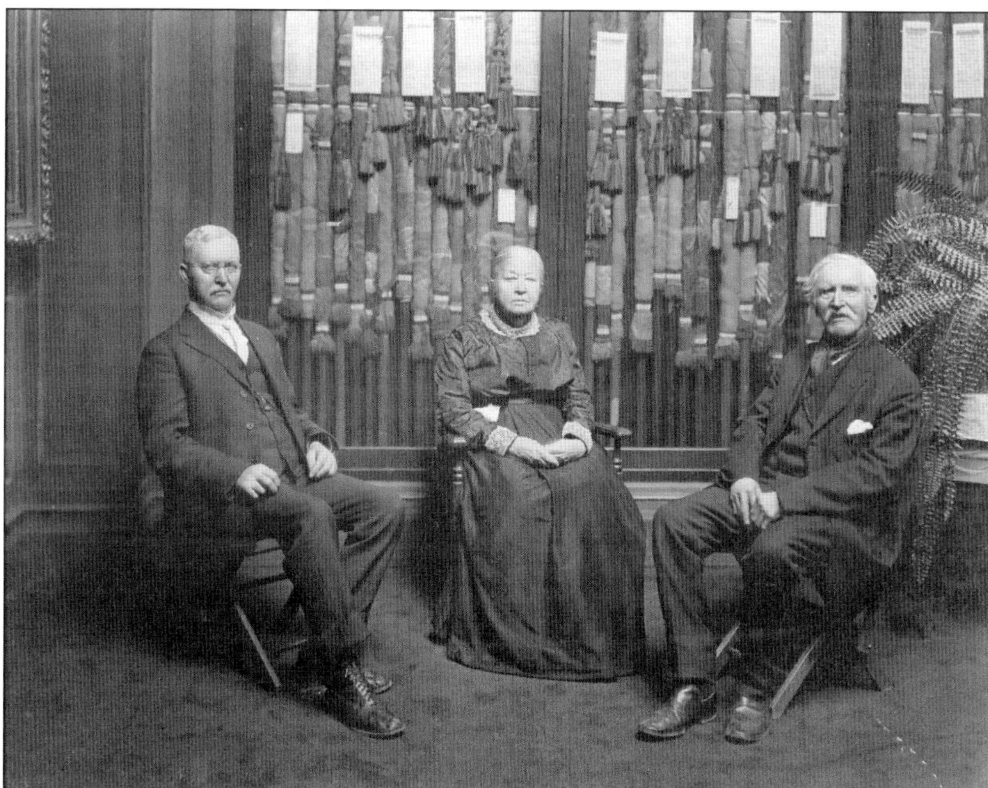

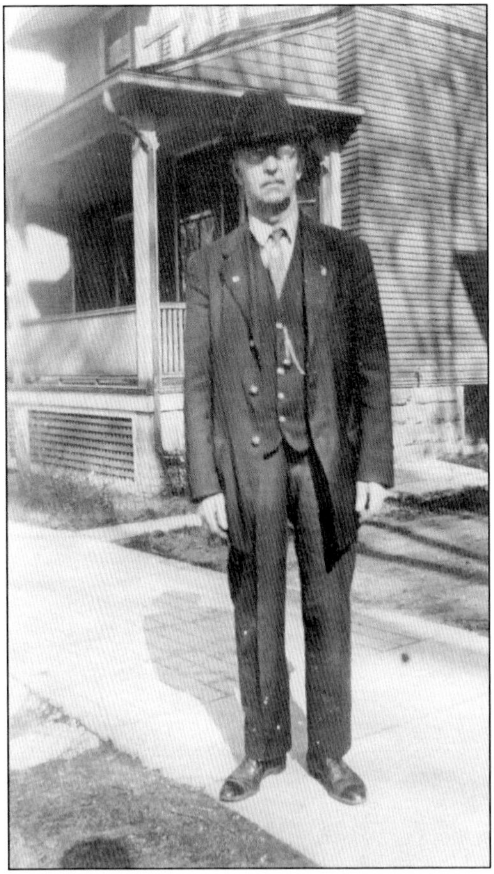

The Civil War began when Edward Gilman Wheeler was merely 15 years old, yet he fought with the 14th Wisconsin Volunteer Infantry, Company K. Standing most likely at his home on 15 East Johnson Street in Madison, Wheeler wears the Civil War dress uniform he would don for parades. Until the 1920 census, he is listed as living at the Westport family farm. (WPL.)

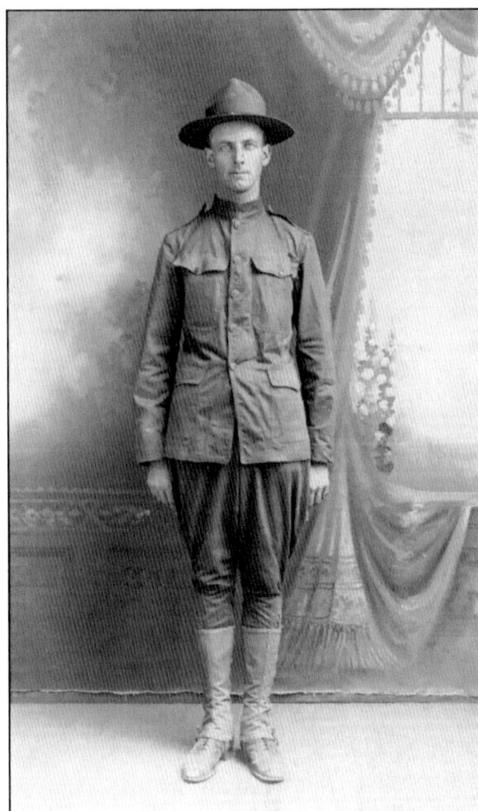

A veteran like his father Edward G. Wheeler, Archie Edward Wheeler poses in uniform August 13, 1917, his second day in service during World War I. Wheeler worked at the Ford garage for A.W. Cameron & Son in Waunakee. When Wheeler's family lived in the Westport farmhouse, the roof was so deplorable that rain would pour through it. After his aunt Ella Wheeler Wilcox sold *Poems of Passion*, she sent money to fix the house. (WPL.)

Henry Lamberty went from farm laborer to construction foreman in the many years he worked for F.C. Raemisch. In 1918, just one week after receiving his World War I draft notice, Lamberty was on his way to Camp Grant. He married Elsa Beck, bought William H. Bernards' house on Grant and Bacon Streets in 1946, and lived to age 73. (Hazel R. Zimbric.)

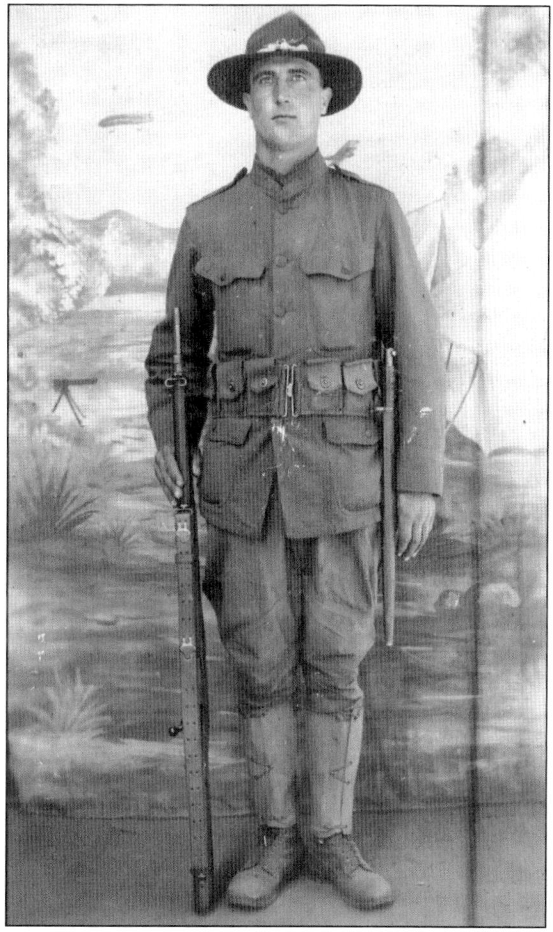

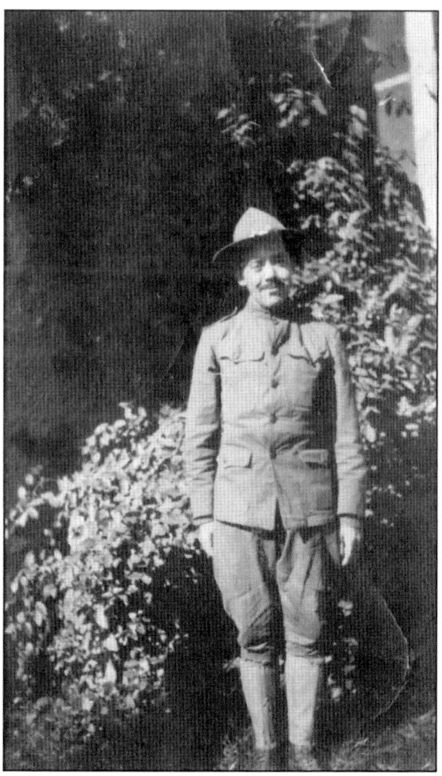

While wearing his World War I uniform, Math Helt Jr. posed for this photograph taken by Hazel Raemisch. Helt had been living in the Raemisch farmhouse in 1923 when he then moved to the Glen Deans house. In 1946, Helt's uncle Math Helt Sr., 95 years old, was the oldest resident of Waunakee. His parents moved to the area years before the village was platted, making their home east of the village. (Hazel R. Zimbric.)

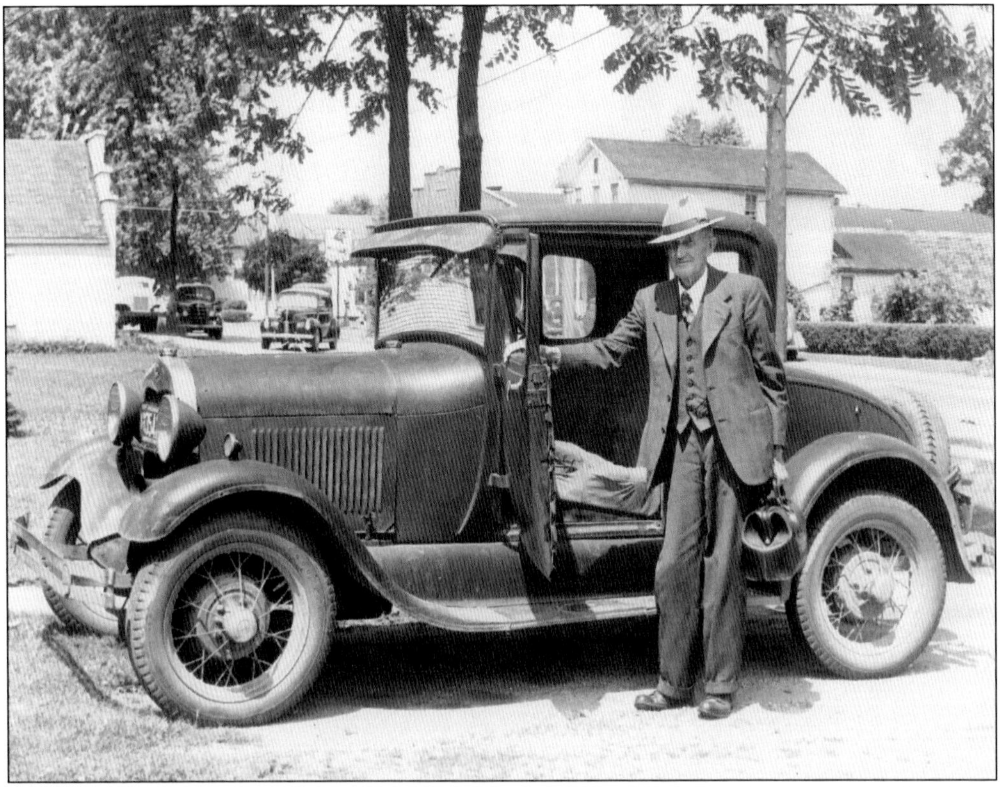

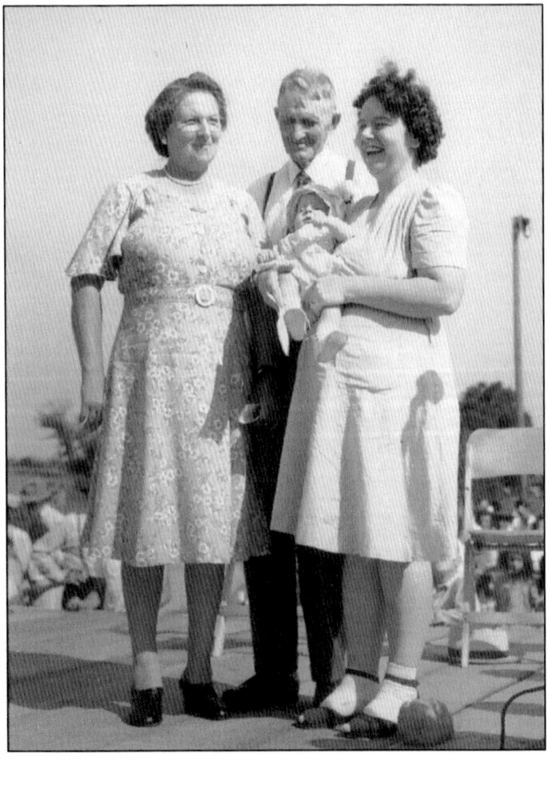

The following photographs of Austin M. Blake, MD, were taken on Sunday, August 10, 1947, which was known to residents of Waunakee as Doc Blake Day. The day commemorated Dr. Blake's 60th year of medical practice in Waunakee. With over 3,000 participants, Doc Blake Day was the largest gathering Waunakee had ever experienced. Blake displays his Ford Model A, which he reportedly described as "the best darned car Ford ever built." (WPL.)

Dr. Austin Blake stands between Margaret Wipperfurth (left), the oldest baby he delivered, and the second youngest baby he delivered, who is unidentified (the youngest had been born the previous night). Wipperfurth was born Margaret Kessenich in December 1888, the same month and year Dr. Blake and his wife married and moved from Lodi to Waunakee. (WPL.)

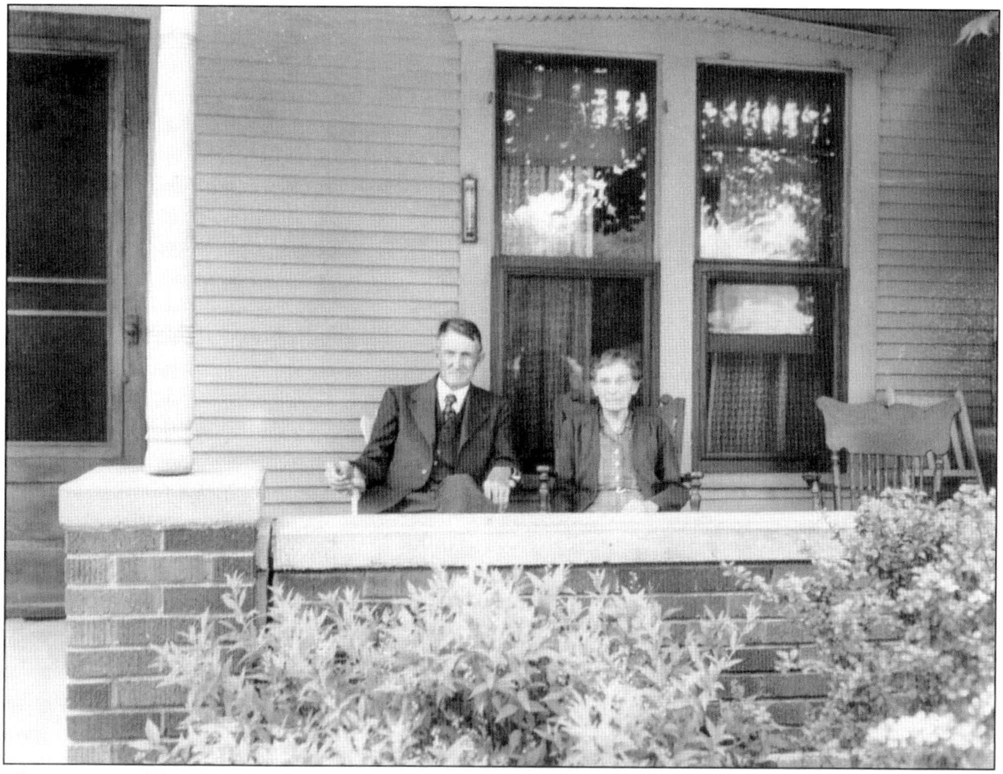

This image of Dr. Austin Blake and his wife, Ida Watson Blake, sitting on the porch of their home is one of the souvenir photographs from Doc Blake Day. The porch had changed from its earlier years, but the house was the same East Main Street home that became Dr. Blake's first office in the 1880s. They had their two children, Ruby and Sam, while living there. (WPL.)

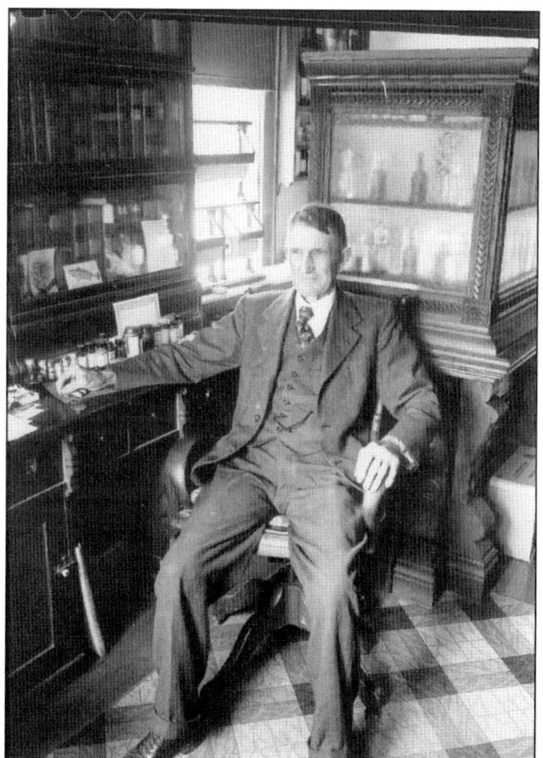

When Dr. Blake died in 1959 at 95 years old, he ranked as one of the oldest and longest-practicing physicians in the country. In his 71 years of service, he accumulated quite the collection of medical paraphernalia, as displayed in another of the souvenir photographs distributed for his 60th anniversary. Though he spent over 70 years working, Dr. Austin Blake's hobbies, including gardening his prize summer Dahlias, kept him busy as well. He also enjoyed baseball, a love he passed on to his grandson Ed Murphy. (WPL.)

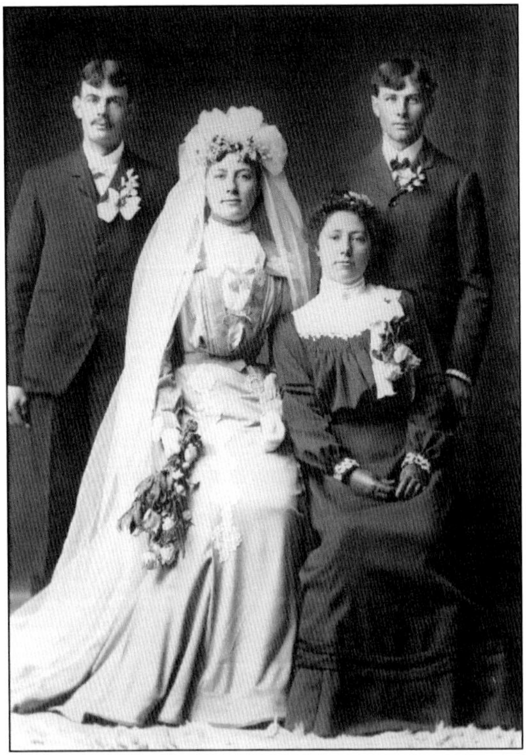

The marriage of F.C. Raemisch and Mary Miller took place at Holy Redeemer Catholic Church in November 1902. Pictured with them are their attendants, Rose Miller Chambers (Mary's sister, second from right) and Ted (T. J.) Hilgers (far right). (Hazel R. Zimbric.)

From the numerous glasses of sudsy drink to F.C. Raemisch sitting on a friend's shoulders, the occasion that brought this group together looks to be a joyous one. The sixth adult standing from the left is Ted Hilgers, wearing the coattails of a groom and standing next to his bride. (Hazel R. Zimbric.)

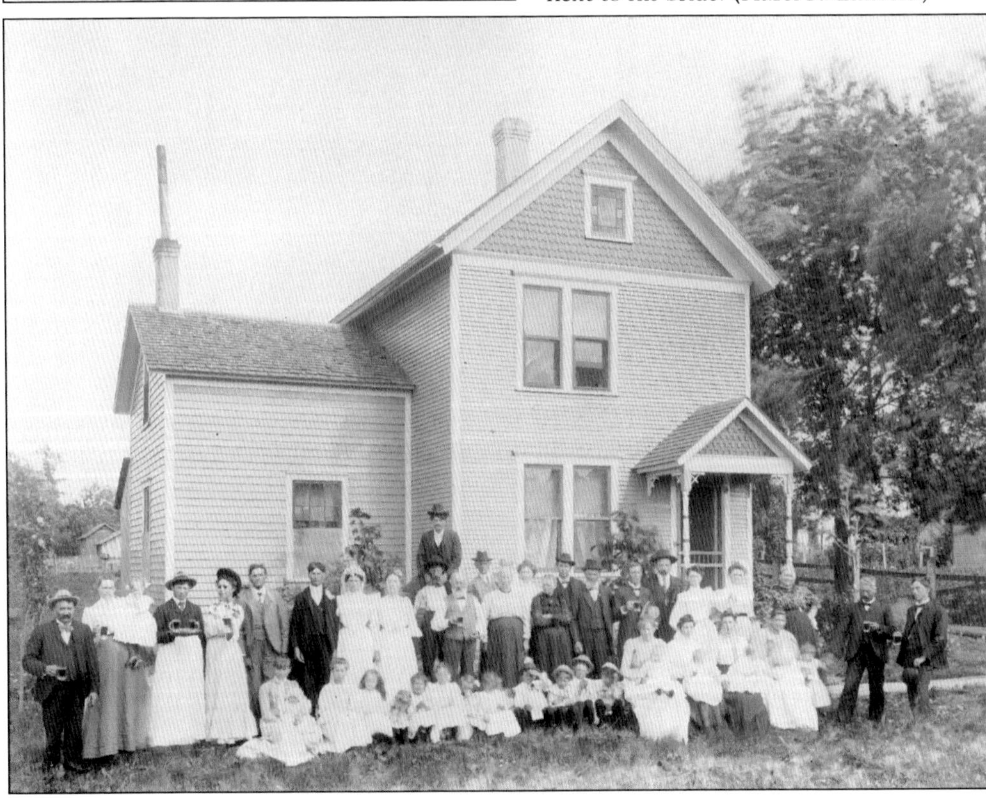

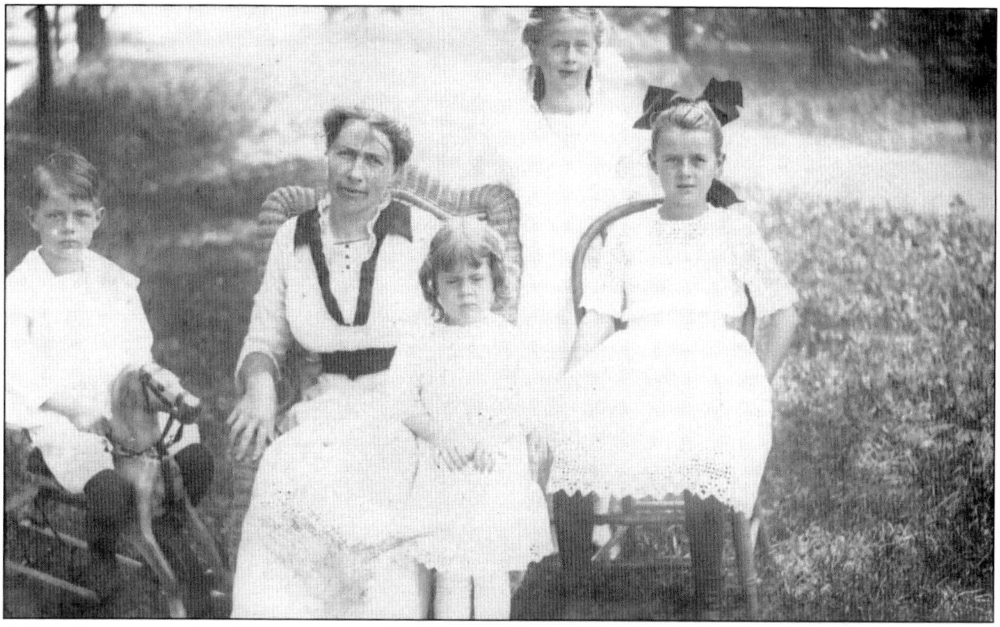

After they married in 1902 and moved into their Bacon Street house, Frank and Mary Raemisch started their family the following year. Pictured from left to right in 1915 is F.C. Raemisch's family as follows: son Gerald, wife Mary Miller Raemisch (pregnant with daughter Loretta), and daughters Hazel, Helenda (back), and Louise. (Hazel R. Zimbric.)

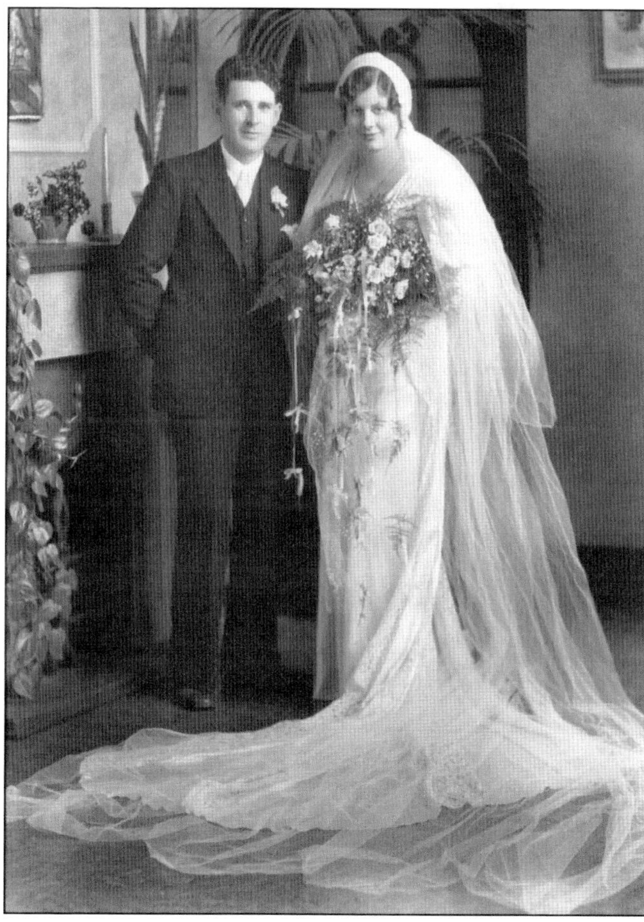

As did many young couples in Waunakee in the 1930s, George Roudebush and Hazel Raemisch enjoyed attending dances in the dance hall above Koltes Lumber Company while they were dating. In 1933, the pair married and then moved to Madison for a while before returning to live in the Truehl house Hazel's father inherited from his stepfather Robert Truehl. When they lived in Waunakee, Hazel was a nurse for Dr. Austin Blake. (Hazel R. Zimbric.)

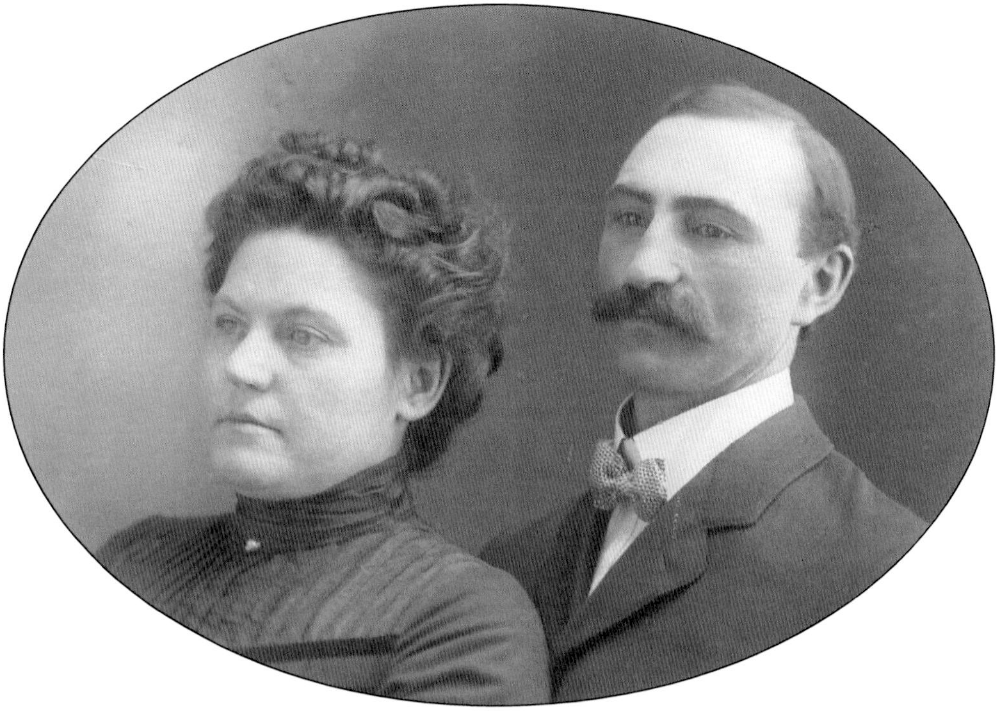

Gertrude Kessenich and Peter Uebersetzig were married around 1900. They lived above their meat market on West Main Street and had eight children. The Uebersetzigs' wedding party was held at the Brausen Hotel, which was purchased in 1939 by Peter and Gertrude's daughter Gertrude and her husband, Pete Miller. (Paul Bernards.)

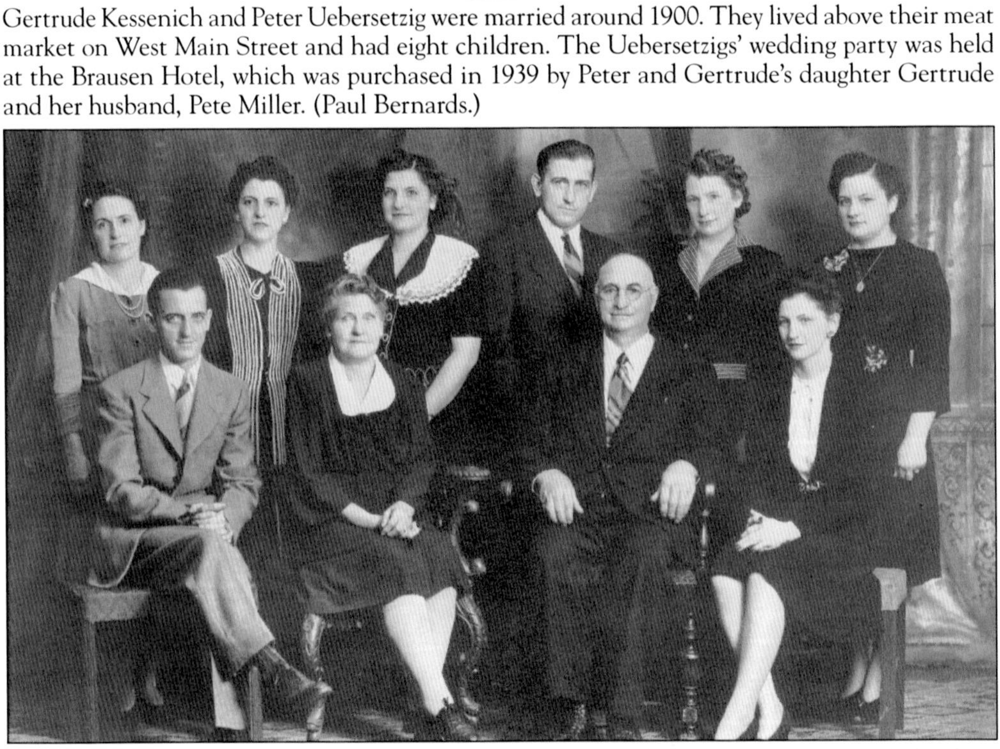

Brought together for a photograph in 1946, the Peter and Gertrude Uebersetzig family includes, from left to right, (first row) Bernard (Ben), Gertrude (mother), Peter (father), and Bernadette; (second row) Christine, Frances, Othilia (Tilly), Raymond, Marsella, and Gertrude. (Paul Bernards.)

The wedding of Catherine Hilgers (left) and Henry Bernards Sr. occurred around 1898. Their families were in business together as tavern and meat market owners. As of 1920, they had eight children: Christina, Werner, Lena, Herbert Walter, Agnes, Edward Henry, William J., and Mary L. In 1931, Henry Bernards Sr. was elected vice president of Farmers State Bank in Waunakee. (Paul Bernards.)

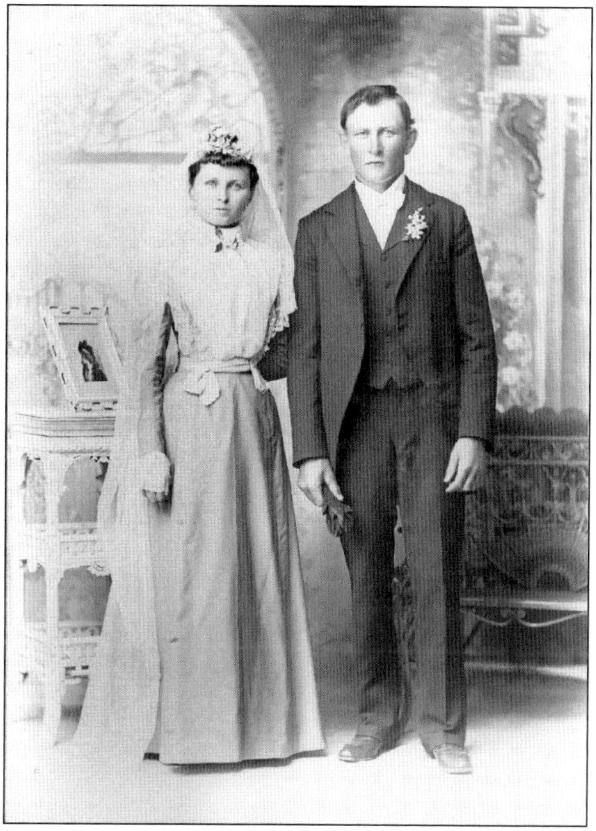

Not only president of an airline, but also a son of Waunakee, Bob Reeve was a logical choice to be the parade marshal for Waunakee's centennial parade in 1971. Paul Bernards (left) sports a beard for the occasion, and both he and Reeve (right) are dressed in centennial garb. Reeve had accomplished much, and his firstborn son, Richard, had also become a pilot by that time. (Paul Bernards.)

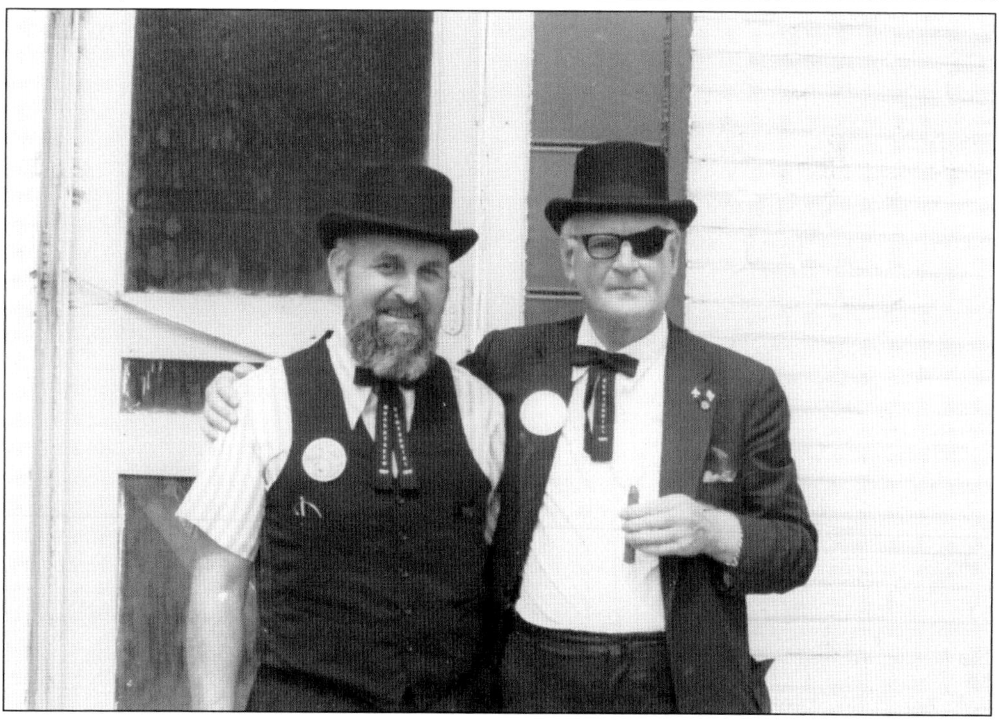

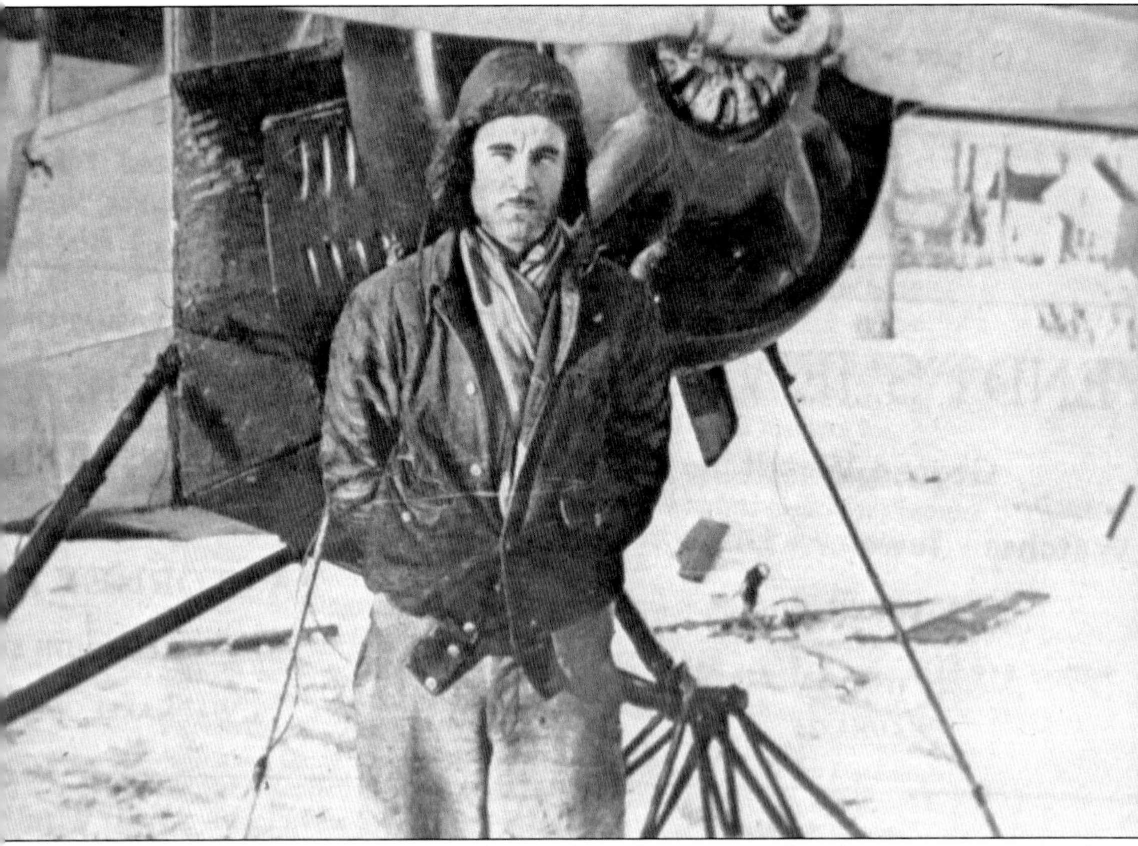

Bob Reeve began his life in 1902 as the son of H.L. Reeve, Waunakee's longest-running railroad station agent, and twin brother to Richard. From the time he first left Waunakee at age 15, he enlisted in the Army, flew a dangerous mail route in South America, contracted polio, and relocated to Valdez, Alaska, in 1932. With money earned flying supplies to the Chisana mines in Alaska, he bought the Fairchild plane shown behind him. In 1938, his brother Capt. Richard Reeve died in a thunderstorm while aboard an Army B-18 in Colorado. The first thing Reeve did was fly, later explaining, "When I heard about Dick, I knew I had to get in a plane—fast—or I never would again." As a civilian during World War II, Reeve flew exclusively for the military, transporting soldiers and "beans, bullets, and booze" to bases not only in the Alaska Aleutian Islands, but also throughout the entire region. After the war, Reeve bought a military C-47 and converted it into a commercial DC-3. Reeve Aleutian Airways was incorporated in 1947 and officially certified in 1956. (WPL.)

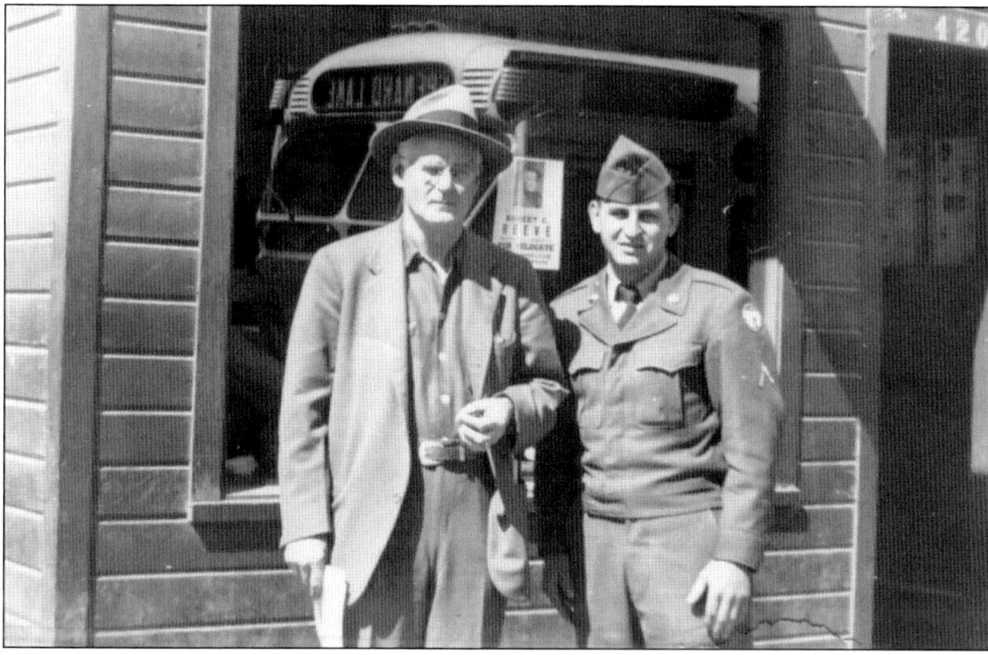

After surviving a heart attack in 1951, Bob Reeve avoided his office for a year, spending time hiking and hunting in an effort to build up his strength and release the stress that had led to his attack. In 1952, he returned to his duties at his Anchorage, Alaska, office where Paul Bernards (right), of Waunakee, visited Reeve (left) the same year. Bernards was stationed in Fairbanks, Alaska, during the Korean War. (Paul Bernards.)

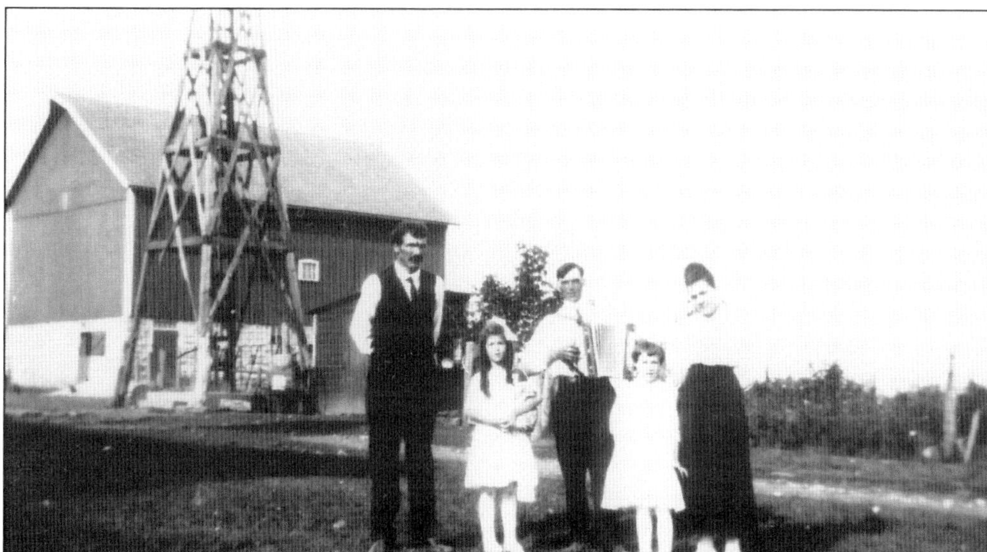

Henry and Eveline Busby Schumacher moved into their white house east of Waunakee on Highway 19 in 1908. The Schumacher family had frequent visitors; assembled from left to right are Henry Schumacher, Marcella Schumacher, Frank Rosa, and two unidentified guests. Around 1913, Frank Rosa came from Serbia and worked for Henry for about three years. Rosa was known for his lively accordion playing. The barn in the background was built by Henry Adler using lumber from Koltes & Riphahn in 1909. (Friends of Schumacher Farm.)

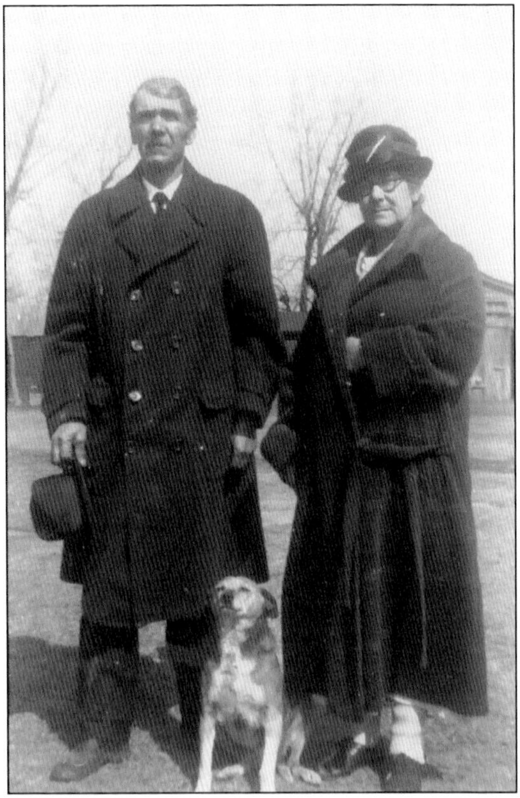

Eveline Schumacher fashioned the clothes for the family, including making her own wool wedding dress. A single dark-gray suit was sufficient for Henry Schumacher to wear to church in both winter and summer. The Schumachers belonged to the Catholic church, though Eveline's parents were Irish and attended St. Mary of the Lake and Henry's parents, George and Clara, were German and thus attended St. John the Baptist. Henry and Eveline Schumacher may well have been on their way to church as they stand with their dog Youknow. (Friends of Schumacher Farm.)

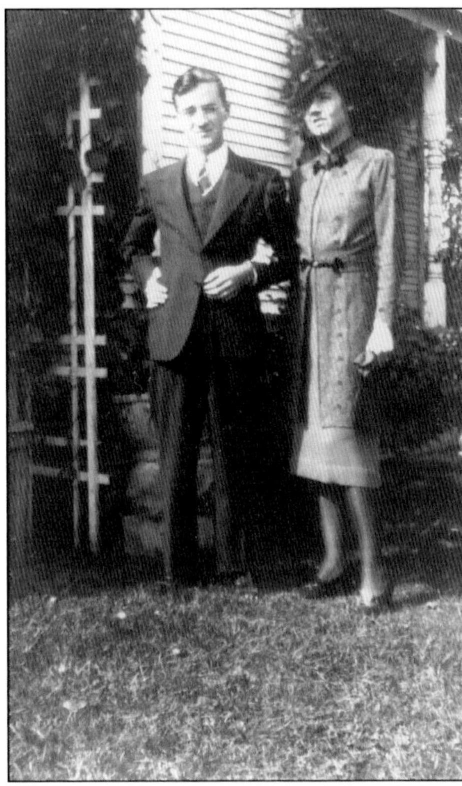

Marcella Schumacher (right) married Rudolph Pendall in 1939. They stand in the yard of Marcella's childhood home, which she returned to after she and Pendall divorced. She taught at Waunakee High School for 15 years until she retired. To preserve the land her father purchased in 1892, Marcella Schumacher Pendall donated her farm to the Dane County Park system for use as a living history farm and nature park. (Friends of Schumacher Farm.)

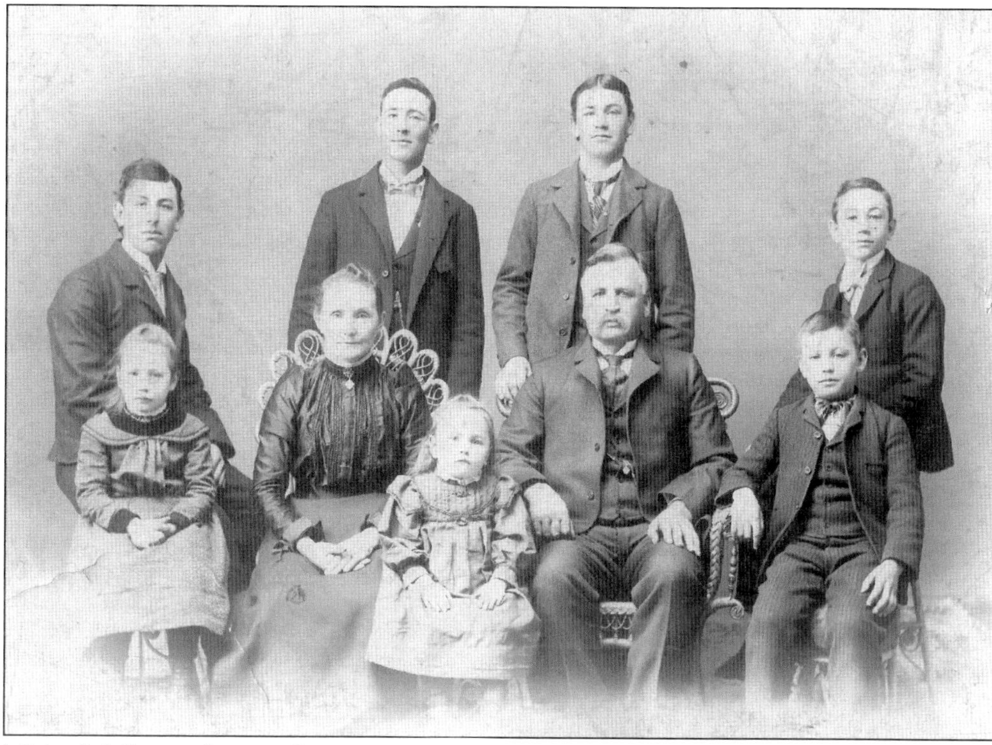

Michael Adler was born in Germany in 1853, and when his father died in 1860 his mother brought him and his brother to Wisconsin. In 1876, Michael Adler married Annie Mergen, and they had 12 children. The seven children who survived infancy are pictured with their parents from left to right as follows: (first row) Mary, Anna Mergen Adler, Anna, Michael Peter Adler Sr., and Joseph Charles; (second row) Henry John, Michael Peter Jr., John Joseph, and Mathias Ferdinand. Michael Adler's 200-acre farm in Cross Plains passed to his son Michael P. before Adler moved to Waunakee. (WPL.)

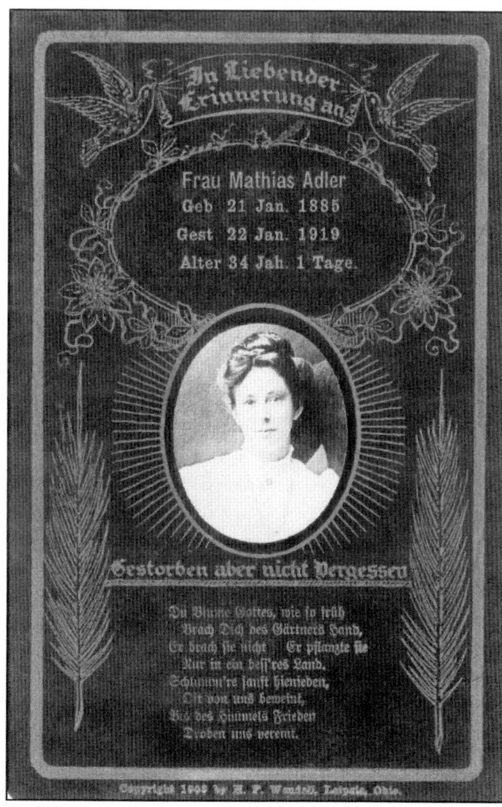

In 1918, influenza spread so much through Waunakee that some of the schools were closed for a time. When Michael Adler was stricken, his son Mathias F. Adler's wife, Josephine Diederich Adler, went to care for him. Michael died and soon after, so did Josephine. When she died in 1919 at age 34, Josephine left four sons as well as her husband. (Kennedy family.)

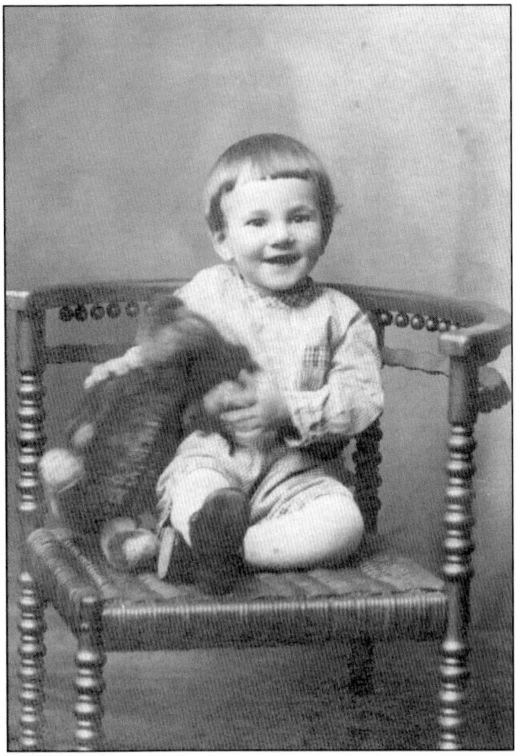

The sons of Mathias F. Adler and Josephine Diederich Adler were Gregory, Sylvester, Leo, and Victor. Victor Adler was born in 1917, and this photograph of him was taken in 1919. Tragically, Victor was killed a few months after he graduated from high school in 1935 when his car hit a culvert on Highway 113. Victor, his half-brother Herman Adler, and friends had just attended a dance in Waunakee. (Kennedy family.)

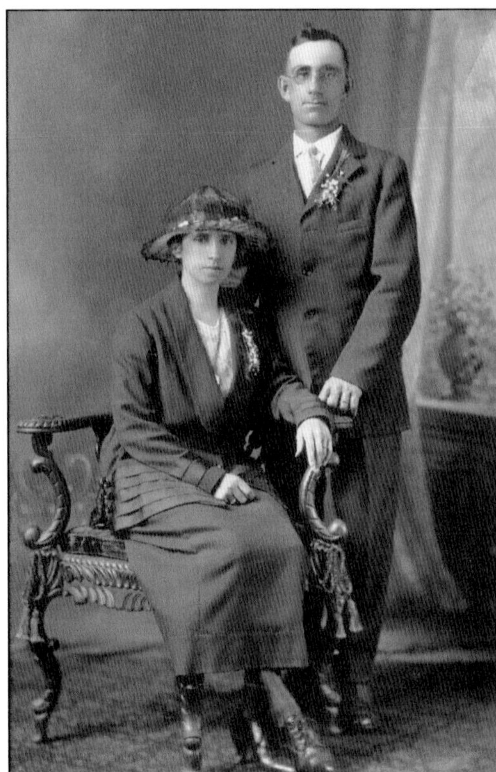

Until Mathias F. Adler married Agnes Virnig in 1920, his four sons from Josephine Diederich Adler were living with other relatives. This wedding photograph of Mathias and Agnes was taken May 25, 1920, in Cross Plains. When they married, Agnes took in the four Adler boys as if they were her own. (Kennedy family.)

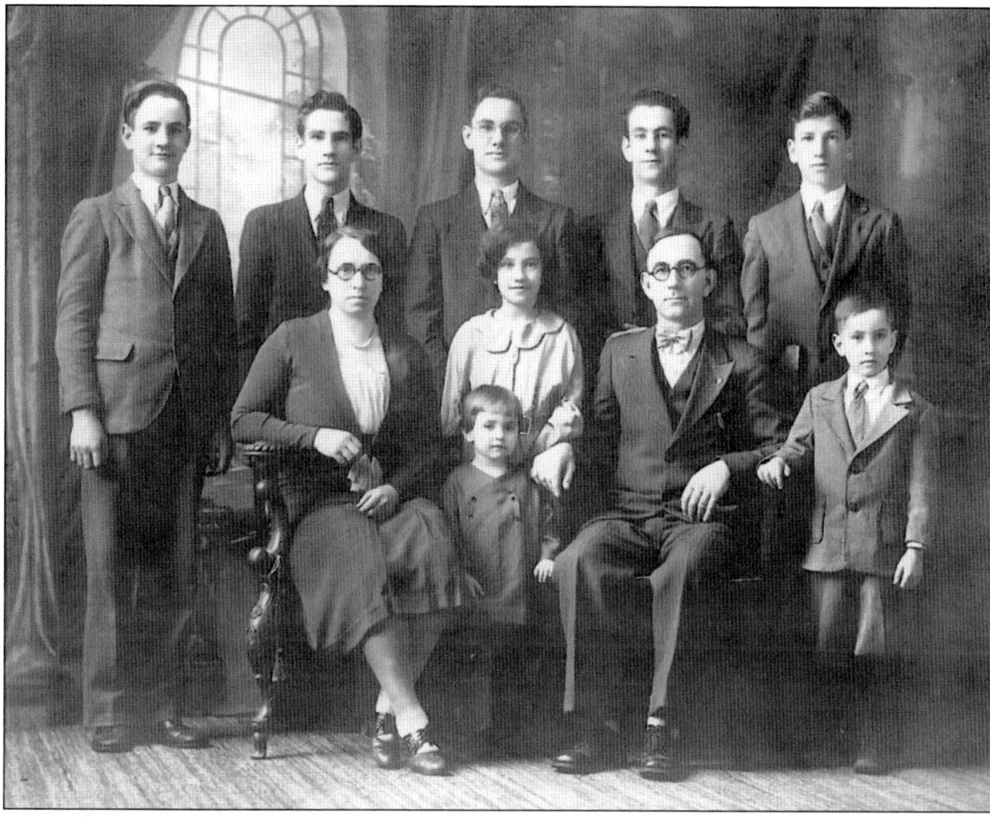

The Adler family in 1931 shows the addition of Mathias F. and Agnes Adler's four children. Pictured from left to right are (first row) Mary Ann; (second row) Agnes Virnig Adler, Louise, Mathias F. Adler, and Mathias M.; (third row) Victor, Leo, Sylvester, Gregory, and Herman. Herman Adler carried on his father's role as postmaster from 1954 to 1971 when he then became a rural carrier. (Kennedy family.)

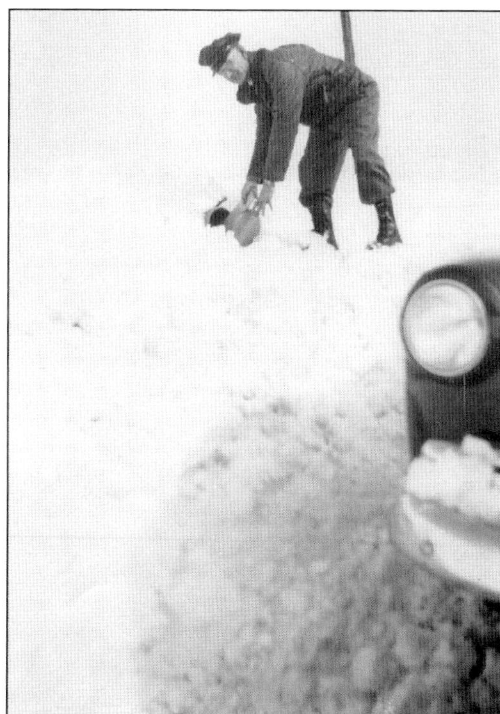

"Neither snow nor rain nor heat nor gloom of night stays these couriers from the swift completion of their appointed rounds." Mathias F. Adler lives up to the postal carrier's unofficial motto by delivering mail after a fierce snowstorm. Adler became the rural carrier for Waunakee in 1934 after a long term as postmaster in town, first at a building on the Koltes property east of the railroad tracks and second at the Adler Michels store in Waunakee State Bank. (Kennedy family.)

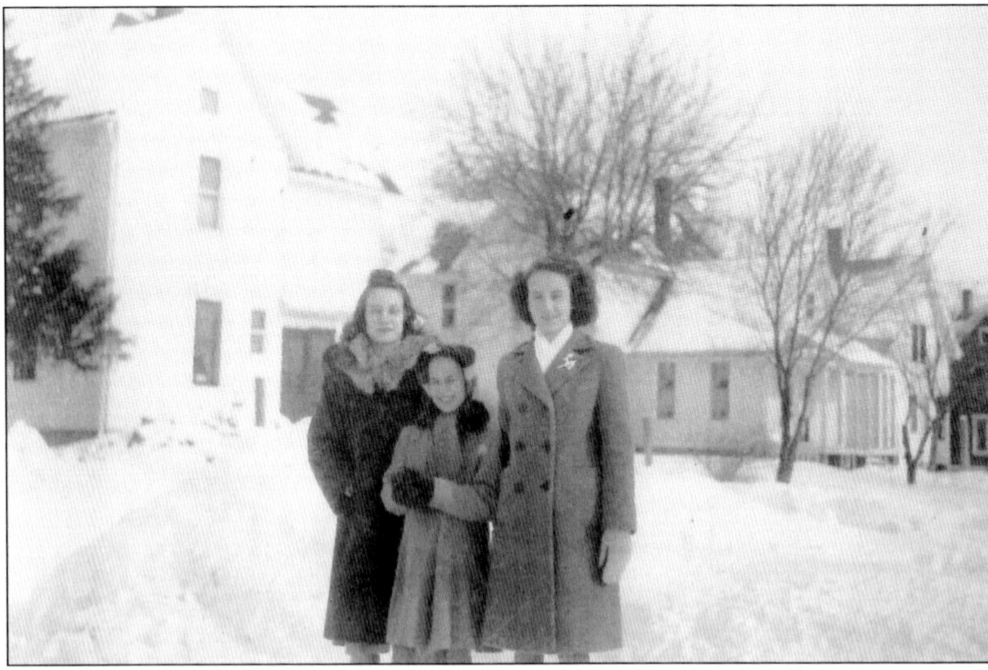

Daughters of Mathias F. Adler and Agnes Virnig Adler stand near their Main Street home in the 1940s. From left to right are Louise, Genevieve, and Mary Ann. (Kennedy family.)

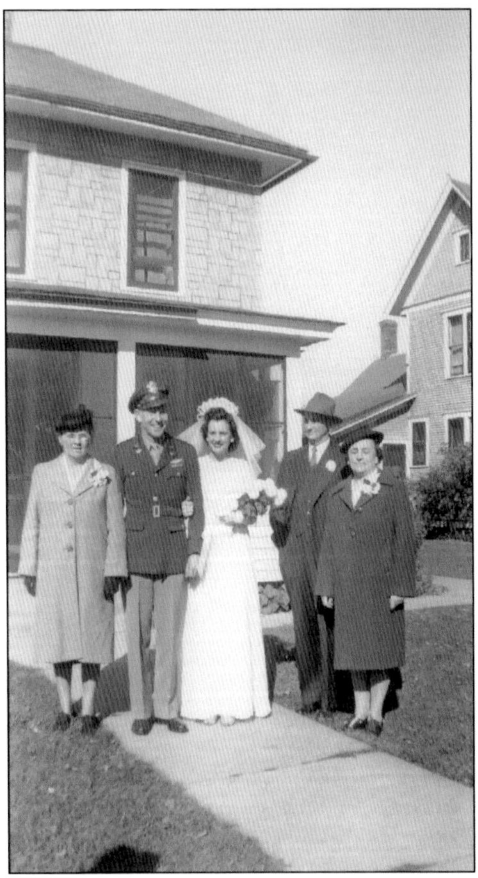

Anna Adler, daughter of Michael Adler and Annie Mergen Adler, married Wayne Bacon. On October 10, 1944, they celebrated their daughter Doris's marriage to Marvin E. Krinke (US Air Force first lieutenant) while he was on 21-day leave as a B-26 Marauder bomber pilot. Standing in front of the Bacon house on Second Street are, from left to right, Mary Krinke, Marvin Krinke, Doris Bacon Krinke, Wayne Bacon, and Anna Adler Bacon. (WPL.)

Eight

COMMUNITY

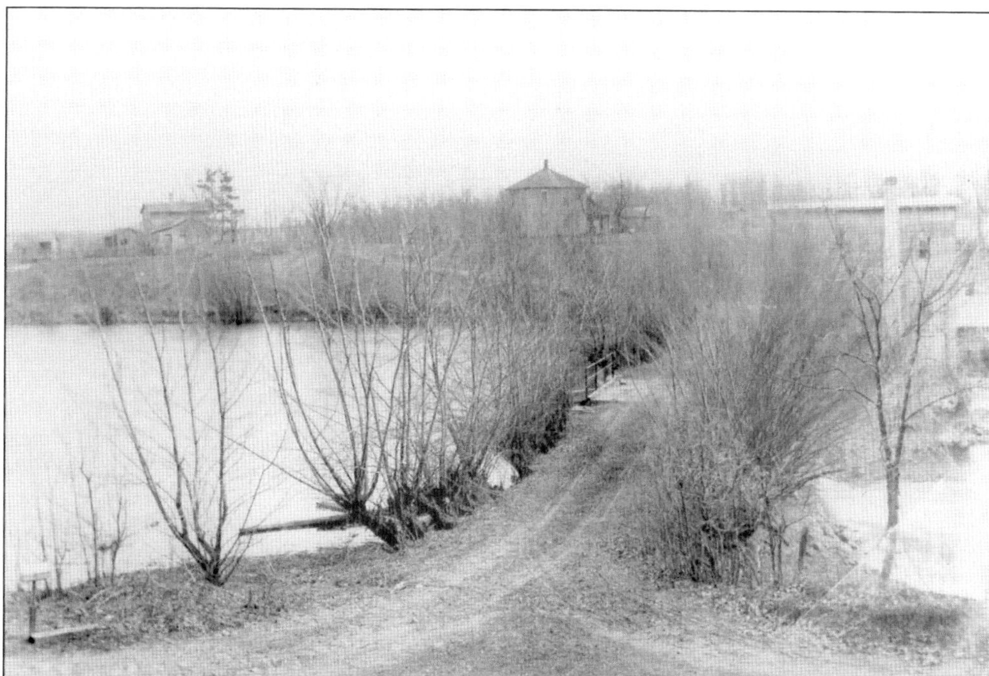

Looking east down the dirt Mill Road, Packham's sawmill is partially obscured by trees on the right. North of the road, Six Mile Creek fills the area and appears much wider than present-day because the creek was dammed for operation of the mill at the time. If not for the famous trio who brought the railroad to Waunakee, this would have become the site for the village. (Village of Waunakee.)

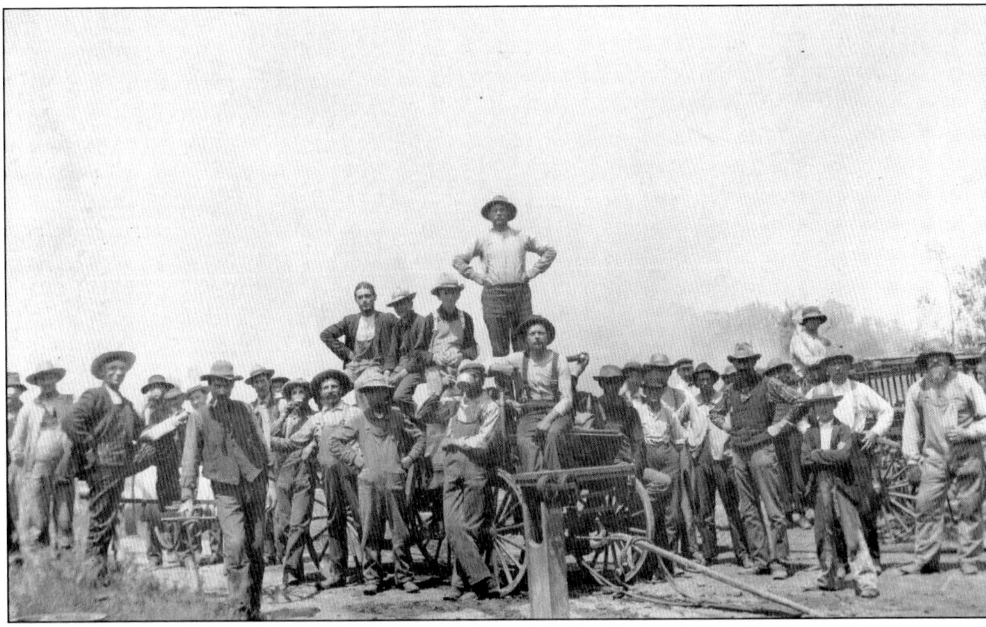

This photograph first appears to be a farming scene, but it turns out to feature an early group of firefighters. From the smoke in the background to the soot-covered faces, the clues seem to indicate that this is a celebration of suppressing a large fire. Stories passed down through generations recount how in southeastern Westport Township near Shillinglaw's tavern, some fires would "accidentally" be set to the marshlands, necessitating a gathering of firefighters—along with a bit of celebratory drink afterwards. (WPL.)

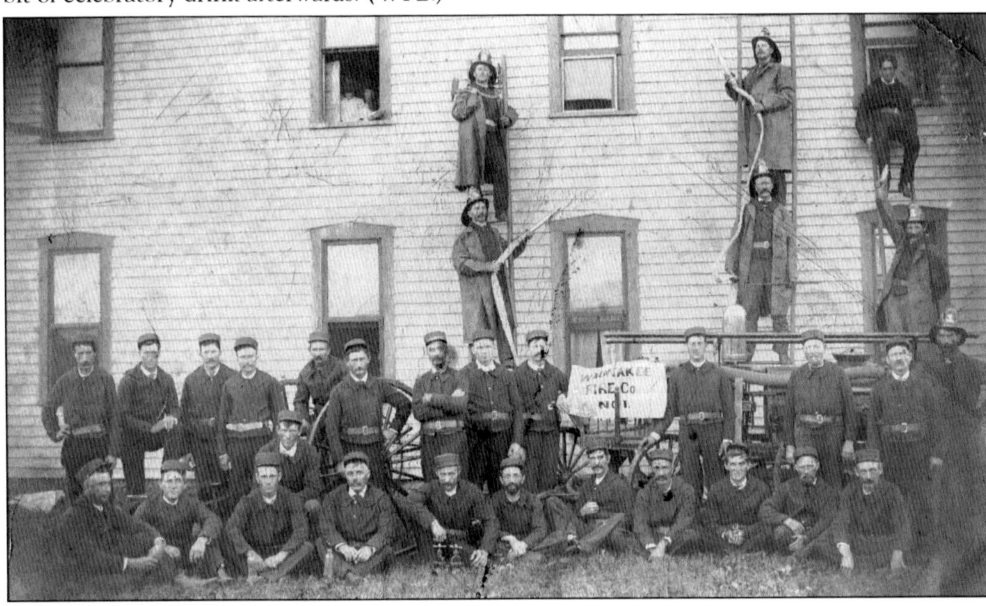

Gathered at the side of the American House (Ryan Hotel), Waunakee's first fire company shows prodigious citizen participation. Though three years too late to save the railroad depot from burning to the ground, the department was organized in 1895 and acquired equipment to prepare for future emergencies. The first officers were H.J. Doll (chief), Jake Feiler (assistant chief), William Flatman (foreman and later chief), and P.R. Riphahn (secretary). (James P. Koltes.)

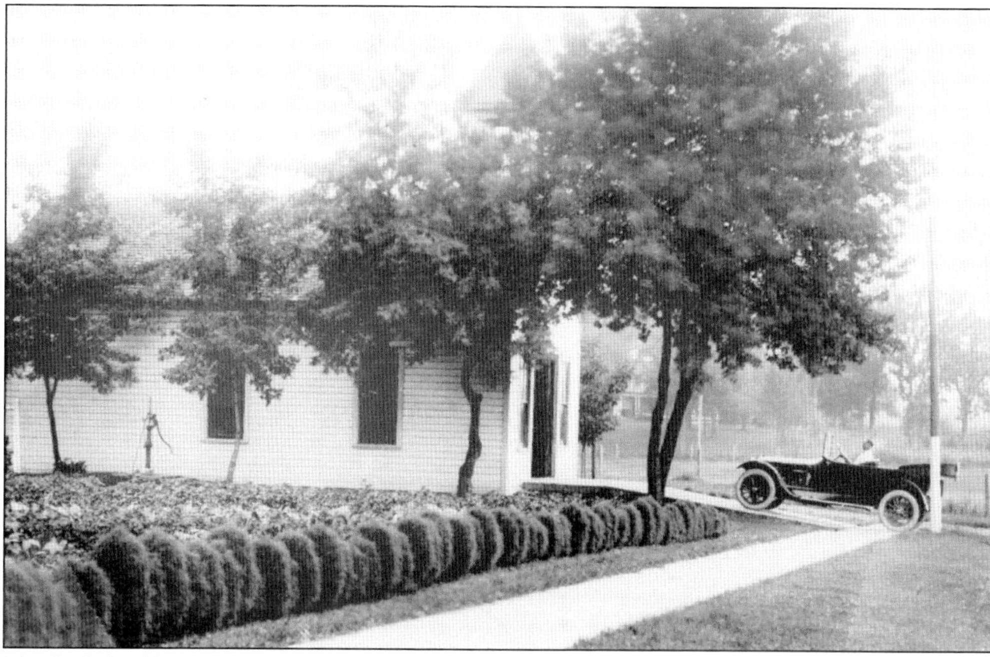

The little building on Baker Street was erected as the village hall in 1895. Soon after, the newly formed fire company, which used the hall to store fire equipment, donated the bell for the bell tower. The need for a firehouse was evident as early as 1898 when the *Wisconsin State Journal* reported that the hall was "shabby" and had no room for village council members to meet. (WPL.)

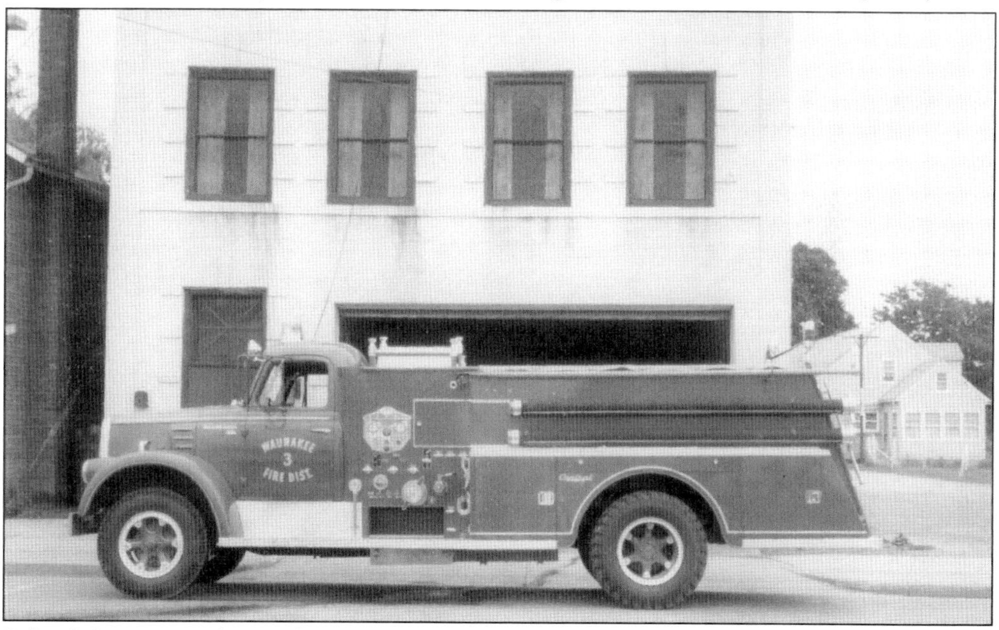

Behind this vintage fire truck on parade is the second village hall, built in 1911. It was the third location for the fire department, which occupied the first floor of the IOOF building from 1904 until 1911. This village hall building served the needs of both organizations until 1965 when the Community Building was constructed to accommodate the fire department, library, village hall, village offices, and police department. (WPL.)

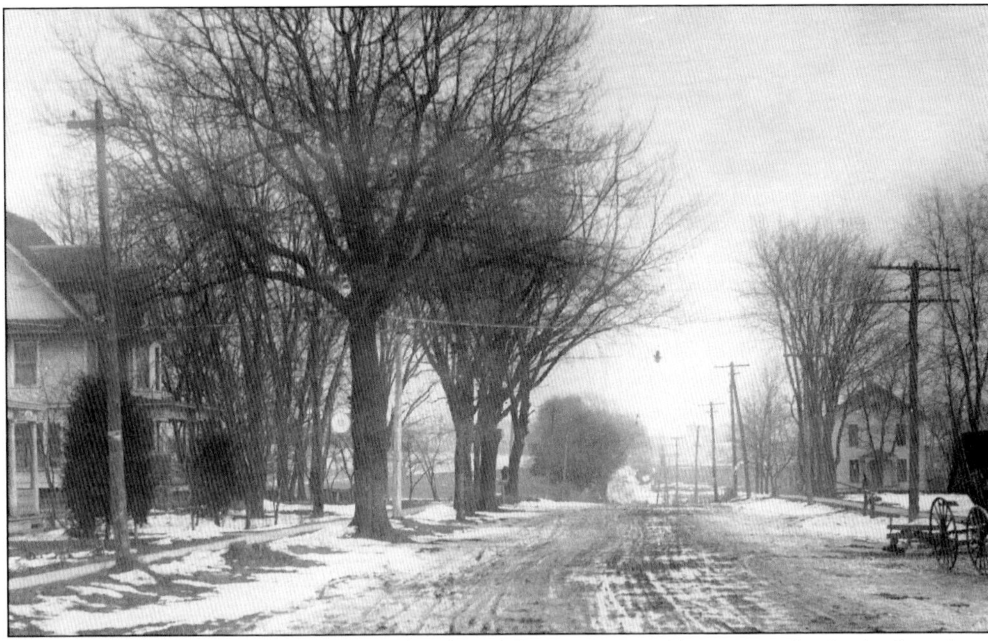

Before paved roads, the streets of Waunakee bared deep ruts carved by wagon wheels. At the edge of town looking east on Main Street, the landscape is dotted with only a few houses. Charles McWatty's house is on the left, and Robert Chambers' Bacon Street house is on the right. (WPL.)

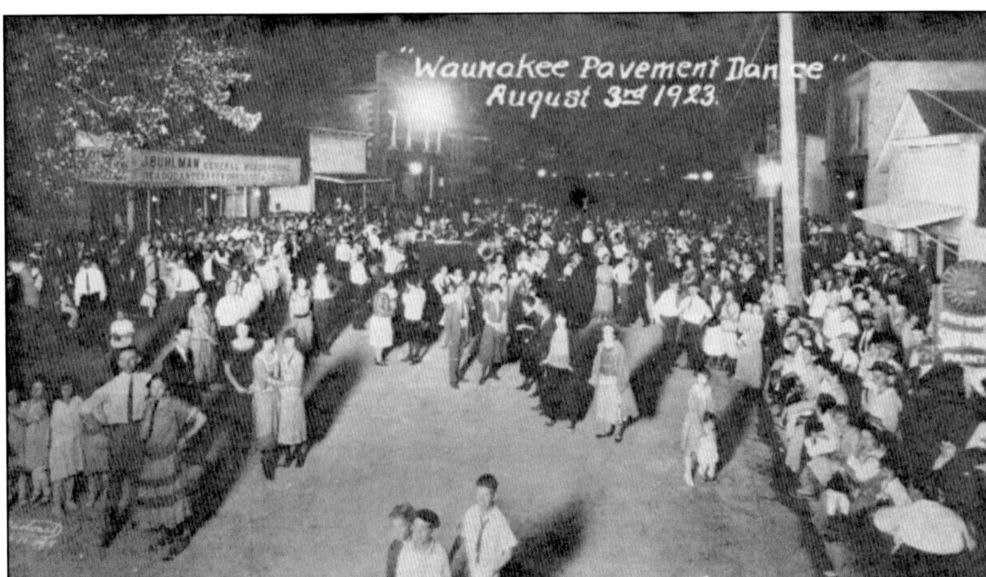

Waunakee's residents dealt with the muddy, often impassable streets until 1923 when Main Street became the first paved road in the village. A few thousand people from Waunakee and surrounding towns came to celebrate during a street dance in August 1923. (WPL.)

After less than a quarter of Waunakee's wells had a clean report in 1927, the village finally settled on a vote to add a water and sewer utility. Hazel Raemisch took this photograph of a worker named Art at one water main installation site, adding her own sense of humor to the situation by writing on the print, "Art at the artesian well, 1927." (Hazel R. Zimbric.)

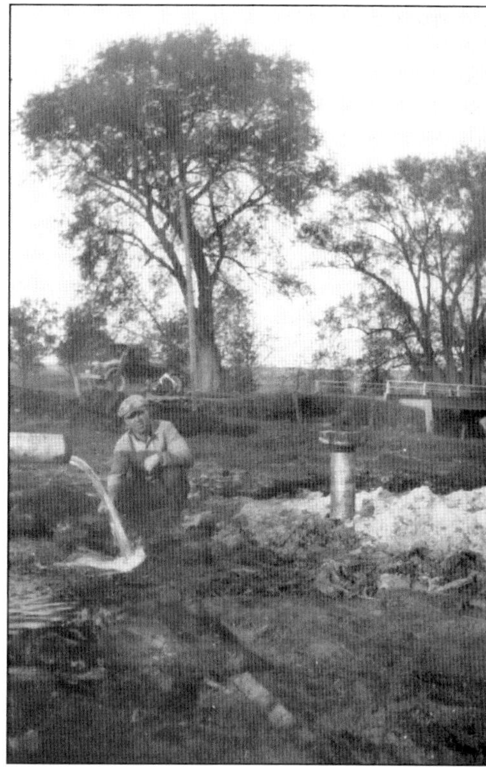

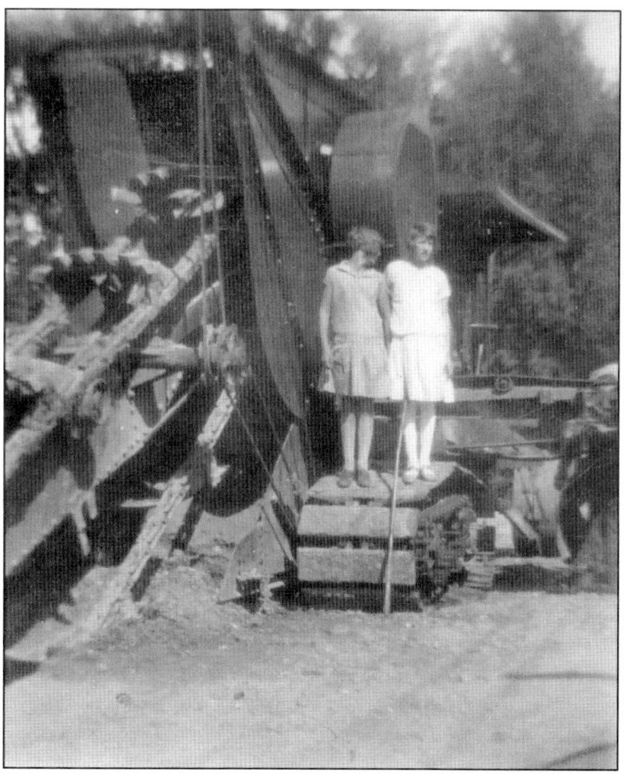

Large machinery lined the streets where sewer lines were placed underground, which proved tempting for local unidentified children. The photograph was taken outside the Raemisch house on Bacon Street in 1927, and the utilities were fully installed by 1928. (Hazel R. Zimbric.)

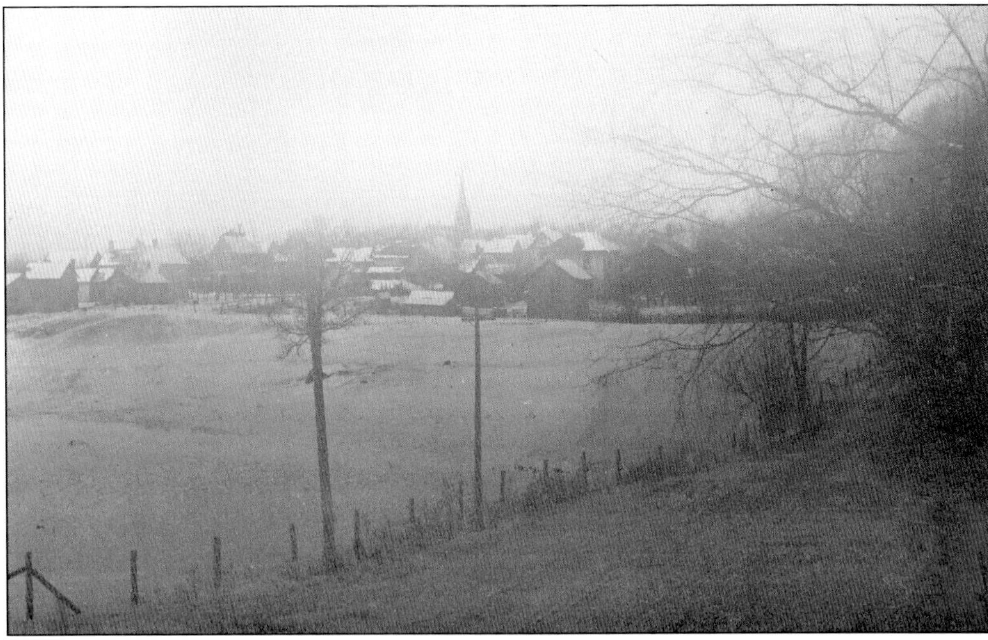

The area east of Bacon Street known as the Cooper pasture was purchased from Earl Cooper Sr. for a community park in the 1930s. The Civil Works Administration (CWA) provided the initial funds in 1933, allowing work for unemployed locals until the park's completion by the Works Progress Administration (WPA) in 1935. The day work began in December 1933, the temperature was 25 degrees below zero. (WPL.)

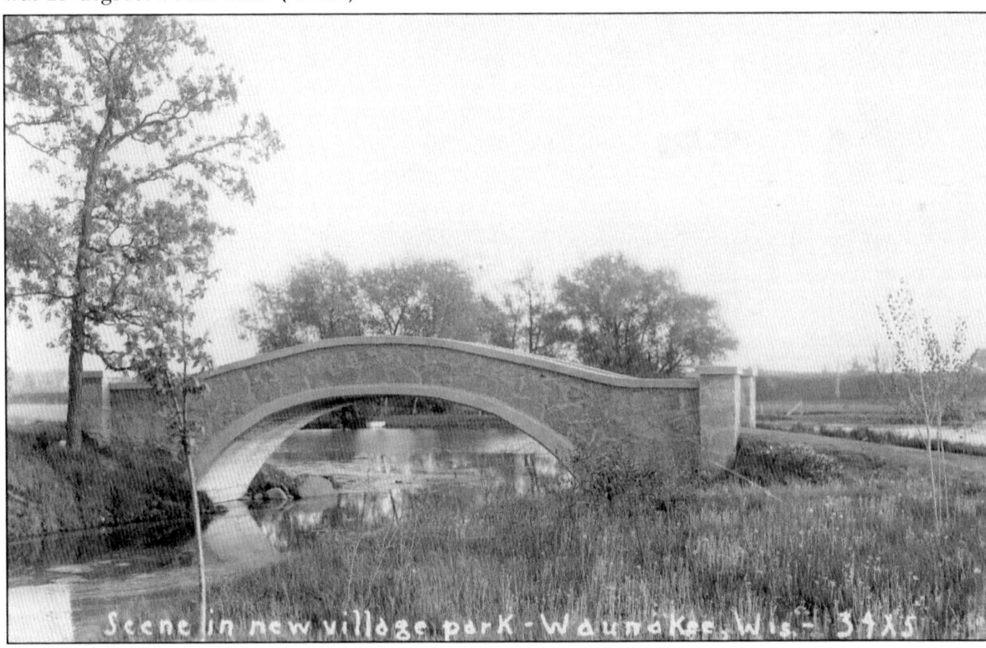

Shown shortly after it was built, a bridge in the Waunakee Village Park spans Six Mile Creek. Henry Adler's building contractors erected the forms for the bridges while the Karls Brothers in Dane constructed them in the style of Madison's Tenney Park bridges. Some trees were purchased from officer George Manthey's nursery, and others were reportedly dug from Baker's field. (WPL.)

The earliest reports of local baseball games were from the mid-1910s. This Westport team includes, from left to right, (first row) ? Hughes, ? Hogan, and Dr. Austin Blake (manager); (second row) ? Williamson, ? Ireland, James J. Kennedy, and ? Williamson; (third row) Richard V. Kennedy and Hank Hurst. (Kennedy family and James P. Koltes.)

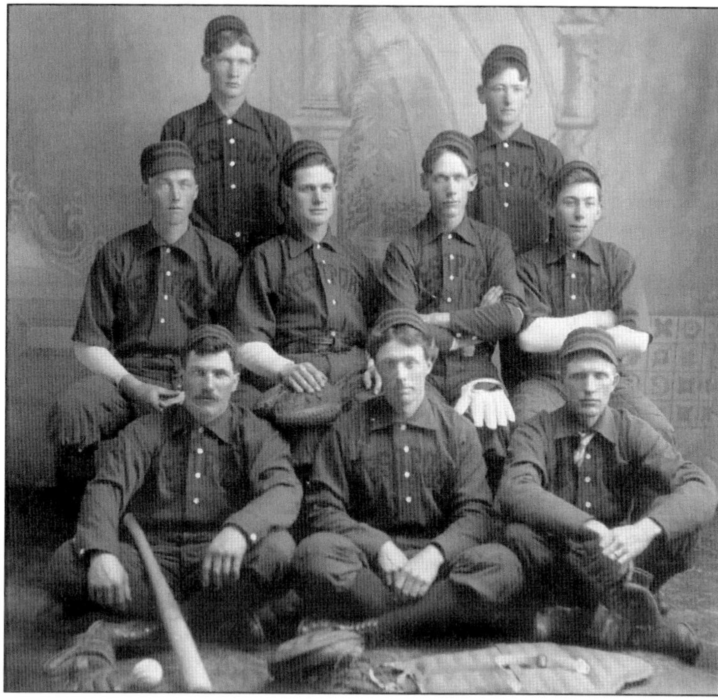

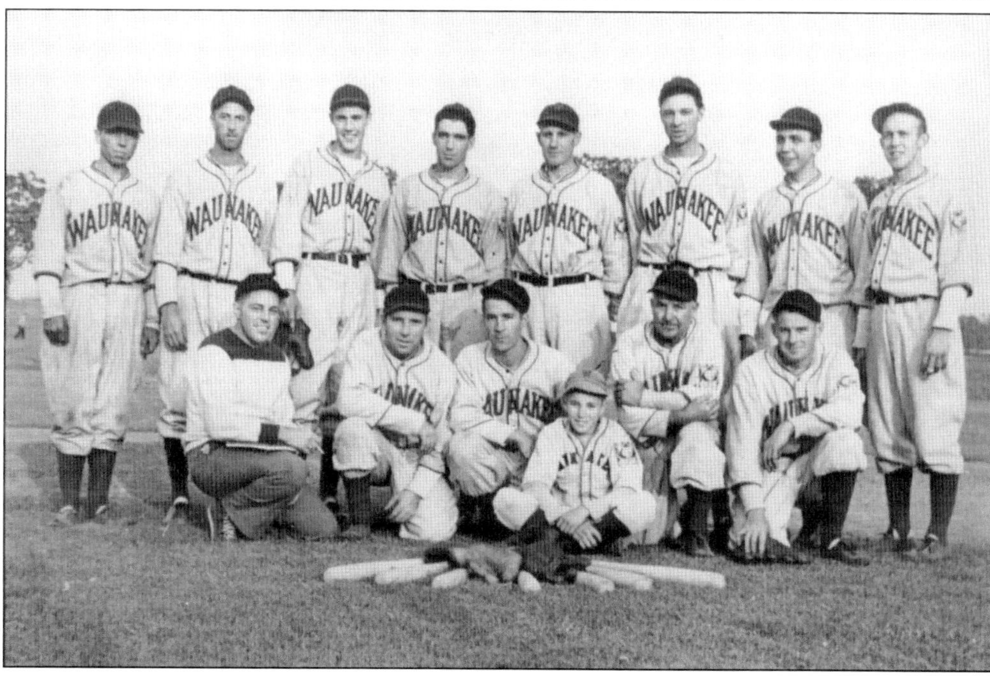

In 1937, baseball continued to be a popular form of recreation for Waunakee residents. The team members that year are, from left to right, (first row) Ray "Doc" Worringer, Pat Bowles, John Kneibuhler, batboy Ed Murphy, manager Pete Brausen, and George Kneibuhler; (second row) Ray Lamboley, Ray Stehr, Howie Cross, Russ Hogan, George Taylor, Carl Hansen, Bob Hilgers, and Harry Hilgers. The baseball field at Waunakee's Village Park was named after Edward Murphy, bat boy, groundskeeper, and all-star shortstop from 1936 to 1971. (Paul Bernards.)

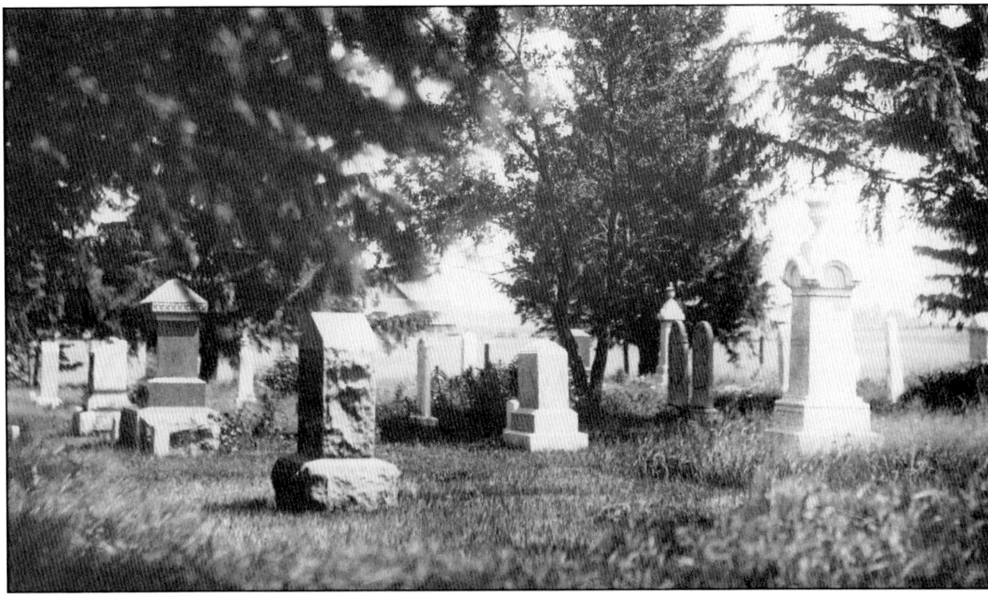

Visiting cemeteries is one way to learn about the area's earliest residents. Pictured is Vienna township's Union Cemetery (also known as Plackett Cemetery and Wilke Cemetery). Based on Ira P. Bacon's gravestone, this photograph was taken before 1929. His wife, Eliza, died that year, and her name was not yet inscribed on their shared stone. As a sad reminder of the hardships families faced, one gravestone in St. John's Cemetery marks the graves of seven Meier children who died in 1887 during the diphtheria epidemic. (WPL.)

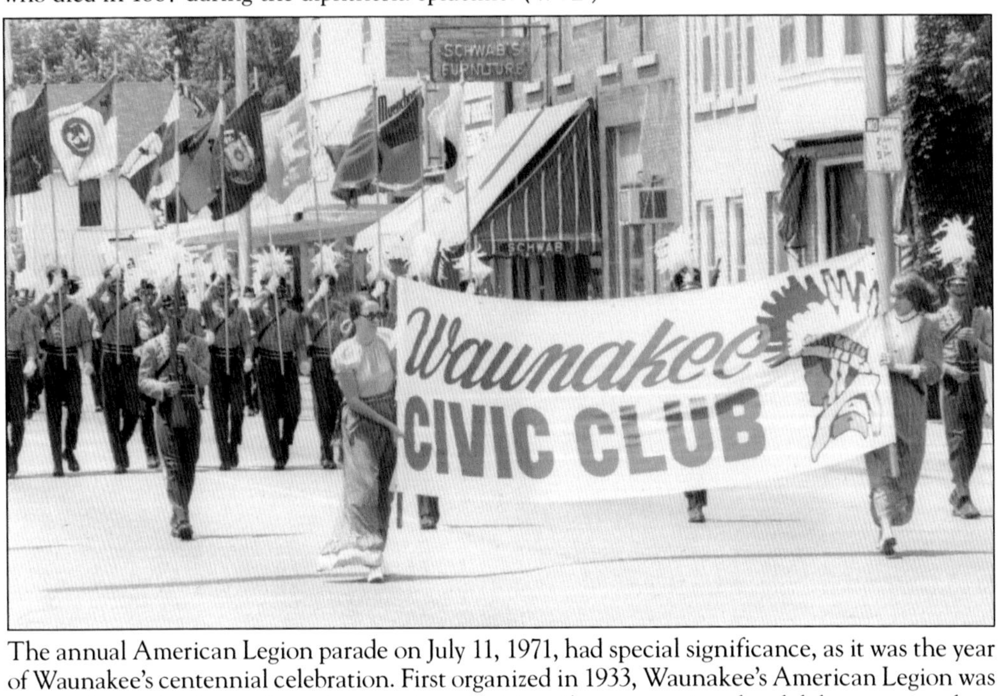

The annual American Legion parade on July 11, 1971, had special significance, as it was the year of Waunakee's centennial celebration. First organized in 1933, Waunakee's American Legion was especially involved in parks and recreation activities. Shown carrying the club banner, members of the civic club created opportunities for recreation and baseball in addition to their primary interest in local trade and industry. (WPL.)

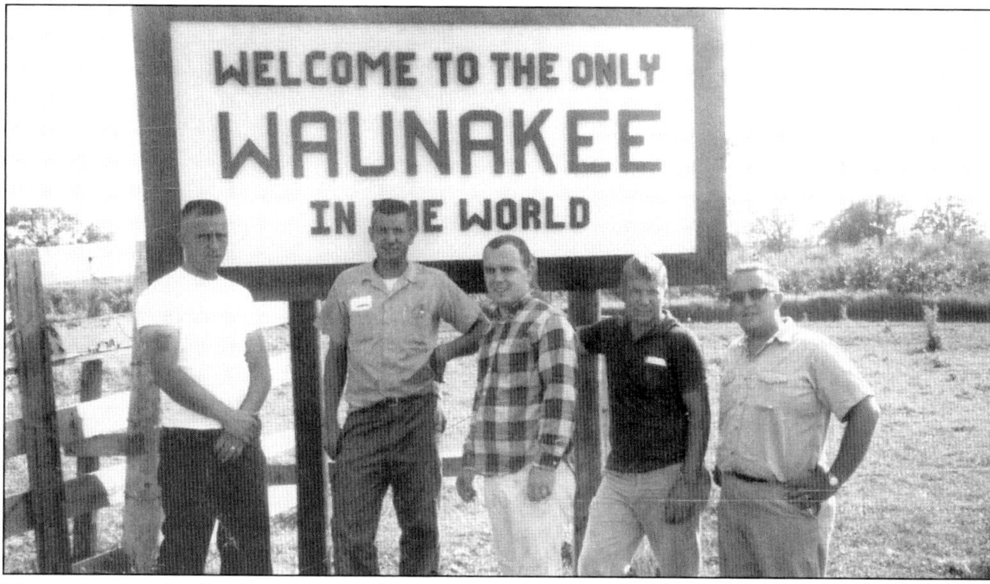

Waunakee received new signs in 1969; this one was set up by the Waunakee Jaycees. President that year was Thayne "Butch" Martin, seen on the left. The remaining members are, from left to right, Ray Statz, Bob Varebrook, Ken Statz, and Myron Wilcox. The Jaycees' mission is to encourage the involvement of area young adults in community improvement through service activities. (WPL.)

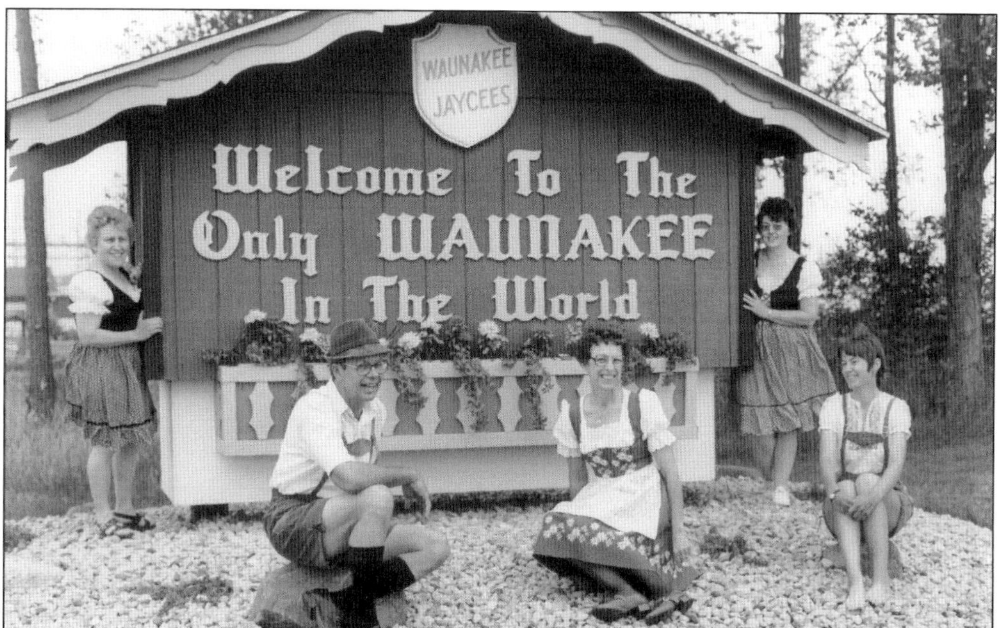

The 1970s were not only a celebration of Waunakee's centennial, but also of the histories and traditional backgrounds of the village's first settlers. Representing that heritage are Waunakee Arts Council members, from left to right, Colette Koltes, Larry Endres, Lee Endres Grub, Betty Barbian, and Kathy van Sistene. They were part of the inaugural Volkfest of the Arts held at the Village Park in 1977. The proceeds from that event were used to restore the railroad depot—one simple structure that led to the development of a treasured community. (WPL.)

BIBLIOGRAPHY

1873 Plat Map of Dane County. www.danecountyhistory.org/1873plat/1873plat.html

Apps, Jerry. *Horse-Drawn Days: A Century of Farming with Horses*. Madison, WI: Wisconsin Historical Society Press, 2010.

Barton, A.O. "History of Waunakee and One of the Early Pioneers. [Mathias H. Schleck]." *Waunakee Tribune*. June 26, 1947.

Biographical Review of Dane County, Wisconsin. Chicago: Biographical Review Publishing Co., 1893. wisconsinhistory.org/u?/wch,1390

Buhlman, Margaret. *An Early History of Village Waunakee*, 1908.

Day, Beth. *Glacier Pilot*. New York: Holt, Rinehart, and Winston, 1957.

Evansen, Russ. *Ordinary People, Extraordinary Faith: The Story of First Presbyterian Church of Waunakee*. Waunakee, WI: 2007.

Freiherr, Margaret, and Marcella Schumacher Pendall. *St. Mary of the Lake Church, Past and Present, 1865–1954*. Westport, WI: 1954.

Gay, Leonard W. *New atlas of Dane County, Wisconsin, Prepared from Actual Surveys and from the County Records*. Leonard W. Gay and Co., 1899. digital.library.wisc.edu/1711.dl/WI.AtlasDane1899

History of Dane County. Chicago: Western Historical Company, 1880. content.wisconsinhistory org/u?/wch,69408

History of Dane County: Biographical and Genealogical. Madison, WI: Western Historical Association, 1906.

Koltes, James P. "The Early History of Waunakee." Seminar paper presented to the graduate faculty, Wisconsin State University-Platteville, 1971.

Ligowski, A. *Map of Dane County, Wisconsin, 1861*. digital.library.wisc.edu/1711.dl WI.MapDaneCo

Loew, Patty. *Native People of Wisconsin*. Madison, WI: Wisconsin Historical Society Press, 2003.

Murphy, Richard, ed. *Waunakee Tribune*. Centennial edition. August 5, 1971.

Noyes, E.L. "Westport and Village of Waunakee." *History of Madison, Dane County and Surrounding Towns*. Madison, WI: Wm. J. Park & Co., 1877.

Paulson, Jerry. *Waunakee Centennial: 1871–1971*. Waunakee, WI: 1971.

Plat Book of Dane County, Wisconsin: Drawn from Actual Surveys and the County Records. Minneapolis, MN: C.M. Foote and Co., 1890. digital.library.wisc.edu/1711.dl/WI.PlatBookDane1890

Ruff, Allen and Tracy Will. *Forward! A History of Dane: the Capital County*. Cambridge, WI: Woodhenge Press, 2000.

Schumacher Pendall, Marcella, and Laura Weis. *St. Mary of the Lake Church, Mine Know Me, 1866–1966*. Westport, WI: 1966.

Schumacher Pendall, Marcella. *Papa, Mama, and Me*. Marcella Madison, WI: 1993.

St. John, Waunakee, Wisconsin, 1874–1974. Charlotte, NC: C.D. Stampley Enterprises, 1974.

Standard Historical Atlas of Dane County, Wisconsin Containing Maps of Villages, Cities and Townships together with Replats of the County. Madison, WI: Cantwell Printing Company, 1911. digital.library.wisc.edu/1711.dl/WI.MPLAtlasDane

Wheeler Wilcox, Ella. *The Worlds and I*. New York: George H. Doran Company, 1918.

INDEX

Adler, 58, 65, 67, 81, 111, 113–116, 122
Bacon, 8, 46, 47, 58, 64–66, 72–74, 76, 103, 107, 116, 120–122, 124
Baker, 8, 20, 62, 63, 119, 122
Bernards, 6, 27, 28, 31, 32, 93, 103, 108, 109, 111, 123
Blake, 16, 23, 25, 34, 57, 66, 67, 71, 104, 105, 107, 123
Borchers, 68, 80, 87, 91
Brausen, 17, 31, 54, 67, 108, 123
Buhlman, 17, 18, 25, 29, 32, 47, 51
Cameron, 33, 34, 80, 102
Chambers, 27, 53, 74, 106, 120
Cook, 71, 85, 86
Cooper, 53, 57, 71, 72, 74, 87, 122
Corcoran, 33, 72, 73
Deans, 17, 53, 57, 103
Diederich, 32, 58, 113, 114
Doll, 16, 57, 118
Endres, 6, 10, 58, 70, 94, 99, 125
Fish, 8, 41, 47, 63
Fisher, 40, 67, 68, 69, 89, 92–99
Flatman, 18, 19, 26, 34, 36, 64, 118
Ford, 33, 34, 72, 73, 102, 104
Francis, 22, 58, 68
Freney, 15, 20, 25, 93
Hilgers, 27, 93, 106, 109, 123
Hogan, 51, 53, 57, 68, 70, 84–86, 88–92, 123
Hohlstein, 17, 29, 32
Hudson, 2, 7, 25, 26, 58
Kennedy, 6, 25, 40, 42, 43, 50, 56, 58, 67–69, 77, 80, 88–99, 113–116, 123
Kessenich, 54, 91, 96, 104, 108
Koltes, 2, 6, 7, 10, 14, 15, 20–26, 33, 35, 50, 51, 55, 62, 66, 69–72, 80, 82–87, 107, 111, 115, 118, 123, 125
McCloskey, 40, 94, 98
McWatty, 34, 37, 38, 64, 65, 97, 120
Miller, 35, 42, 57, 74, 83, 106–108
Montandon, 7, 89
Murphy, 58, 105, 123
O'Malley, 7, 26, 29, 30, 42, 51, 57, 61–63, 65, 77–81, 89
Oncken, 55, 72, 87
Packham, 7, 8, 14, 16, 64, 117
Plackett, 7, 45, 124
Raemisch, 21, 36, 39-40, 57, 73, 74, 103, 106, 107, 121
Reeve, 53, 61, 109–111
Riphahn, 20, 22–25, 27, 32, 83, 111, 118
Ripp, 15, 21, 54
Schleck, 14, 15, 17, 20, 54
Schmidt, 16, 48, 53, 62
Schumacher, 2, 6, 7, 11, 29, 39, 42, 43, 51, 66, 75, 111, 112
Schunk, 18, 19, 26, 29, 34, 36, 54
Schwab, 30, 69, 97
Shaw, 13, 53, 61, 67, 80
Shillinglaw, 50, 58, 86, 91, 118
Simon, 29, 30, 35, 48, 51, 53, 57
Statz, 28, 34, 36, 54, 125
Tierney, 7, 15, 27, 42, 50, 57, 70, 71, 83–86
Truehl, 16, 73, 107
Uebersetzig, 13, 28, 29, 81, 108
Walsh (Welsh), 7, 57, 58, 68, 77, 94
Wheeler, 7, 14, 53, 57, 66, 75, 100–102
Wilke, 7, 49, 53, 124
Wipperfurth, 17, 54, 104
Worringer, 19, 57, 123